An Annotated Bibliography
of
Texts on Writing Skills

Garland Reference Library of the Humanities (Vol. 38)

An Annotated Bibliography
of
Texts on Writing Skills

*Grammar and Usage, Composition,
Rhetoric, and Technical Writing*

Shannon Burns
Mark Govoni
M.D. McGee
Lois Burns

Garland Publishing, Inc., New York & London

1976

Copyright © 1976

by Shannon Burns

All Rights Reserved

Library of Congress Cataloging in Publication Data
Main entry under title:

An Annotated bibliography of texts on writing skills.

    (Garland reference library of the humanities ; v. 38)
    Includes index.
    1. English language--Rhetoric--Bibliography.
2. English language--Grammar--1950-   --Bibliography.
3. College readers--Bibliography. I. Burns, Shannon.
Z2015.R5A55 [PE1408]   016.808'042   75-24096
ISBN 0-8240-9968-0

Contents

Preface

We have designed this bibliography to be a research tool for teachers of writing. Often, the process of selecting a text becomes a time-consuming and frustrating ordeal simply because of the difficulties involved in obtaining, sorting through, and cataloging advertisements from scores of publishers. So many times an instructor will spend hours evaluating a text once it has been obtained only to find that it is not, after all, applicable to the particular course or to the taste of the instructor. How does one, for example, begin the search for a basic grammar text for use in a section of remedial English? We can examine countless publisher's flyers, browse through bookstores and libraries, ask our colleagues if they can recommend a text, or perhaps methodically pore over the subject listing of *Books in Print*. Since the nature and character of the text determines, in some part, the success or failure of a class, research into available material should be more systematic and thorough. In order to bring some order to this chaos, in this bibliography we have alphabetically arranged and described texts and readers which pertain to traditional college-level English courses. Our categories include texts in grammar and basic usage, rhetorics and advanced composition books, basic composition materials, readers, guides to writing about literature, texts on language and style, guides to technical writing, and a few miscellaneous selections. Hopefully, an instructor consulting this bibliography will be able to avoid much of the haphazard and helter-skelter activity that so often attends textbook selection. We do not intend that our guide be used as the sole basis for text selection; rather, we have attempted to give a clear, accurate, and fair synopsis of each text included so that the individual teacher, on the basis of that description, may decide whether or not he would like to examine personally an individual text. There is no substitute

PREFACE

for the instructor's personal and considered evaluation.

Each entry includes standard bibliographical data—author(s), title, edition, publishing information, and date—plus the number of pages, the price, and a following notation of (P) or (H) to designate paperback or hardbound. When no price was available, usually because of recent publication, NPA (no price available) appears. The annotations are objective descriptions of those writing texts. We have made no attempt to make value judgments about the quality of the texts; indeed, we have actively attempted to avoid any kind of subjective evaluation with full knowledge that each teacher has his own approach and individual taste.

In annotating these texts we have not adhered to a specific or rigid formula. However, we have included in each entry certain common data we feel will be helpful: a statement of purpose or quotation from the preface or introduction of the book, a description of the contents of the book and its order and method of presentation, and classification by format (workbook, handbook, reader, and so on). If the book itself contains no reference to the primary audience addressed, we have indicated what group we feel the text might best serve. These comments are in no way to be taken as prescriptive; we have merely tried to present our best judgments concerning the general intended audience. Ultimately, the instructor must make his own decision as to whether a particular text suits his aims. A guide to the technical format of these annotations can be found in the How to Use This Bibliography section of the book.

This bibliography in no way includes every text currently in print. The 443 entries represent a substantial percentage of the available materials, but the actual number of composition and rhetoric texts on the commercial market is indeterminable and constantly changing. We have made every attempt to compile a complete bibliography, knowing all the while the magnitude of such a task. Specifically, we have contacted over 220 publishers, advising them of our project and requesting examination copies of texts currently in print that we did not have in our possession or had not personally read and annotated. Our only criterion for including a text in this bibliography was that

PREFACE

we actually see the book and be able to spend some time in writing an accurate description of it. Only those books currently in print were considered. Certainly by the time this bibliography is published new editions and titles will have appeared, and some titles included will have gone out of print. Nevertheless, the great majority of titles should be available.

We would like to acknowledge our many debts. We thank Arthur Woolley, Director of Freshman English at Ohio University, for his generous assistance in allowing us access to his library of composition texts. Professors Jim Davis and Tony DeJovine also deserve our gratitude in this regard. We would also like to thank the entire staff of Ohio University's Student Development Center—Carolyn Bubenzer, Suzanne Hunter, Judy Klare, George Staley, Gary Tolliver, and Cynthia Holderby—for their patient support and advice given over the course of this project. Special thanks to Deborah Sillery, who devoted considerable time in preparing the book in its initial stages, and to Stephanie Goldsberry for her extremely professional preparation of the manuscript. We wish also to thank James S. Hartman, coordinator of the Student Development Center, for a generous and timely grant that made the completion of this bibliography possible.

Shannon Burns
University of Arkansas
  at Little Rock

Mark Govoni
Memphis State University

M.D. McGee
Ohio University

Lois Burns
University of Arkansas at Little Rock

How to Use This Bibliography

This bibliography is not designed to be read cover-to-cover but selectively in accordance with the specific needs of the writing instructor. We saw the necessity, therefore, for an alternative to an alphabetical listing. Consequently, we have designated eight descriptive categories and have placed each entry into one or more categories:

Grammar and Basic Usage: This section has four sub-divisions—Traditional Text, Handbook/Reference, Work-book, and Programmed Text. All texts which are primarily addressed to the problems of correct usage, information about grammar, sentencing, and word usage are placed in one of these subdivisions.

Composition: This category is divided into Fundamental and Standard texts. The former section includes texts whose primary focus is on the first steps of composition (i.e., sentences into paragraphs, paragraphs into themes) which are designed for the beginning writer. The latter classification includes texts with primary emphasis on writing the whole essay, considering organization, unity, tone, audience, etc.

Advanced Composition and Rhetoric: This category includes texts which assume basic writing skills and offer a more sophisticated level of instruction, particularly those texts which investigate the various forms of composition (i.e., description, narration, persuasion, etc.). Readers which contain substantial amounts of instruction in principles of rhetoric are also included in this classification.

Writing About Literature: This category includes texts which address themselves to the problems of writing about literary topics. These texts are usually suggested as supplementary texts for general literature courses.

Readers: These source books contain no formal instruction

on composition or rhetorical principles, although they may include discussion questions, suggested topics, and formal writing assignments.

Language and Style: These texts are studies of semantics, language development, history and usage, and the fine points of style (e.g., S.I. Hayakawa's *Language in Thought and Action, Elements of Style* by Strunk and White).

Technical Writing: This category includes technical writing texts, general and specific.

Miscellaneous: We annotated four texts that did not fit into the designed categories.

Each text is listed by number under at least one category; some, because of their scope, are listed in several categories. Texts which have handbook, workbook, or programmed formats are designated by (H), (W), and (P), respectively. Those entries followed by an asterisk (*), in our judgment, are suitable for use in high schools.

We found that categorizing these texts was often quite difficult because many have broad appeal while others are so unique that traditional classifications do not apply. This guide is intended as a means to facilitate the use of this text, and in no way is it intended as a prescriptive categorization.

GUIDE

Grammar and Basic Usage

38, 58*, 97, 111, 120, 144*, 148, 267*, 269, 279, 356, 378, 424.

Handbook/Reference

29, 36*, 40, 45, 51*, 53, 54*, 88, 91, 112, 116, 118, 119, 123, 183, 196, 198, 210, 226*, 240, 262, 273, 278*, 294, 295, 300*, 302, 303, 304, 310, 318, 353, 379, 409, 427.

Workbook

7, 32*, 43, 87, 129, 139, 154, 159, 161, 166, 167, 197, 199, 207, 239*, 290*, 309*, 319, 338, 385*, 392, 419*, 426, 428.

Programmed

49*, 50, 70*, 151*, 152*, 195, 203, 277, 328, 443.

Fundamental Composition

24(P), 25, 26, 31*(W), 39*(P), 60*, 65*, 66*, 67, 74, 84*, 87(W), 108*, 113, 115*, 131, 152(P), 159(W), 161(W), 169*(W), 172(W), 173, 176*, 194*, 198, 205, 214, 224, 225(W), 239*(W), 250*, 279*, 293, 294, 296, 297, 299, 316, 321, 323, 332*, 334, 347, 354, 355, 357*, 360(W), 376, 382(W), 390, 396, 398, 404*, 413*, 419*, 420*(W), 421*, 422, 423, 428(W), 431, 436*.

Standard Composition

2*, 4*, 5, 12, 16, 18, 23, 19(W), 37, 43(W), 45, 47(W), 52, 53, 57, 67, 68, 74(W), 82*, 85, 86, 87(W), 92, 94*, 97, 98, 101, 104, 106,107, 117, 119, 133, 137, 138, 140, 143, 146,

13

148, 150, 163, 164, 165, 168*, 169, 170, 171, 172, 179, 183, 184, 185, 187, 189, 190, 191, 192, 200, 204, 212, 214, 229, 230, 231, 233*, 235, 242, 253, 254, 257, 259, 263, 264, 268, 274, 280, 281, 282, 283, 291*, 296, 297, 299, 302, 303, 304, 306*, 314, 316, 318, 319, 320*, 321, 325, 326*, 329*, 332*, 333, 337, 339, 345, 346, 348, 352, 354, 366, 367, 369, 373, 375, 380*, 382(W), 383, 384, 386, 396, 399*, 405, 409, 411, 412, 418, 420*(W), 421*, 422, 423, 425*, 426, 231, 433, 435, 438*(W).

Advanced Composition/Rhetoric

1, 8, 9, 11, 13*, 15, 16, 17, 20, 27, 28, 30, 33, 34, 35, 41, 42, 44, 56, 61, 62, 71, 79, 86, 89, 90, 92, 93, 95, 99, 102, 103, 105, 106, 110, 126, 128, 130, 136, 141, 142, 145, 153, 158, 164, 170, 174, 180, 189, 190, 191, 192, 201, 202, 204, 215, 217, 222, 228, 236, 241, 242, 245, 246, 253, 254, 256, 260, 271, 284, 286, 292, 308, 313, 317*, 324, 335, 336, 337, 341, 342, 343, 344, 351, 361, 362, 370, 371, 372, 374, 388, 393, 395, 407, 408, 411, 414, 429, 430, 432, 440, 442.

Writing About Literature

3, 8, 22, 59, 80, 81, 96, 101, 104, 141, 147, 211, 272, 294, 322, 327, 394.

Readers/Source Books

14, 63, 69, 72, 75, 76, 109, 122, 125, 127, 132, 134, 135, 149, 155, 161, 162, 169, 186, 188, 193*, 206, 209, 213, 216, 219, 220, 223, 227, 232, 234, 238, 244, 248*, 249, 251, 252*, 255,

258, 261, 265, 275*, 285, 288, 289*, 311, 315, 340*, 349, 363, 364, 365*, 377, 387, 389*, 391, 397, 402, 403, 410, 417, 434, 437, 441.

Language/Style

6, 73, 76, 93, 114, 121, 122, 177, 182, 266, 287, 350, 359, 377, 386, 400, 442.

Technical Writing

10, 21, 48, 55, 64, 77, 78, 83, 100, 124, 156, 157, 175, 178, 208, 218, 237, 243, 270, 276, 298, 307, 312, 331, 358, 368, 381, 401, 406, 415, 416, 439.

Miscellaneous

221, 247, 301, 305.

BIBLIOGRAPHY

1   Adams, Maurianne. *Autobiography*. Indianapolis: Bobbs-Merrill, 1968. 64 pp. $1.50 (P)

    This book is part of *The Bobbs-Merrill Series in Composition and Rhetoric*. See listing under Johnson, Falk S. for the complete annotation.

2   Adams, Royce W. *TRRPWR: Think, Read, React, Plan, Write, Rewrite*. New York: Holt, Rinehart and Winston, 1975. 316 pp. NPA (P)

    This workbook provides explanations followed by exercises. The text consists of thirteen units, each of which presents a topic for analysis: Education, Marriage, Alcoholism, and Television, for example. Each of these thirteen larger units is divided into six parts. Part one asks the student to give his opinions about specific points which the essay (part two) covers. Part three is a series of questions dealing with the content and vocabulary of the essay. Part four gives instruction in planning the essay--from selecting topics to the essay as a whole. Parts five and six discuss the actual writing. The text is a book on basic composition which begins with prewriting activities and moves toward more complex and sophisticated questions. Planning, topic sentences, introductory paragraphs, transition, agreement, parallelism, and logic, among other topics, are specifically discussed. The concept of attacking reading comprehension, vocabulary, logic, and writing skills at the same time is clearly presented. This text requires active participation in the learning process and allows the student to think on his own and give his own opinions. The text is aimed at basic composition courses from high school to college. For those students with problems in basic grammar a handbook should, perhaps, be used as a companion text.

3   Allen, Eliot D. and Ethel B. Colbrunn. *A Short Guide to Writing a Critical Review*. rev. ed. Deland, Fla.: Everett/Edwards, 1975. 32 pp. NPA (P)

    This text is designed primarily as a reference work for students although it could be used more formally in class. The first third of the book consists of short explanations about the steps of writing a critical review (i.e., What Is a Critical Review?, Reading the Work, About the Author, Preparing the Outline, and Documentation). The second third gives suggestions for various types of review (The Novel, Other Non-Fiction Prose, and The Poem), and the final third gives sample outlines on various types of literature and a sample review. Students could expand the sample outlines into their own reviews and use the information for oral reviews also.

This text is a short reference work for composition courses based on writing about literature or literature courses with papers.

4   Allen, Eliot D. and Ethel B. Colbrunn. *The Student Writer's Guide*. rev. ed. Deland, Fla.: Everett/ Edwards, 1970. 172 pp. $3.50 (P)

The authors state that this text "is intended to be used as a textbook in composition classes and as a refer- ence book for the individual student." The book is divided into two main sections; the first is on the whole paper (i.e., Writing Themes, Writing Research Papers, Writing Critical Reviews). The second covers the parts of a paper (paragraphs, sentences, usage, punctuation, mechanics, and manuscript form). There are groups of exercises with tear-out pages at the end of the text for each of the sections. The book includes examples of the different types of paragraphs, an index at the end, and a list of editing marks which refer the student to page numbers in the text. A reference book for classes in which composition is taught in conjunction with litera- ture, the revised edition conforms in manuscript form to the 2nd ed. of *The MLA Style Sheet*.

5   Allen, H. G. *Fundamentals of English: Reading, Writing, Grammar*. Dubuque, Iowa: Wm. C. Brown, 1970. 273 pp. $4.50 (P)

This text is designed to be "a complete course in beginning college English." The first and last sections in the text are readings, stories by John Steinbeck, A. J. Cronin, H. Fredricka Allen, and Paula Frederickson. Following the first set of readings are tests; follow- ing the last set are examples of seven different types of writing--a character sketch, a personal narrative, a humorous satire, a humorous story from a true account, an example of gobbledygook, a journalistic piece, and an editorial--designed to produce either discussion or writing ideas.   The second section is on writing a paper, including units on sentence development and punctuation and a unit on the complete paper; exercises and discussion topics follow each part. The third section covers grammar and mechanics with exercises also following each unit. Appendices include a checklist for mechanics, a spelling section, a chart for punctuation, and a chart for the pronoun. The author suggests that the text can be used selectively.

6   Allen, Harold B., Enola Borgh, and Verna L. Newsome, eds. *Focusing on Language: A Reader*. New York: Thomas Y. Crowell, 1975. 284 pp. NPA (P)

Not a conventional composition or rhetoric text, this book is a source of information on the English language-- its sources, development, structure, dialectic variations, and usage. The editors suggest that the book may be used by itself or as a supplement but urge that its contents be discussed in the presented order. Each of the eight chapters deals with a principle of language. Chapter one offers four essays on the nature of language, including a passage from Helen Keller's autobiography, descriptions of language by Wallace L. Chafe and William G. Moulton, and George Orwell's "The Principles of Newspeak." Chapter two has essays by L. M. Meyers and Harold R. Hungerford on the development and change of language while chapter three presents three essays on the alphabet and spelling. Chapters four and five deal with grammar, grammars, and usage, including essays by Kenneth Wilson, Kellogg Hunt, and Bergen Evens. Chapter six examines American dialects (Jean Malmstrom) and the Southern dialect (Cleanth Brooks). Chapter seven offers three essays on words and diction- aries, including a dicussion of sexism in the English language. The final chapter consists of essays on the contemporary use of the language. There are twenty-five essays in all, and each is followed by lists of questions for study and discussion and suggested activities. The editors point out that the exercises are both cumulative and interlocking. This book is designed for advanced classes, either in linguistics or rhetoric, although the exercises are clearly worded and supply fundamental instruction on each subject.

7   Allen, Robert, Rita Pompian, and Doris Allen. *Working Sentences*. New York: Thomas Y. Crowell, 1975. 165 pp. NPA (P)

The purpose of the text, as the authors state in their preface, is "to provide the student with experience in writing sentences that exhibit the features of edited English," that is, polished prose. It is based on "sector analysis," a method by which the sentence is viewed as consisting of a sequence of positions (sectors) which can be filled by various constructions, for example, phrases and clauses. Each construction has its own sequence of positions for other constructions functioning on a lower level of structure. Hence, the focus is on syntactic relationships, not on individual words. The grammar in the text attempts to make the student aware of these constructions and the ways they are put together. The first five units review the major constructions of written English and their functions: X-Words (am, do, can, will), More About Subjects, Agreement, Writing about Past Time, and Sentence Trunks. The following ten concern "sentence-combining techniques of high utility in edited English": Shifters (parts of sentences that can come before or after the sentence trunk), Compounds, Included Clauses, One-and-a-half Sentence, Making Connections (linking sentences and/or ideas), Noun Clusters, Expanding Noun Clusters, Other Nominals (clauses and predicates), Time Relationship in Clauses, and Adding Something Extra (appositives, inserts, and so on). Each unit has basic instruction, usually illustrated with some form of diagram, "practices" to develop the skill on tear-out pages, and a series of "tasks" applying the principles. The authors also include several lists of common words (X-Words, Includers) to facilitate learning. This text would, perhaps, be best suited for basic skills courses with emphasis on sentence development rather than the whole essay.

8 Altick, Richard D. *Preface to Critical Reading*. 4th ed. New York: Holt, Rinehart and Winston, 1965. 326 pp. $7.00 (H) $6.00 (P)

This text is designed to teach the student how to read critically. The fourth edition has increased the emphasis on writing: "The intimate relationship between critical reading and effective writing, hitherto left more or less implicit, is now specifically defined and analyzed." The text is divided into five chapters: Denotation and Connotation, Diction, Patterns of Clear Thinking, Sentences and Paragraphs, and Tone. The chapters consist of explanations of principles with examples and exercises in which the student uses these principles. Selections for the students to read as examples are varied in style and content, and the exercises often have the student analyze passages provided. Metaphor, symbol, allusion, irony, sentimentality, and restraint are discussed in the chapter on tone, and examples and exercises are provided. This text would be appropriate in an advanced English college-level course in which the instructor wished to teach interpretation of literature and critical reading of all varieties as well as good writing. It does not specifically teach principles of writing such as sentence structure or outlining.

9 Amend, Victor E. and Leo T. Hendrick, eds. *Readings from Left to Right*. New York: The Free Press, 1970. 497 pp. $5.25 (P)

This reader presents essays in groups of three, offering opinions on the left, right, and middle ground of certain issues. The authors state, "It is the aim of the following groups of readings to present, as it were, three minds in collision" as a means of stimulating discussion. The groups of essays are entitled Civil Rights, The Individual in Modern Society, Civil Disobedience, The Revolt of Youth, Equality, Religion, Technology, Poverty, and so forth. A table of contents of rhetorical

topics is also included for reference. Rhetorical elements illustrated are definition, description, narration,
comparison and contrast, cause and effect, and argument.
Each essay is followed by a short group of exercises on
the rhetorical devices used in the essay, a group of
discussion questions, and suggested topics for writing.
The book is best suited, perhaps, for the composition
student who is grounded in basic theme writing and
mechanics.

10 Andrews, Clarence A. *Technical and Business Writing.*
    Boston: Houghton Mifflin, 1975. 243 pp. $9.50 (H)

    Although this basic text in technical writing does not
contain sections on mechanics and grammar, it presupposes
a knowledge of these subjects in the material and language
used. The author recommends that the *Practical English
Handbook* by Floyd C. Watkins be used in conjunction with
this text unless the student is well grounded in basic
English. Following an introductory chapter on definition
of "Technical Software" and language, the author includes
paragraphs on The Technical Sentence Pattern and Patterns
in the Technical Paragraph. With these basics discussed,
"The book proceeds from the simplest pattern--the face-
to-face or telephone report--to the most complex--the
feasibility report or the magazine article." Chapter
four, Person to Person: The Letter, covers most types
of letters as well as telephone calls, memoranda, and the
art of diction. Each chapter is broken up into smaller
packets of information followed by its own set of study
questions. Some of the study questions call for written
assignments while many can be used for class discussion.
Chapter five, Retrieving Technical Information, covers
use of the library in all of its aspects and includes a
bibliography of guides, handbooks, and manuals as well as
limited special information on sampling and polling the
general public and interviewing the individual. Chapter
six--Standards, Properties, and Specifications--defines
these terms as they apply to technical information,
teaches the student to write a production parts list or
bill of materials, and discusses the exploded drawing and
schematic drawing as they might be used in such an assignment. Chapter seven, Defining Technical Words and
Phrases, includes the logical or formal definition,
partial definitions, the operational or process definition, the extended definition, and also deals with when
to use a technical definition. Chapter eight teaches
description by a method the author calls the "information
block" which consists of predicting what you are going
to write, developing your prediction point by point, and
summarizing what you have written. Chapter nine, "How-
to-do-it" Information, deals with giving directions or
instructions. Chapter ten, The Routine Technical Report,

gives an introduction to report writing in general and to such specific reports as the telephone report, reports of meetings, trip reports, and reports to groups. Chapter eleven presents examples and types of the informal report; and chapter twelve covers such formal reports as the progress report, the feasibility report, the proposal report, and the report based on literature search. Chapter thirteen, Writing for Magazines, is quite brief, consisting mainly of examples. The final chapter deals with technical illustrations, their function, placing, and explanation. A large number of examples of such graphics are given here and throughout the body of the book. The appendices included in the book consist of examples of student-written instructions and various types of reports.

11 Andrews, Clarence A. *Writing: Growth Through Structure.* Beverly Hills, Ca.: Glencoe Press, 1972. 340 pp. $5.95 (P)

   This text consists of expository chapters, beginning with one on the question of voice and going on to material on collecting information, discussions of the language, order and knowledge, motion, patterns of persuasion, definition, description and narration, evaluating, judging and directing, organization of language, structure, and finally some suggestions of things to write about. There is an appendix containing essays by T. H. Huxley, Randolph Bourne, E. B. White, and Ring Lardner. The text discusses general principles and has short examples, questions, and exercises scattered throughout the material. There are many class projects and assignments for writing throughout the chapters. Lists of further readings conclude some chapters. This text is basically a rhetoric; it contains no sections on grammar, punctuation, or mechanics. It is suitable for freshman or advanced college composition.

12 Arapoff, Nancy. *Writing Through Understanding.* New York: Holt, Rinehart and Winston, 1970. 230 pp. $5.25 (H)

   The author states in the preface that "This text is based on the following precepts: that one learns language via a discovery process; that one's use of language is a demonstration of the discoveries he has made about the written language which differentiate it from the spoken one." This text is set up to help the student make and understand new discoveries about his language and then to make the student use these new discoveries. The text is divided into three main sections: Discovering Differences between Speaking and Writing (Direct Address, Indirect Address, and Factual Account), Discovering Meaning Relationships in Writing (Cause-Effect Relationships,

Clarifying Relationships, and Comparing Relationships),
and Discovering How to Summarize. Each section begins
with a short (about two pages) introduction of the concepts which the student will discover in that section.
Each part within the sections also begins with a short
introduction of the concept to be discovered through
exercises. There are two selections for the student,
then a section to read, and a group of questions which
cause him to discover the particular principle. The
questions are sometimes lengthy. The student then goes
on to a section in which he writes--either rewriting
sections provided or writing selections of his own. The
chapter ends with a section in which the student has
further practice on the principles he has learned. This
text could be used in a composition course in which the
instructor deals with students who are having difficulty
making the transition between spoken and written language
since the exercises deal heavily with this transition.

13   Archer, Jerome W. and Joseph Schwartz. *Exposition*. 2nd
       ed. New York: McGraw-Hill, 1971. 346 pp. $4.50
       (P)

       This rhetoric/reader, for the most part, uses contemp-
orary essays as examples of different kinds of rhetorical
approaches. Chapters include essays illustrating such
principles as definition, example, comparison and contrast, process analysis, classification and division,
cause and effect, and a combination of methods. Although
two essays in each section have no study questions--"for
the benefit of the instructor who prefers at times to
prepare his own questions"--all other essays contain
1) questions contained in footnotes and 2) questions at
the end of each selection, including vocabulary exercises.
This text could be used in advanced high school composition classes as well as college classes in standard, and,
perhaps, advanced writing courses, depending on what
selections are chosen to be studied and to what depth the
discussions are considered.

14   Arny, Mary Travis and Christopher R. Reaske. *Ecology: A*
       Writer's Handbook with a Full Glossary of Ecological
       Terms. New York: Random House, 172. 112 pp. $2.50
       (P)

       This text could be used in writing classes at the
beginning college level. The authors state in the preface that "This book is designed to aid the college student writing about ecology. We have tried to make the
book about good writing in general, as well as about some
of the special considerations in writing about ecology."
The text is divided into seven sections: Writing for
Your Life (introducing the importance of writing about

ecology); Selecting the Topic; Restricting and Developing the Topic; Technique, Style, and Persuasion; A Glossary of Ecological Terms; Essential Usage (a list of frequently misused words and how to use them); and Mechanics. There are black and white photographs scattered throughout the text. Although there are suggestions for student projects in the text, this is basically a book of explanations and examples; there are no exercises or theme topics included.

15 Bain, Robert and Dennis G. Donovan, eds. *The Writer and the Worlds of Words.* Englewood Cliffs, N.J.: Prentice-Hall, 1975. 369 pp. NPA (P)

The editors emphasize the practical orientation of the text and call the writers whose works are included "wordworkers": journalists, poets, advertising writers, and linguists. The text addresses the problem of diverse ways of seeing and saying by examining each writer's concern for the way "that language shapes meaning and attitudes, conveys our profundities and perversities, reveals or conceals our feelings and ideas." The readings are arranged in six sections; the first, The Worlds of Work, examines how naming things affects the way we see the world and how our ways of seeing affect our language. Authors represented in this section include Lewis Carroll, Emily Dickenson, S. I. Hayakawa, and Shakespeare. Section two treats the writer as "See-er and Thinker," examining the difference between looking at experience and seeing it and the difference between perceiving something and understanding it. Authors represented include Ezra Pound, Virginia Woolf, Robert Frost, and Marchette Chute. Section three discusses the writer's roles as worldmaker and word-maker with readings that stress the writer as the shaper of words, ideas, and feelings and poses questions about audience and style. Section four includes selections that place emphasis on media language and its deceptive power. Section five studies how our words, once we leave them, can be perceived in many different ways. The final section centers on man's capacity to convey his feelings and ideas. All selections are followed by a series of exercises on words and sentences, ideas and implications, rhetorical strategies, and suggestions for writing. An alternate table of contents lists the readings by rhetorical type.

16 Baker, Sheridan. *The Complete Stylist.* 2nd ed. New York: Thomas Y. Crowell, 1972. 397 pp. $6.95 (H) $5.95 (P)

This text is designed to be a "comprehensive book that would serve as both basic text and handbook throughout the college years." Chapter one introduces the student

to the general area of rhetoric and is followed by a
chapter on finding a thesis. Chapter three discusses how
to arrange the middle part of the essay--the orders of
space, time, cause and effect, comparison and contrast,
and inductive and deductive forms, for example. Chapter
five analyzes outlines; six and seven discuss paragraphing. Eight and nine cover basic sentence structure; ten
deals with punctuation while eleven discusses words.
Chapter twelve introduces essays: the autobiographical,
the terrible, the ironic, and the critical review.
Thirteen deals with logic; fourteen with the research
paper. Appendices include a grammar, a glossary of usage,
and rhetorical devices. Each chapter concludes with
brief exercises. For fuller exercise work Sheridan Baker
and Dwight Stevenson's *Problems in Exposition: Supplementary Exercises for The Complete Stylist and The Practical Stylist* (New York: Thomas Y. Crowell, 1972), 154
pp., is available (see separate entry). This text is
perhaps too long for use on a quarter system unless one
is dealing with a two or three quarter sequence. However,
it seems easily adaptable to semesters as it allows for
selectivity of assignments according to the instructor's
purposes.

17 Baker, Sheridan. *The Essayist*. 2nd ed. New York:
     Thomas Y. Crowell, 1972. 370 pp. $3.95 (H)

     This rhetoric/reader, as the author states in his
preface, "aims for the one practical point: how to write
an essay. . . . Each of the twelve sections takes up a
rhetorical problem and holds to it until the end, for-
going for the moment other targets of opportunity." Thus,
each section contains several essays that illustrate the
general section topic, and each section concludes with
suggestions for writing which directly relate to the
preceding readings. The sections are entitled Thesis:
The Argumentative Edge; Structure: Middle Tactics;
Middle Tactics: The Vector of Interest; Paragraphs:
Beginning, Middle, End; Sentences: A Note Book of Styles;
Sentences in Exposition; Words: The Figurative Dimension;
The Autobiographical Essay; The Horrors of Exposition:
Too Much or Too Little; The Ironic Essay; The Critical
Review; and Evidence and the Author's Voice. The authors
range from George Bernard Shaw to Charles E. Wyzanski,
Jr. to Norman Mailer.

18 Baker, Sheridan. *The Practical Stylist*. 3rd ed. New
     York: Thomas Y. Crowell, 1973. 182 pp. $3.95 (P)

     This text assumes that the basic problems in writing
come down to two general areas: form and style. Form,
the author states, is really spatial style; and "Since,
in general, writing well is writing in style, I have found

it practical to teach writing almost as a tactile act, in which the student learns how to shape his material and bring out the grain to best advantage." This text assumes that the argumentative paper is one of the easiest to teach and learn, so it begins with this type of essay in the first chapter. Following chapters are entitled Structure, Paragraphs, Evidence, Writing Good Sentences, Correcting Bad Sentences (this chapter is about style, not grammar), Punctuation, Words, The Research Paper, and three appendices: A Writer's Grammar, with exercises for the student; Spelling and Capitalization; and A Glossary of Usage. The chapters are short and designed so that the student can read them in one sitting. The exercises at the end of every chapter include writing sentences, paragraphs, and short themes, practicing the principles taught in the chapter. A sample research paper is provided in the final chapter along with a sample outline, notecards, footnotes, and bibliography. There is a list of editing symbols for common errors on the back cover with brief explanations and references to page numbers in the book. Examples in the text are usually a sentence long; there are no complete essays used as examples of techniques. The author states that this text is primarily for freshman English and is a shorter version of the author's *The Complete Stylist*.

19 Baker, Sheridan and Dwight Stevenson. *Problems in Exposition: Supplementary Exercises for The Complete Stylist and The Practical Stylist*. New York: Thomas Y. Crowell, 1972. 154 pp. $2.95 (P)

This workbook is designed to accompany *The Practical Stylist* and *The Complete Stylist* (Baker) and provide further exercises for the student using these texts. The practices in this workbook follow both texts chapter by chapter. There are twelve chapters in the text: The Written Voice; Stating the Thesis; Basic Structure: Middle Tactics; The Middle: Other Arrangements; Outlines; Paragraphs; More about Middle Paragraphs; Sentences; Punctuation; Words; The Research Paper; and Straight and Crooked Thinking. The chapters each begin with short introductions concerning the material dealt with. The exercises involve both the student's rewriting sentences and paragraphs provided and writing his own sentences, paragraphs, and themes on suggested topics. The exercises are all on tear-out pages, and there is an answer key available. The exercises are almost all subjective and involve the students in writing and rewriting according to their own inclinations, following instructions in the workbook.

20 Banks, P. M. and V. M. Burke. *Black Americans: Images in Conflict*. Indianapolis: Bobbs-Merrill, 1970. 64 pp. $1.00 (P)

This book is part of *The Bobbs-Merrill Series in Composition and Rhetoric*. See listing under Johnson, Falk S. for the complete annotation.

21 Barnett, Marva T. *Elements of Technical Writing*. Albany, N.Y.: Delmar, 1974. 232 pp. NPA (P)

This text was written specifically for two-year colleges and vocational schools, but it can be used in the last two years of high school "for students preparing to enter industry as tradesmen and technicians. It can also be used in correspondence-study programs or as a self-teaching textbook." The preface holds that the material is "presented in the same simple, direct style of writing that it recommends. Most of the sentences are short, the words are carefully chosen, and the style is primarily objective." Examples given in the Suggested Activities are from electromechanical fields. The text comes with an instructor's guide which includes concepts and guidelines for evaluating written and oral communication. Section one, Guidelines to Technical Writing, contains an introduction to technical writing and a review of its definition, basic principles, and importance. This section also includes a review of grammar and mechanics. Section two, Planning the Report, contains units on definition and classification in reports, uses and kinds of graphic aids, as well as how to integrate graphic aids with the text. Units on the physical format of material and writing an outline are also included. Section three deals with the report itself, each unit covering a different type of report. Included are the descriptive report, the process report, the analytical report, the troubleshooting report, the examination report, interoffice reports, and oral reports. Section four, Report Supplements, covers material included in addition to the informative body of the report. In this category the text treats letters of transmittal, tables of contents, tables of tables, and abstracts as well as research data and methods of obtaining such data. Section five, Writing Letters, begins with a look at the general objectives of letter writing and what can be conveyed by the writer's attitude, language, and format. This section goes on to treat The Positive Letter, The Persuasive Letter, The Negative Letter, The Data Sheet, and the Letter of Application. All sections contain some examples and a brief selection of suggested activities.

22 Barnet, Sylvan. *A Short Guide to Writing about Literature*. 3rd ed. Boston: Little, Brown, 1975. 244 pp. NPA (P)

This text has writing about literature as its primary aim, and the author assumes a knowledge of fundamental usage. Chapter one gives an overview of critical writing and discusses three approaches: explication, analysis, and review. Also included in this chapter are discussions of organization and topic selection. Chapter two discusses style and format, dealing with words--denotation, connotation, concreteness, for example--effective sentences, paragraphing, manuscript form, and use of quotations. Chapter three discusses plot, character, symbolism, point-of-view, and theme in relation to fiction. Chapter four centers on writing themes about drama, including types of plays, theme, plot, conventions, and characterization. Chapter five discusses poetry: the language of poetry, explication, imagery, structure, and rhythm and structure. Chapter six discusses writing about film. Appendices cover research papers and essay exams. The text includes examples of essays dealing with the particular topics. Each of the last four chapters includes a student essay and two professional essays. This book would be useful in courses on all levels--high school through college--which require students to write essays about literature.

23 Barnet, Sylvan and Marcia Stubbs. *Barnet and Stubb's Practical Guide to Writing*. Boston: Little, Brown, 1975. 319 pp. $4.95 (P)

This college-level composition text would be most appropriate for freshmen. Although the chapters are related, the authors have attempted to make them self-contained enough so the teacher of composition can take them in any order, or he can assign specific chapters to students who need them. The text is divided into four major units: Writing, Revising, Editing, and Acquiring Style and Fluency. In the unit Writing there are chapters on finding a topic, analysis, outlining, paragraphs, exposition and definition, argument and persuasion, and the research paper. Under Revising there are chapters on conciseness, clarity, and emphasis. Editing has chapters on manuscript form, punctuation, and usage. Under the unit Acquiring Style and Fluency there are chapters entitled Defining Style and Acquiring Fluency. There is a subject index at the end and a list of commonly used editing marks on the inside of the back cover. Chapters consist of explanations and discussions of principles in composition, examples from literature, and exercises. The exercises are sometimes in the form of questions which could be used for class discussion or appear as suggested writing assignments. There are no exercises in the chapters on mechanics; the exercises in this book are designed to get the students to think about writing and to write. A teacher's manual which offers advice to new instructors on teaching writing as well as suggested answers to exercises and suggestions on how to spend class time on each chapter is provided. Examples scattered throughout this text include poems, excerpts from stories, journalism, novels, and other literary works. Examples from student journals are given at the end.

24 Barrett, Blair, programmer. *Writing Skills I: A Program for Self-instruction.* New York: McGraw-Hill, 1970. 109 pp. $3.25 (P)

This programmed text is one of three parts in a series devoted to writing skills instruction and part of a larger system of instructional materials--*The McGraw-Hill Basic Skills System: Tools for Learning Success.* It is "aimed at college-bound high school students, and junior college and college students who need to improve those skills necessary for academic success." The topics covered in this volume are sentences and clauses, verb tenses, singular and plural, subject and object pronouns, adjectives and adverbs, capitalization, and punctuation.

25 Barrett, Blair. *Writing Skills II: A Program for Self-instruction.* New York: McGraw-Hill, 1970. 114 pp. $3.25 (P)

The second in this series (see preceding annotation), this programmed text includes chapters on clause and phrase placement, parallelism, perfect verb tenses, adjective and adverb comparison, possession, and punctuation.

26 Barrett, Blair. *Paragraph Patterns: A Program for Self-instruction.* New York: McGraw-Hill, 1970. 106 pp. $3.25 (P)

The third in this series, this programmed text includes chapters entitled How a Paragraph Forms, Topic Sentences, Development Sentences, Concluding Sentences, Paragraph Series, and Rewriting and Editing.

27 Beardsley, Monroe C. *Literature and Aesthetics.* Indianapolis·: Bobbs-Merrill, 1968. 63 pp. $1.00 (P)

This book is part of *The Bobbs-Merrill Series in Composition and Rhetoric.* See listing under Johnson, Falk S. for the complete annotation.

28 Beardsley, Monroe C. *Modes of Argument.* Indianapolis: Bobbs-Merrill, 1967. 64 pp. $1.00 (P)

This book is part of *The Bobbs-Merrill Series in Composition and Rhetoric.* See listing under Johnson, Falk S. for the complete annotation.

29 Bell, James K. and Adrian A. Cohn. *Handbook of Grammar, Style, and Usage*. Beverly Hills, Ca.: Glencoe, 1972. 125 pp. $2.50 (P)

This text is a brief handbook with items arranged in alphabetical order; no table of contents is provided. The authors state that the text "aims first of all at practicality and succinctness in presenting what American students need to know about effective writing." As a reference book, this text provides quick, easy-to-find explanations of questions concerning grammar, punctuation, and usage. However, because of the concise approach, problems of organization, thesis statement, and paragraphing are only generally treated. This text would, perhaps, be most useful in standard and advanced composition classes in which the student needs a quick reference text.

30 Bell, James K. and Adrian A. Cohn. *Rhetoric in a Modern Mode with Selected Readings*. 2nd ed. Beverly Hills, Ca.: Glencoe, 1972. 424 pp. $6.95 (P)

The second edition of this college-level rhetoric is considerably revised from the first. The first half of the text has new examples and revised exercises and is divided into chapters entitled Unity in the Paragraph, Development in the Paragraph, Organization in the Paragraph, Continuity in the Paragraph, From Paragraph to Essay, and The Art of the Essay, which contains three sample essays. Each chapter includes brief explanations and examples and exercises. The student learns by a step-by-step process which involves repeated practice. The readings, which take up over half of the book, are by Marya Mannes, George Orwell, Herbert Gold, Gloria Steinem, Norman Cousins, Richard Wright, and Ashley Montagu, among others. The last eight readings are all in a more classical mode; some authors represented here are Montaigne, Bacon, and Swift. After each selection appear "reading helps" such as vocabulary lists, questions on rhetorical devices, questions about content, and questions on ideas and implications in the work. Since the text moves from paragraphs to essays, it teaches using the good paragraph as a model for the essay.

31 Bellafiore, Joseph. *English Language Arts Workbook*. New York: Amsco School Publications, 1971. 418 pp. $2.10 (P)

This fundamentally oriented workbook addresses itself to three phases of language: the written word, the oral word, and reading. Unit one has sections on grammar, usage, sentence structure, spelling, and mechanics. Unit two deals with building vocabulary and gives particular attention to homonyms, synonyms, antonyms, prefixes, suffixes, and stems. Unit three, Training in Written Expression Skills, has sections on practical writing (reports, notes, business letters) and creative composition (stories, poetry, newspaper writing, reviews, personal narratives). Unit five treats developing speaking abilities and contains sections on public speaking, interviews, and role-playing. A reading comprehension unit follows which concentrates on types of reading, dictionary use, and library skills. A brief unit on understanding and enjoying literature, focusing on techniques in genres, comes next, and a reading list follows. The final unit studies other types of communication: mass media, propaganda, films, television, radio, magazines, and comic books. Explanations of principles and discussions of topics are brief. Exercises of all types are included.

32 Bellafiore, Joseph. *Essentials of English Workbook.* New York: Amsco School Publications, 1971. 247 pp. $1.70 (P)

This workbook, according to the author, is designed to motivate the student to improve "expressional ability by pointing out the acceptable form and the Wrong Way" to say things. The text is divided into six units. The first deals with sentence structure and contains subsections on putting together parts of sentences, identifying kinds of sentences, and avoiding fragments and run-ons. Unit two covers the parts of speech; unit three, punctuation and capitalization. Units four and five deal with spelling and vocabulary, respectively. The final unit is a series of achievement tests. Each unit defines and discusses the various rhetorical elements, points of grammar, and so on, and diagrams are often used for illustration. The primary parts of each unit are a series of exercises. Space is provided for answers, and the pages can be torn out. Each unit has review tests at its end. The approach is basic; the text is primarily for high school and remedial college English classes.

33 Bellamy, Joe David, ed. *Apocalypse: Dominant Contemporary Forms.* Philadelphia: J. B. Lippincott, 1972. 415 pp. $5.50 (P)

In the preface the editor states that this reader "is a collection of diverse prose forms in contemporary idioms, chosen for their relevance to crucial (apocalyptical) contemporary issues and (potentially apocalyptical) phenomena, and chosen also for their relation to age-old human dilemmas, situations, miseries, celebrations." There are two tables of content, the first according to content and the second according to form. The major units in the first table are entitled Cataclysm in America, Man's Origins and Aggression, Nuclear Catastrophe,

Ecological Catastrophe, The Electronic Revolution, the
Biological Revolution, The Sexual Revolution, Revolution
in Education, Revolution in Religion, Dominant Art Forms,
People, and The Future. The forms listed in the second
contents are entitled The Diary, The Review, The Interview, The Modern Informative Magazine Essay, The Modern
Persuasive Book-length Essay (excerpts), Non-Fiction
Fiction, Fiction, The Critical Essay, and Combinations.
Each section begins with an introduction which deals with
the content of the various forms of writing in that
section. Each selection also has a short biographical
sketch about the author. There are discussion questions
and suggestions for writing after each selection, but
they are not specifically theme topics. Rather, they are
questions designed to make the student think about what
he has read. Selections are from a variety of authors
using a variety of forms. Some authors included are
Norman Mailer, Tom Wolfe, Marshall McLuhan, John Hold,
Vance Packard, and Kurt Vonnegut, Jr.

34 Bergmann, Fred L. *Essays*. 2nd ed. Dubuque, Iowa: Wm.
       C. Brown, 1975. 338 pp. NPA (P)

       In the preface the author states, "In the revision of
this collection, originally entitled *Essays: Method,
Content, Conscience,* more than half of the essays are new
to this edition, and half of those first appeared in the
'70's." The text is divided into two main parts, with
an introduction before the first part which discusses
what an essay is and includes a short discussion of the
process of essay writing. The first part is on the forms
and methods of the essay and includes a section entitled
Forms of Discourse (narration, explanation, description,
and argument and persuasion) and a section on Methods of
Exposition (example, definition, comparison and contrast,
cause and effect, and classification and analysis). The
second part has examples of various types of essays:
biography, the review, the literary essay, satire, humor,
and the familiar essay. Each group of essays begins with
a short introduction which discusses the particular form.
After each essay there are a list of questions and problems which could be discussed in class, suggestions for
writing which usually involve writing on a topic related
to the essay just read, and a list of suggested further
readings. There is an index at the back which lists
authors, titles, and types of essay, with page references.
Authors included in this collection are George Orwell,
Grace Brown, Dylan Thomas, Gloria Steinem, George
Santayana, Samuel L. Clemens, and others.

35 Berke, Jacqueline. *Twenty Questions for the Writer: A
       Rhetoric with Readings*. New York: Harcourt, Brace,
       Jovanovich, 1972. 528 pp. $6.20 (P)

This reader is designed to be the complete and self-contained text in a college writing course; it includes readings, writing assignments, a style guide, and exercises. The order of the book is sequential, in order of increasing complexity. The author states that the text contains sufficient material to "be used simultaneously in two different sections of a course without duplicating either the readings or the writing assignments." The text draws its title from the first section, Writing a Short Paper, which employs the premise that all writing begins with questions, and the author uses these questions to develop twenty types of theoretical papers. Examples of chapters from this section are What Does X Mean? (definition), How Can X Be Described?, How Does X Compare to Y?, and so on. Each chapter has readings, exercises, and topics for writing. Section two, Writing a Long Paper: Research and Organization, includes material on four types of term papers: Extended Analysis, Description-Narration, Extended Characterization, and Extended Argument. The material about these types of papers consists mainly of examples and assignments. Section two also includes material on researching and organizing the paper. Section three, Principles of Style: A Guide, gives the student an additional hundred pages on language and words, writing a meaningful sentence, and developing the paragraph.

36 Bernstein, Theodore M. *Miss Thistlebottom's Hobgoblins: The Careful Writer's Guide to the Taboos, Bugbears and Outmoded Rules of English Usage*. New York: Farrar, Straus and Giroux, 1971. 260 pp. $7.95 (H)

The author states in his preface that "The purpose of this book is to lay to rest the superstitions that have been passed on from one generation to the next by teachers, by editors and by writers--prohibitions deriving from mere personal prejudice or from misguided pedantry or from a cold conservatism that would freeze the language if it could." The bulk of the text is an alphabetical listing of those words and expressions which often cause questions in terms of usage and explanations on how to use them properly. There are a number of appendices in which the author reproduces past attempts to fix the usage of the language, including William Cullen Bryant's *Index Expurgatorius*, the "Don't List" of the New York *Herald* under James Gordon Benett, and Ambrose Bierce's *Write It Right*. As a reference text this book could be used by any college-level writing class, perhaps even by high school classes.

37 Berry, Thomas Elliott. *The Craft of Writing*. New York: McGraw-Hill, 1974. 196 pp. $2.95 (P)

The author states that "Broadly speaking, the book aims to provide answers to the two all-important questions: What is effective writing? How can I acquire that kind of writing?" Part one, The Elements of Writing, contains chapters entitled Your Writing Style; Right Words for Emphasis; Writing Sentences; Rhetorical Devices; Humor, Mild Satire, and Parody; Undesirable Conditions in Expression; The Nature of the Paragraph; Attributes of the Paragraph; The Structure of the Paragraph. Part two, The Forms of Writing, contains chapters on description, narration, exposition, and argument. Part three, The Writing Process, has chapters entitled Formulating Your Thoughts, Planning Your Paper, From Rough Draft to Final Copy. An appendix, Rules for the Use of the Comma, is included. The author states that "This book is intended to serve as a guide for the person who seeks to improve his writing" and thus is not intended solely or exclusively for the student in a class. The approach of the text is similar to that of a handbook, and no exercises are included.

38   Berry, Thomas Elliott. *The Most Common Mistakes in English Usage*. New York: McGraw-Hill, 1971. 146 pp. $1.95 (P)

The author states two purposes for the text: "(1) to serve as an analysis of the errors most commonly made in spoken and written English and (2) to present clear explanations of how to correct these errors." There are eighteen sections to the book covering errors in usage (nouns, pronouns, case, verbs, adjectives and adverbs, predicate adjectives, modifiers, prepositions, conjunctions, comparisons, punctuation), redundancy, stylistic faults, vague wording, and miscellaneous errors. The index is cross-referenced. Each section consists of a list of errors with brief explanations. There are no exercises. The author suggests that the book be used as a text or a handbook.

39   Bigby, John and Russell Hill. *Options: A Program for English*. Boston: Houghton Mifflin, 1972. Two books of 100-150 pp. and eight pamphlets.

This program consists of a number of books and pamphlets which deal with different approaches to language. The authors state in the preface that "*Options* is a set of observations about how language works. . . .*Options* is a guide book for explorations." There are two books which could be used as material in a composition course: *Language Is a Way of Seeing* ($4.95), "a series of observations and questionings about language and how language connects people to their worlds and to each other," and *Language Is a Way of Hearing* ($4.50), six "artifacts" from our civilization which are "significant examples of the use of language in our time." *Language is a Way of Seeing* is set up as a programmed text which asks the student to answer questions about language. However, the authors say in the preface that this is not programmed in the sense that there is one "right" answer to each section; rather, there could be many right answers. There are chapters in this text on perception through words, language changing, dictionary use, decoding words, and how language affects perception. *Language Is a Way of Hearing* is a series of readings and photographs for the student to react to. These selections include poetry, essays, cartoons, songs, and stories, and authors represented include Lenny Bruce, Ralph Ellison, Walt Whitman, and Judy Collins, among others. The eight pamphlets entitled *Language Is a Way of Saying* require the student to read explanations and examples of a variety of types of writing and then to produce his own writing. Types covered are entitled the Interior Monolog, Autobiography, Memoir, Biography of an Event, Profile, Chronicle, and Words and Things (poetry). The basic audience is the college student, but the advanced high school student could also use this text.

40 Birk, Newman P. and Genevieve B. Birk. *A Handbook of Grammar, Rhetoric, Mechanics, and Usage.* Indianapolis: Odyssey, 1972. 148 pp. $2.75 (P)

In their introduction the authors state that "This handbook is essentially Part Three of Birk and Birk, *Understanding and Using English,* Fifth Edition. It is printed as a separate volume at the request of teachers who want their students to have a basic guide to conventions of grammar, rhetoric, mechanics, and usage, but who are reluctant to ask students to buy the longer combined rhetoric and handbook."

41 Birk, Newman P. and Genevieve B. Birk. *The Odyssey Reader: Ideas and Style.* Indianapolis: Odyssey, 1968. 905 pp. $6.50 (H)

This rhetoric/reader begins with a section entitled An Introduction to Rhetorical Analysis which discusses ways of ordering ideas and experience, clarity, coherence, audience, assumptions, tone, persona, style, and how to read for ideas and style. The text proper is divided into three main parts. Part one, Ways of Ordering Ideas and Experience, includes essays which exemplify the topics Thesis and Examples, Thesis and Reasons, Generalization and Qualification, Narration, Analysis, Contrast and Comparison, Cause and Effect, Question-to-Answer or Problem-to-Solution, and Definition. In this first part only one essay per topic is presented. The other two parts include several selections under each subsection.

Part two presents essays under the general heading Ideas
and Values, and subsections include Education and the
Inquiring Mind; The Quest for Values; Some Timeless
Philosophies; The Quest for Values: Some Later Views;
Human Nature and the Human Situation; Language; Literature and the Arts; Science and the Modern World; Men and
Events; and Current Problems and Attitudes. Part three,
the shortest section, is entitled Autobiography and
Personal Essays. Authors represented in this text range
from classical to contemporary writers. Each selection
is followed by a section entitled Comment and Questions.

42 Birk, Newman P. and Genevieve B. Birk. *The Odyssey
Reader: Ideas and Style.* shorter ed. Indianapolis:
Odyssey, 1969. 515 pp. $3.95 (P)

This text is a shorter version of *The Odyssey Reader*
and differs from the longer book in that there are fewer
essays, and part three of the full version has been
deleted.

43 Birk, Newman P. and Genevieve B. Birk. *Practice for
Understanding and Using English.* Indianapolis:
Odyssey, 1972. 162 pp. $1.95 (P)

This workbook was designed to accompany the authors'
Understanding and Using English, fifth edition, and
follows the general organization of the handbook section
of that text. Page references to that text are given at
the beginning of each exercise. However, the authors
suggest that the workbook may be used with any rhetoric
or handbook. Also, the book can be used independently or
as part of supervised work. There are eighty exercises;
most are objective tests, but some call for revision or
rewriting and are geared toward improving style. The
book's purpose is to supply a range of material which
will provide knowledge of syntax, conventions, and
rhetorical principles. There is no instruction; the text
is a series of tests subdivided into four major sections:
sentence elements and their relationships, style and
rhetoric, punctuation and mechanics, and dictionary use.

44 Birk, Newman P. and Genevieve B. Birk, eds. *Readings for
Understanding and Using English.* Indianapolis:
Odyssey, 1959. 433 pp. $2.75 (P)

This rhetoric/reader is designed for college students
taking composition courses, but it is primarily for students beyond the level of many freshman composition
classes. The text is divided into six sections, a
glossary of rhetorical terms, and an index. Each section
contains essays and excerpts from longer works that
illustrate the type of reading presented by the section
title. Sections are entitled Reading Informative Prose;

36

Reading Evaluations; Reading Persuasion; History and Biography: Information and Evaluation; Reading for Ideas and Values; and Simple Narrative, Autobiography, and Informal Essays. Pieces are by such authors as George Orwell, Carl Sandburg, Virginia Woolf, John Henry Newman, William Faulkner, and E. B. White. Further, there is included an Organization of the Readings by Theme which is broken down into seven sections: Human Nature and the Human Situation; Freedom of Thought and the Inquiring Mind; Education and Mental Enlargement; The Individual and Society; Language, Literature, and the Arts; Science, and Science and Religion; and Religion and Morality. After most of the entries appear Comment and Question sections which ask the student to respond to the essay he has just read.

45 Birk, Newman P. and Genevieve B. Birk. *Understanding and Using English*. 4th ed. Indianapolis: Odyssey, 1965. 560 pp. $6.50 (H)

There is a 5th edition (1972) which was not available for annotation. The price of the 1972 edition is $6.50 and there are two paperback supplementary workbooks which may be used with the 5th edition: *Practice for Understanding and Using English* and *Readings for Understanding and Using English,* both of which appear in this bibliography. This text is a complete writing and grammar handbook. Part one, Using English Effectively, opens with two chapters dealing with the working of language and the principle of appropriateness; the next three chapters deal with sentence structure, style, and paragraphs. Chapter six analyzes an essay to demonstrate the principles considered in earlier chapters. Chapters seven and eight treat the informal theme and the research paper, and the last chapter of part one reviews everyday uses of English, including taking notes, writing examinations and business letters, and public speaking. Each chapter concludes with a brief review section and a section of exercises. Part two, Understanding Types and Forms, consists of introductions to informative, evaluative, and persuasive prose; to descriptive writing; to autobiography and simple narrations; to literature; and to particular genres of literature. Part three, Understanding Conventions: A Handbook of Grammar, Rhetoric, Mechanics, and Usage may be assigned or used as a reference. Each section in this part aims at being self-contained so that a student may use only one section. The text concludes with a appendix on plagiarism with an appendix of suggested writing assignments.

46 Birk, Newman P. and Genevieve B. Birk. *Using English Effectively*. Indianapolis: Odyssey, 1965. 301 pp. $3.25 (P)

This text is part one of the fourth edition of Birk
and Birk's *Understanding and Using English* which is
annotated in this bibliography.

47   Birkley, Marilyn, James Birkley, and Louis Rivers. *Pat-
     tern Practices to Learn to Write By: Level II*. New
     York: College Skills Center, 1972. 268 pp. NPA (P)

This text begins with basic sentence patterns which
slowly get more complicated. The format of each section
is explanation, examples, and exercises. There are
answers to the exercises in the back and tests at the end
of each section which only the teacher can grade. The
lessons are short; most of the book consists of exercises
and tests. The tests are on tear-out pages. Sections
are on sentence patterns, paragraphs, rhetorical types,
development, style, and spelling and mechanics. The
student is encouraged to follow models in the examples.

48   Block, Jack and Joe Labonville. *English Skills for Tech-
     nicians*. New York: McGraw-Hill, 1971. 210 pp.
     $6.50 (P)

This text is designed for those entering occupations
which demand writing such as composing operational manuals
and writing reports. The authors have included a range
of technical writing topics with numerous examples from
many fields plus discussions of some rhetorical, syntactic, and grammatical devices. The introduction offers
a general discussion of the problem of writing; chapter
two gives instruction on the design, placement, and function of purpose statements. Chapter three deals with
content, including subsections on definitions, selection
of facts, static and dynamic description, analogies, and
other topics. The next chapter covers organization--
long and short papers, introductions, conclusions, transitions, notecards, and bibliography. A section on
written reports follows which includes subsections on
status reports, progress reports, travel reports, just-
ification reports, and evaluative writing. Oral reporting is reviewed in chapter six; then a substantial chapter on job seeking is given with information on letters
of application, resumés, and researching. The final
chapter is a review of grammar. Exercises emphasizing
major points and demanding writing (with space provided
for response) accompany each chapter. A bibliography of
texts on related topics is also included. This text is
suitable for basic technical writing instruction.

49   Blumenthal, Joseph C. *English 2600: A Programmed
     Course in Grammar and Usage*. 4th ed. New York:
     Harcourt, Brace, Jovanovich, 1973. 488 pp. $4.60
     (P)

This text is basically the same as *English 3200* with slightly more elementary information. Also, the units are arranged differently with different titles. Units are The Verb and Its Subject; Patterns of the Simple Sentence; The Work of Modifiers; Building Better Sentences; Understanding the Sentence Unit; Using Verbs Correctly; Agreement of Subject and Verb; Choosing the Right Modifier; Using Pronouns Correctly; How to Use Capitals; Learning to Use Commas; and Apostrophes and Quotation Marks. The audience for this text is basically the same as for *English 3200*, but the present text is aimed toward the remedial college student and the high school student. See Blumental, *English 3200,* listed in this bibliography.

50 Blumenthal, Joseph C. *English 3200: A Programmed Course in Grammar and Usage.* 2nd ed. New York: Harcourt, Brace, Jovanovich, 1972. 550 pp. $4.95 (P)

This programmed text is divided into twelve units: Patterns of the Simple Sentence, The Process of Compounding, The Complex Sentence to Show Relationship, Other Devices of Subordination, Achieving Sentence Variety, Recognizing the Sentence Unit, The Smooth-Running Sentence, Making Subject and Verb Agree, Solving Your Verb Problems, Using Adverbs and Adjectives, Solving Your Pronoun Problems, and Skill with Graphics. Each of these units is further broken down into specific lessons relating to the area of the unit. The particular subject under discussion is given a page number as the starting point. In addition the frame numbers are given. For example, The Semicolon as a Connector begins on page 247 and includes frames 395-437. A student will find the page number where his lesson begins and locate the frame. If a lesson begins with the first frame on the top of page 5, the next frame in the lesson is on the top of page 7, the next on page 9, and so forth. Answers are given for any frame at the beginning of the following frame so the answers do not appear on the same page as the questions. This text is designed basically for self-instruction, and a teacher may assign only those units or lessons he wishes to. Primarily, this text is for remedial instruction on the college level or for use as a self-teaching text.

51 Bossone, Richard M. and James M. Reif, Jr. *The Handbook for Basic English Skills.* Lexington, Mass.: Xerox College Publishing, 1971. 370 pp. $5.75 (P)

This programmed text, as the author states in To the Student, is designed to develop the skills of analyzing, evaluating, and revising one's own writing. It consists of four parts: Sentence Structure, Common Errors, Punctuation and Mechanics, and Spelling. An appendix

consists of a review of grammatical terms and twenty-five
tests on tear-out sheets. An answer mask is provided on
the back cover. Each part consists of several skills and
sub-skills presented through a standard instructional
format followed by a class-preparation exercise. A
variety of correction charts are also provided. This
text can be used on the high school or remedial college
levels and is also adaptable to individualized instruction.

52 Braddock, Richard. *A Little Casebook in the Rhetoric of
      Writing*. Englewood Cliffs, N.J.: Prentice-Hall,
      1971. 108 pp. $2.50 (P)

The author states in A Warning to Instructors that
"this little casebook presents writing problems which
each student can approach from his direct experience or
from a modest amount of reading and interviewing he con-
ducts to gain the knowledge he needs for a particular
paper." The text contains no prescriptive discussions
concerning how to write a paper; rather, each short
chapter begins with a writing assignment, goes on with a
few examples of completed papers following such an assignment, and concludes with discussion questions. The
chapters build on each other; thus, the first chapter is
A Sharply Focused Description which is followed by A
Description Written with a Different Voice and An
Analytical Comparison. All the problems are designed to
produce rather short papers except for the last chapter,
A Proposal to Resolve a Controversy, which is designed to
give the student practice in writing a longer paper.
Primarily, this text is designed for a first-year college-
level composition course.

53 Brennan, Maynard J. *Compact Handbook of College Compo-
      sition*. 2nd ed. Lexington, Mass.: D. C. Heath,
      1972. 158 pp. $2.95 (P)

The author states in the preface that this text is
"simply a book concerned with fundamentals; it identifies
and defines basic grammatical terms; it provides many
hints about what not to do and some hints about what to
do. A familiarity with the contents will not guarantee
that the student emerges a polished, imaginative, even
correct, writer; but it may help him to become a better
writer than he was before he read the book." The text is
divided into two main sections. The first section covers
usage, including grammatical terms, punctuation, sentence sense, the pronoun, strange or troublesome verbs,
and diction. Section two deals with paragraphs, including a general introduction and explanation of methods of
development followed by explanations and examples of
specific types of paragraphs such as definition and

description; illustration and example; comparison, contrast, and analogy; reasoning; space, time, narration; and opening and closing paragraphs. Section one includes short explanations, examples, and conventional exercises. Section two also has brief explanations and a number of examples and is often accompanied by questions designed to help the student understand concepts. There are no writing drills.

54 Briggs, Frances M. *English Grammar: A Handbook for Everyday Usage*. Durham, N.C.: Moore Publishing, 1970. 215 pp. $4.95 (H)

This handbook, according to the author, is "designed to help the student become self-directive in his written and oral communication. It is a ready reference which may serve an individual throughout years of study." As such, this text is not specifically designed to be a teaching text. Rather, it is intended to serve as a book that the student can refer to whenever he encounters some problems in his writing. Consequently, no exercises are provided. The first chapter deals exclusively with the parts of speech, first by a brief definition of the term under consideration and then by providing examples of the term. Chapter two covers phrases and clauses; chapter three discusses sentences and includes common errors, faulty pronoun reference, misplaced modifiers, and parallelism. Chapter four covers punctuation and mechanics while chapter five is devoted to a discussion of spelling. Six is a glossary of usage, and chapter seven deals with social and business letters, notation, and other types of practical writing. This text could be used as a handbook in composition courses on both the college and high school levels, and the author states that "The layman, businessman, secretary . . . will find this book useful."

55 Brogan, John A. *Clear Technical Writing*. New York: McGraw-Hill, 1973. 213 pp. $6.55 (P)

This programmed text involves no more than sixteen hours of individual study, according to its author. It is designed to cure common faults by moving the student rapidly through many short and easy learning steps. The author developed the text from extensive analysis of unclear sentences by technical writers. There are four major parts. Part one, Removing Redundancies, includes chapters on technical terms (time words, quantity words, dimension words, activity words, and object words), nontechnical words for emphasis and propriety, function words (by, as, of), verbs, and long redundancies. Part two, Unleashing Verb Power, discusses the active voice and elimination of weak verbs. In part three the focus is on using lean words and eliminating ponderous writing. Part four, Stressing What Is Important, has chapters on eliminating *it* and *there*, being personal or impersonal, punctuation, emphasis and subordination, and locating modifiers effectively. A list of recommended books on style and technical writing concludes the text. In the exercises problem sentences are on the right, clues for solving the problems and answers on the left. Review exercises conclude each chapter. This text would be suitable for any student who will confront technical writing assignments and would be helpful to businesses which wish to improve the quality of personnel writing.

56 Brooks, Cleanth and Robert Penn Warren. *Modern Rhetoric*. shorter 3rd ed. New York: Harcourt, Brace, Jovanovich, 1972. 440 pp. $5.95 (P)

This shorter version, as the authors states, is not intended to replace the longer one "but to serve the instructor who requires less explanatory material and who prefers to choose his own readings." The book's basis rests on "the cultivation of an awareness of the underlying logical and psychological principles." Part one studies the necessary tools and attitudes for making a beginning. Chapter one deals with the relationships among language, thinking, feeling, and rhetoric. Chapter two treats finding a subject, and the main elements of themes--notes, outlines, introductions, and so forth. Applications usually come at intermittent periods in the text rather than only at the end of each chapter. The third chapter treats units, coherence, and emphasis. Part two begins with an introductory chapter on intention and different types of discourse. Each following chapter deals with methodology. Chapter five deals with six different methods of exposition--identification, comparison/contrast, illustration, classification, definition, and analysis--with each of these discussions containing a sample writing, diagrams, commentary, and applications. Chapters six through nine each deal with a particular method: argument, persuasion, description, and narration. Chapter ten studies several points on paragraphing and sentencing; the next three chapters deal with diction, metaphor, tone, and stylistic considerations. Part four is a separate section on term paper writing; an appendix covers the book report, summary, and précis. The emphasis in this text is on the applications; examples are numerous. The book is aimed at advanced-level writing classes.

57 Brown, Harry M. *The Contemporary College Writer: Patterns in Prose*. New York: Van Nostrand Reinhold, 1971. 244 pp. $3.75 (P)

The author states in his preface that "The book stresses the notion of *patterns* in prose--fundamental patterns to be discovered in the work of expository writers not only today but yesterday, fundamental patterns that the student can adapt to his own purposes in writing." Part one, The Paragraph, discusses in some detail three main concerns of the paragraph: the central idea, proper development, and coherence. Part two is a brief section on the essay. These two parts of the text include exercises which apply the principles discussed. The third part of the book is entitled Patterns in Prose; twelve patterns are presented, and each pattern is illustrated by three essays. The patterns are entitled Parts and Wholes, An Event and Its Meaning, A Scene and Its Features, The Meaning of a Term, Likes and Unlikes, How a Thing is Done, Tracing a Development, Tracing a Cause or a Consequence, Information and Application, Error and Truth, Weighing the Matter, and Problems and Solutions. Each of these patterns is introduced briefly, and after each selection exercises appear. These exercises include drills on finding the thought pattern, writing with a pattern, and a group of suggestions for essay writing. The primary audience of this text is the beginning college writer.

58   Brown, Harry M. and Karen K. Colhouer. *Checking Your English*. San Francisco: Boyd and Fraser, 1974. 357 pp. $4.95 (P)

This text focuses on common errors. It has fifty-seven units, and each unit, in general, has four parts: Illustration--an application of a particular concept of English usage; Concept--a statement of principles, including examples, and techniques for correction; Exercise with answers (answers are in the back of the book); and Exercise without answers (answers are in Teacher's Manual). The authors use a visual approach with concepts illustrated by sketches, cartoons, ads, and news stories. Most illustrations are related to the expressions and slogans in our culture. It avoids grammar terminology, stays basic, and patterns of usage, not prescriptions, are given. There are seven major parts: The Mother Tongue (kinds of English, parts of speech, etc.), Word and Sentence Goofs (subject/verb agreement, pronoun case, etc.), Sentence Goofs (e.g., incomplete thoughts), Cool Words (exactness, concreteness, freshness, and brevity), Sense and Nonsense (generalization, emotional appeal, etc.), Putting in Signals (punctuation and mechanics), and Spelling. The text is suitable for high school or remedial college work and is basically self-explanatory.

59 Bryan, Margaret B. and Boyd H. Davis. *Writing about
    Literature and Film.* New York: Harcourt, Brace,
    Jovanovich, 1975. 192 pp. NPA (P)

This text is intended "to help the student bridge the
gap between the ability to read a work of literature or
view a film, and the ability to write about a work with
some confidence." The book offers four genres for study:
poetry, short fiction, drama, and film. Each section
consists of a series of steps concerning elements basic
to interpreting each genre, and the selections are usually
brief. The last step of each chapter focuses specifically on the types of writing that employ the analytic
techniques discussed in the preceding steps. The
authors use six basic patterns or types in their discussions of writing: analysis of a single aspect of a work,
analysis of multiple aspects, comparison and contrast,
explication, exploration of a problem, and evaluation.
Student themes are used to illustrate the principles discussed, are followed by suggested topics, and are
arranged by type of writing and keyed to the analytic
step that the student must have mastered to write a paper
on that topic. Section one covers poetry with specific
sections on reading carefully; discovering meaning;
analyzing rhyme and meter; analyzing patterns like
couplets, ballads, and sonnets; and analyzing imagery,
rhetorical devices and symbols. Section two covers short
fiction, including steps on analysis of point of view,
setting, characterization, plot, imagery, symbolism, and
rhetorical devices. The drama section studies conflict
and plot, structure, irony, language, etc. In the discussion on film the following issues are considered: how
to respond to the genre, multiple viewing, how to deal
with what happens, analyzing shooting and editing techniques, and recurrent imagery. The student papers are on
American Graffiti and *Death Wish*, and the final part is a
checklist for documentation. The authors suggest three
ways of using the book: as a self-contained, introductory
textbook; as an accompanying text to an anthology of
literature, filmscripts, or films; or as an individualized
self-paced text.

60 Burhams, Clinton S., Jr. *The Would-be Writer.* 3rd ed.
    Waltham, Mass.: Xerox College Publishing, 1971.
    379 pp. $5.95 (H)

The author states in his preface that his book "makes
no pretense at being either a rhetoric, a logic, a
glossary, a handbook, or a reader. Neither is it an
attempt to be all of these at once. It is simply and
only a basic course in writing. . . ." The text is
divided into four main sections: Pre-Writing, Writing,
Re-Writing, and a collection of about forty essays.

There are short essay examples within each major section
by both established authors and students. Exercises and
writing assignments at the end of chapters in the first
two main sections give the student a chance to apply the
principles discussed. Essay assignments are not given
until near the end of the second section; hence, the
sequence of writing assignments begins with sentences,
then short paragraphs, and concludes with essay writing.
The text starts with sections of developing and organizing ideas (e.g., Exploring Your Language, Free Association and Exploring Your Language, The Categorical List).
The second section focuses especially on structure and
organic unity with individual chapters centering on the
paragraph, the introduction, and the conclusion. The
Re-Writing section discusses the question of usage and
common errors in mechanics and style and does not include
exercises. General rules are given and discussed with
examples. The essays at the end of the text include both
student papers and works by nineteenth and twentieth
century artists.

61 Burke, Virginia M. *The Paragraph in Context*. Indianapolis: Bobbs-Merrill, 1969. 64 pp. $1.00 (P)

   This book is part of *The Bobbs-Merrill Series in Composition and Rhetoric*. See listing under Johnson, Falk
   S. for the complete annotation.

62 Burt, Forrest D. and E. Cleve Want. *Invention and Design:
   A Rhetorical Reader*. New York: Random House, 1975.
   334 pp. NPA (P)

   The authors begin by defining *invention* as "the orig-
   inating and discovering of ideas, illustrations and
   relationships through the accumulated knowledge that the
   writer has" and *design* as "the ordering and structuring
   of that content into its most effective form." Thus,
   the book is intended to coordinate imagination and the
   mechanics of writing. There are four major sections to
   the text. Part one deals with illustration, including a
   discussion of what is "good writing," how to develop a
   subject, writing with a purpose, how to establish a
   thesis and support it, the writer's obligations, and the
   importance of making abstractions concrete. The subdivisions in the sections concern simple illustration,
   extended illustration, multiple illustration, and complex
   illustration. Each subsection contains a brief discussion of principles, a writing sample from literary
   and popular writers, questions on the content of each
   essay and its rhetoric and style, and applications of the
   principles discussed. This format is sustained throughout. Part two deals with comparison and contrast. Part
   three covers analysis--parts and wholes, division,
   synthesis--with subsections dealing with classification,

process analysis, and causal analysis. Part four discusses argument--sensitivity to audience, rebuttal, evidence, and purposes for argument--with subsections covering emotion, reason, and complexity. The authors state that the selections need not be taken in the presented order but that each succeeding unit incorporates previously learned units. The text includes an alternate table of contents by subject (growing up; a sense of place; individuals and stereotypes; past, present, future; male and female; society and culture; science and nature; the arts; problem-solving; law and justice; religion and ethics; love and brotherhood; and living and dying). The primary audience is the college freshman.

63 Callin, Diane Tomcheff, Gilbert Tierney, and Daniel Tomcheff. *Perceptions and Reflections: A College Reader*. Dubuque, Iowa: Wm. C. Brown, 1973. 325 pp. $4.95 (P)

The works included in this reader are designed to give the student variety in subject matter, approach, and length on a variety of topics. The authors state in their preface that "The plan of the book calls for a scope that is historical in perspective and within which one can trace an individual's life, from birth through death and beyond death, through the discovery and creation of a sense of values." Following this plan, the text is divided into sections called Looking Back--Recollections of Things Past, Looking In--Realizing One's Self, Looking Out--Recognizing Others, Looking at Death, and A Sense of Values. Authors included in this anthology are Walt Whitman, Jean Jacques Rousseau, Mary Swenson, Li Po, Spiro T. Agnew, Aristotle, and many others. Each section begins with a short introduction by one of the editors discussing the themes in the selections. After each one there are general questions for discussion, questions which require close analysis of the work, and suggested theme topics. A black and white reproduction of a painting, such as Van Gogh's "Self Portrait," begins each section. An alternative table of contents is included at the back which lists the selections according to rhetorical type: Reporting, Analysis, Process, Analogy, Figurative and Symbolic, Cause and Effect, Evaluation, Persuasion, Biography, Personal Statement, and Potpourri. An author index and a title index conclude the text.

64 Campbell, John M. and G. L. Farrar. *Effective Communications for the Technical Man*. Tulsa: The Petroleum Pub. Co., 1972. 273 pp. $11.50 (H)

The authors state in their introduction that this volume is more specialized than some in that it is directed not as a general text but rather as a guide for the professional working in the petroleum industry. Although this emphasis will limit the use of the book in some situations, there are aspects of the material which could be useful to specialized courses in technical schools. The book begins with a section entitled Clearer, More Effective Writing which covers such basics as action verbs, dangling modifiers, and a range of grammatical and mechanical concerns. It goes on to discuss the whole manuscript in terms of division into sections, conclusions, appendices, etc., and then gives information and samples of report writing. Technical papers for publication and short written communications are also discussed. There are chapters on the inclusion of mathematical presentations and the use of figures and illustrative material. A short chapter on the philosophy and psychology of reports is included as well as detailed information on the professional presentation of information verbally. The final chapters are the most specialized and include empirical analysis of data, error analysis and dimensional analysis, and the theory of models. There are two appendices: one on grammatical mechanics and another listing standard abbreviations in the petroleum industry. Exercises are provided, including some in which the student must understand a body of data, draw a conclusion, and write a report. Suggested readings are included.

65 Canavan, P. Joseph. *Effective English: A Guide for Writing.* Encino, Ca.: Dickenson, 1970. 291 pp. $4.95 (P)

The author states in his preface that "The organization proceeds, in three parts, from the word to the group of words; from the simple, topic-sentence type of paragraph to the complex paragraph; and, finally to the composition." Part one, Background to Effective Communication, centers on basic grammar--parts of speech, groups of words, diction, the sentence, capitalization, punctuation, manuscript form, mechanics, and spelling. This first part comprises over 200 pages of the text. Part two, Writing the Paragraph, discusses the simple paragraph (definition, characteristics, unity, order, coherence, and completeness), special kinds of paragraphs (introductory, transitional, and concluding), and the complex paragraph (comparison and contrast, analysis by various methods, definition, and analogy). Part three, Writing the Composition, focuses on finding a subject, gathering material, limiting the subject, outlining, introductions, developing the middle, conclusions, and revising the essay. This text does not include any

exercises. Its primary audience seems to be those persons, both students and non-students, who wish to master
basic grammar and basic techniques of essay writing.

66 Canavan, P. Joseph. *Elements of College Writing and
    Reading*. New York: McGraw-Hill, 1971. 234 pp.
    $5.50 (P)

This text works under the assumption that reading and
writing are closely connected skills which must be
improved simultaneously. "Offering a simple but detailed
presentation of the writing and reading processes, it may
be used in the traditional classroom, in the various
laboratory or study-skills improvement programs, or by
the student himself working independently." The first
unit deals with organizing the simple paragraph. Succeeding units are entitled Reading Paragraphs Efficiently,
Developing the Thought, Breaking down the Subject,
Skimming for Study, and Writing and Reading the Essay.
Appendix A is Dominant Types of Essay Development, and
Appendix B contains suggested topics for writing. Each
unit consists of an explanation of basic principles,
examples which are discussed and analyzed, writing assignments relating to the subjects under discussion, and
exercises which generally ask the student to read some
short passage and answer questions about it. Answers to
the exercises are at the end of each chapter. The exercises also involve vocabulary and comprehension questions, and the author provides charts to determine reading speed. The text would be most appropriate in either
high school or lower-level college classes designed for
students who need help in preparing for college writing
and reading.

67 Canavan, P. Joseph. *Paragraphs and Themes*. 2nd ed.
    Lexington, Mass.: D. C. Heath, 1975. 345 pp. $4.95
    (P)

This basic composition text begins with general discussions of both the short and the long essay stressing
the organization of the separate parts--introduction,
middle, conclusion--moves to a detailed treatment of different kinds of paragraphs, and concludes with a chapter
devoted to prewriting activities. The stress is on
writing to explain and inform. The first three chapters
are entitled Viewing the Whole, Structuring the Paragraph,
and Planning the Whole Paper. Following chapters are
entitled Moving through Time--Narration; Moving through
Space--Description; Explaining and Informing--Comparison,
Analogy, and Contrast; Explaining and Informing--Analysis;
and Explaining and Informing--Classifying, Defining, and
Combining. Each chapter contains sample essays, stories,
and from one to four sets of exercises on tear-out pages

which are related to the items under discussion or to the readings. The readings are contemporary and include selections by Sylvia Porter, Norman Cousins, and John Steinbeck, in addition to student essays. Suggested essay topics are also included in each chapter. The text's basic audience is the standard freshman composition class.

68 Canavan, P. Joseph. *Rhetoric and Literature*. New York: McGraw-Hill, 1974. 392 pp. $5.95 (P)

In his preface the author states that "This book was written to help the student who wishes and needs to organize his thought effectively for written communication in college." After a brief introductory chapter on writing, chapter two discusses writing the paragraph in general, then introductory, middle, transitional, and concluding paragraphs. Chapter three, Planning the Paper, treats how to select a subject, limit a subject, gather material, organize and outline, write and revise the first draft, and prepare the final copy. Chapter four deals with narration and description while chapter five discusses comparison, contrast, and analogy. Chapter six centers on process and classification, and seven focuses on partition and causal analysis. Eight discusses defining and combining; nine discusses persuasion. Approximately the last 100 pages are selections from contemporary literature. Each chapter has several assignments such as writing topic sentences and limiting the subject. Discussion questions addressing the readings from each chapter are included periodically, and the answers for these are provided at the end of each chapter.

69 Carpenter, Jack. *Destination Tomorrow*. Dubuque, Iowa: Wm. C. Brown, 1972. 453 pp. $5.95 (P)

In his preface the author states that "Although *Destination Tomorrow* contains much material about man's fate on this little spaceship we call Earth, it is not a doomsday book about the future and the shocks that await us there. It is a book of readings about basic human experiences, the kind of experiences that we face today and will face again each tomorrow." The text is divided into eight sections: The Health of the Nation--Diagnosing the Ills; Some Old Wounds--Black, Red, and Sore; What Do Women Want?; Love, Marriage, Family--Couples, Coupling, and Communes; A Place to Live--Sodom, Gomorrah, or the Hog Farm; Doors of Education, Doors of Perception; The Good Life--Making It with Style; and Utopia or Apocalypse? A brief introduction precedes each section; discussion and writing assignments and quotations for discussion or writing are included at the end of each. Poems, stories, and photographs supplement the essays. Some of the authors represented are Benjamin DeMott, Jesse Jackson, Rollo May, Walt Whitman, Germaine Greer, Issac Asimov, and Frederick Pohl.

70   Casty, Alan. *Building Writing Skills*. New York: Harcourt, Brace, Jovanovich, 1971. 273 pp. $3.95 (P)

The author states in his preface that a writer must learn to recognize the working parts of sentences and paragraphs then apply his knowledge of these parts in order to be able to write clearly and effectively. This is a programmed text in which the chapters are divided into two parts--Examining, recognizing and understanding parts; and Using, applying principles in construction problems. Part one has seven chapters on sentence constructions: Verbs and Conjunctions, Subjects and Prepositions, Coordination and Independent Clauses, Single-Word Modifiers, Phrase Modifiers, Clause Modifiers, and Building Sentences with Coordination and Subordination. Part two studies Sets and Levels of Abstraction, Topic Sentences, Paragraph Development, Paragraph Organization, and Paragraph Coherence. There is a list of the key topics covered at the end of each examining section and a set of review exercises at the end of each chapter. Answers appear at the end of the book. The text is suitable for high school or college and could be used in individualized learning.

71   Cherry, Richard L., Robert J. Conley, and Bernard A. Hirsch. *The Essay: Structure and Purpose*. Boston: Houghton Mifflin, 1975. 473 pp. NPA (P)

In their preface the authors state that "The primary purpose of this book . . . is to explore the essential rhetorical modes and methods of prose, mainly nonfiction prose, and thereby to provide an understanding of the strategies that underlie good writing." The text is divided into five parts: Exposition, Description, Narration, Argument and Persuasion, and Essays for Further Reading. Each of these sections contains readings; more than eighty are included in the text. Part one, Exposition, is divided into separate chapters which treat process analysis, example and illustration, definition, comparison and contrast, analogy, division and classification, and cause and effect. Each of the essays included in this text is followed by questions for discussion; both the essays and the sets of discussion questions are in general fairly brief. A wide range of authors is included, literary and popular, contemporary and traditional.

72   Cherry, Richard L., Robert J. Conley, and Bernard A. Hirsch, eds. *A Return to Vision*. 2nd ed. Boston: Houghton Mifflin, 1974. 437 pp. $6.25 (P)

This rhetoric is divided into five sections. Part one, The Fear, contains essays, poems, and fiction (as do all five sections) dealing in some way with "chaos, disorder, and man's response to it." Part two, The Word, contains selections that deal with man's language and his use of it. The third part, Toward Oneness, contains pieces dealing with universal truths. The fourth part, With What We Have, concerns itself with society and man in relation to universalities. The final section, A Return to Vision, deals with art as a means of imposing order on experiences. Most of the essays included are followed by a paragraph of thematic analysis and one of structural and stylistic analysis. In addition, a series of questions on concepts and ideas and on structure and style are presented. Poems and fiction are followed by paragraphs of commentary and sets of questions for discussion. An alternate table of contents places pieces in standard rhetorical catagories with some essays appearing under more than one catagory. The text is aimed primarily at college-level writing classes in which a reader is desired, and the readings themselves range from classical to more contemporary selections.

73 Chisholm, William S., Jr. and Louis T. Milic. *The English Language: Form and Use*. New York: David McKay, 1974. 496 pp. $6.95 (P)

This text centers on the English language, its history, its form, and its use. Part one, Form, is divided into three sections. Section one contains nineteen chapters on topics such as language families and origins, syntax, sentence combining, and negatives. Section two contains chapters on the English language in America, American regional dialects, social dialects, and standard written English. The third section of part one is a short history of the English language. Part two, Use, contains four sections: English Words, Figurative Language, Structures, and Form and Style. The great majority of the individual chapters, sixty in all, end with exercises for the student and are printed on tear-out pages. In their preface the authors state that the preliminary versions of this text were used in freshman English classes, and the primary audience of the book seems to be writing classes on the beginning levels.

74 Christensen, Francis and Marilynn Martin Munson. *The Christensen Rhetoric Program: The Student Workbook*. San Francisco: Canfield, 1969. 239 pp.

This program operates on the assumption that the most interesting and significant feature of sentences is what Christensen calls "free modifiers" or sentence modifiers. These modifiers are the principal working unit of the professional writer, and "It is these modifiers, not subordinate clauses, that give him his most useful options and make it possible for him to say much in little--to make his writing concrete and specific without making it prolix, to get the movement or rhythm that is the life of prose." This program starts with four basic principles, proceeds to a review of the grammatical con- structions used as free modifiers, and then builds up the student's repertoire of constructions and sentence types, covering descriptive, narrative, and expository writing. All the examples used in the program are taken from well-known professional writers so that the student might get a realistic idea of well-written prose. *The Student Workbook* consists of brief informative material combined with a large number of exercises. The instructor works from a set of transparencies on an overhead pro- jector. The material could be used for any standard composition course. The entire program includes 195 transparencies with script and manual, and the price is $295.00.

75 Clare, Warren L. and Kenneth J. Ericksen. *Multimediate: Multi Media and the Art of Writing*. New York: Random House, 1972. 256 pp. $5.95 (P)

The authors state in their preface that students often find it easier to write about films and songs than essays and that a multi-media approach to writing can teach the student that the same principles are used in both. "The following pages reflect the belief that awareness of how composition works in one medium can lead to awareness of how it works in another." The book contains examples from many media, including excerpts from movie scripts, poems, song lyrics, comic strips, magazine advertise- ments, paintings, photographs, and caricatures. The text is divided into seven sections: Conflict, Transition and Unity, Image and Symbol, Point of View, Irony and Satire, Style, and Themes of the Seventies, each of which discusses how some element of composition can be used in various media. Each chapter contains short explanations by the authors of the examples included and a list of projects to complete which involve questions, short exer- cises, and suggestions for essay topics. This text could be used in any lower-level composition course in which the instructor wished to have the students learn how to criticize literature by having them apply critical prin- ciples to many different media.

76 Clark, Virginia P., Paul A. Eschholz, and Alfred F. Rosa, eds. *Lán guảge: Introductory Readings*. New York: St. Martin's Press, 1972. 558 pp. $5.95 (P)

This text is divided into five main parts: Language,

Thought, and Culture; The Systems of Grammar; Words,
Meanings, and the Dictionary; Americans Speaking; and
Space and the Language of the Body. Writers included in
the work are Peter Woolfson, Nelson Francis, Noam Chomsky,
and Julius Fast, among others. Each selection concludes
with a number of questions for discussion and review,
and each of the five parts ends with a list of projects.
Finally, there is a selected bibliography of further
references after each of the main parts. This is not a
reader which teaches composition; it is a book of readings about language in which there are a number of
possible composition assignments. This college-level
text could be used in an English class in which the
instructor wished to emphasize recent developments in the
study of language.

77 Clarke, Emerson. *A Guide to Technical Literature Produc-
    tion: A Concise Handbook of Production Methods*.
    River Forest, Ill.: T. W. Publishers, 1961. 194 pp.
    $3.00 (P)

This book is not a classroom text; it is a guide to
the professional production of technical literature but
could serve as a supplementary guide for an upper-
division student who plans a career in technical writing.
The book is divided into two parts. Part one describes
the elements of production such as the organization, operation, and management of technical literature production
groups. Considerable material is given on professional
technical writing as the job of groups of specialists
which, in addition to writers, may include draftsmen,
photographers, artists, and printers. Methods for organizing such groups are described. Information on literature for military agencies is incorporated, and the
author includes a chapter on technical writing agencies.
Part two deals with the technical writer as an individual.
There are sections on recruiting the technical writer,
evaluating the writer, increasing the writer's efficiency,
and the liaison between engineer and writer.

78 Clarke, Emerson and Vernon Root. *Your Future in Technical
    and Science Writing*. New York: Richards Rowen
    Press, 1972. 162 pp. $3.99 (P)

This book is not intended solely as a classroom text
but as a supplementary reference for the student who may
wish to make a career of technical writing. The authors
discuss the various fields which require a staff in pro-
fesssional writing including medicine, industry, aerospace
defense, government positions, journalism, and trade
magazines. Free lance technical writing is also discussed. Technical and science writing are treated as two
separate fields, and a brief chapter on women in the

technical writing field is given. Other information
includes salary ranges, applying for jobs, technical
associations, and information on various methods of
training for a future in technical writing.

79 Cobb, Charles M. *The Shapes of Prose: A Rhetorical
    Reader for College Prose*. New York: Holt, Rinehart
    and Winston, 1975. 339 pp. NPA (P)

This reader is designed for use in both "'fundamental'
and 'English One' courses." The reading selections range
from Plato to E. M. Forster to Richard Brautigan. The
text is divided into four main sections: Narration,
Description, Argumentation, and Thematic Contents, each
of which is further divided into subsections (i.e., Using
Cause and Effect under Argumentation) which contain
three essays as illustrations. The reader is encouraged
to notice overlapping rhetorical techniques in the selections. Each main section begins with an introduction
and discussion of the particular rhetorical mode and ends
with writing suggestions. There are discussion questions
after each selection which address points of diction,
rhetoric, and style. Terms which may need explanation
are printed in bold faced type and discussed in the
glossary at the end. Both selections and questions are
graded according to difficulty; therefore, the text could
be used by both beginning and advanced students.

80 Cockelreas, Joanne and Dorothy Logan. *Writing Essays
    About Literature: A Literary Rhetoric*. New York:
    Holt, Rinehart and Winston, 1971. 244 pp. $3.95 (P)

This text is designed for the student of introductory
courses in literature and offers a three-step plan for
learning to understand a work of literature: "1. Discovering the dramatic experience (what happens and to
whom) 2. Discovering the author's presentation of the
dramatic experience (the techniques the author employs
to enrich with meaning the human experience he sets
before the reader) 3. Synthesizing the two steps above
to discover, narrowly, what the author has to say about
a particular human experience, or, more broadly, what he
has to say about the human condition in general." The
first two sections of the text discuss the steps listed
above; then sections three, four and five examine fiction,
poetry, and drama, respectively, in terms of the principles of analysis established. Examples are included
periodically to illustrate literary principles such as
symbolism, point of view, tone, etc., and the major works
offered for analysis in the final three chapters are
"Araby" by James Joyce, Shakespeare's "Sonnet CXLVI,"
"The Rival" by Sylvia Plath, and *The Leader* by Eugene
Ionesco. Several sample essays follow these works to
illustrate various approaches to literature, i.e., using

voice and tone, using evaluation, using myth and arche-
type, and using structure. Suggested assignments for
writing about each genre are also included (ten for each).
The text concludes with a glossary of literary terms.

81   Cohen, B. Bernard. *Writing about Literature*. rev. ed.
     Glenview, Ill.: Scott, Foresman, 1973. 273 pp.
     $4.35 (P)

The author states that "*Writing about Literature* was
the first text designed to assist students not only to
interpret literary works but also to channel their
insights into effective essays." The text is divided
into two sections. Part one, About Literature, deals
with responses and fundamental principles involved in the
analytical reading of literature. There are six chapters
in this section. The first, Responses and Attitudes,
deals with understanding and interpreting literature.
The remaining chapters deal with genres and perspective;
setting; characterization; style; and structure in fiction, drama, and poetry. Part two, Writing about Literature, discusses the writing process, applying the terms
and concerns of analyzing literature. This section begins
with a chapter on the importance of clear reading and
note-taking. Chapter eight deals with evolving a thesis
statement as related to content and structure. Chapter
nine, Solidity of Content, warns of the problems of generalization, summary, misreading of details, and super-
ficial analysis. It also contains a three-step procedure
to insure solid content in the essay. Chapter ten works
with organization and chapter eleven with style. The
final chapter introduces the topic of research in literary interpretation, including biography and interpretation of criticism. The text also contains an essay on
writing about film, a selection of literary works which
may be used as topics for essays, and a glossary of terms
commonly used in literary interpretation.

82   Cohn, Jill Wilson. *Writing: The Personal Voice*. New
     York: Harcourt, Brace, Jovanovich, 1975. 214 pp.
     NPA (P)

The author establishes in the preface several premises
for the text. First, "the process of learning to write
is similar to the process of maturation." The students
must "explore the details of their immediate experience
with themselves and their world, to discover appropriate
language, and to develop authentic voices," examine their
relationships with places and people, and consider
issues, ideas, and sources for their opinions. Another
premise is that "learning to write is an ongoing process
that continues throughout our lives." The author suggests
that the book be used as "a guide and source of motivation.'

The first two chapters provide an introduction on the nature and function of writing and our response to it. Chapter three discusses self-encounter and provides a number of examples (mainly student models) within the context of explanations of principles. A list of subjective writing modes follows the discussion (interior monologue, immediate responses, sense impressions, free writing, and journals). Most chapters have this feature as well as a list of writing assignments dealing with free associations and sense impressions. The next two chapters treat the writer's reaction to his environment. Chapter six discusses the autobiography and student models and includes a list of possibilities for organization. The last three chapters also deal with specific aspects of writing: exploring issues, criticism, and fiction writing. The author suggests a grammar handbook for those who need one. This text could be used on the advanced high school level as well as the college level.

83 Coleman, Peter and Ken Brambleby. *The Technologist as Writer: An Introduction to Technical Writing*. New York: McGraw-Hill, 1969. 356 pp. $6.95 (P)

The authors note the uniqueness of this text because it is "an introduction to the field (technical writing) and a casebook which provides data for assignments, thus obviating the need for extensive and time consuming research." It is divided in two: Handbook and Casebook. In the former part the selection, arrangement, and presentation of data are discussed with individual chapters entitled The Nature of Data, Tests of Evidence, The Use of Evidence, Fallacies in Logic, Exposition--Description of Hardware, Exposition--Description of Processes, Argument and Persuasion, Style, Formats, Specifications, and Graphic Aids. Appendices offer a sample technical report and standards for graphic presentation. The latter section offers eight cases on such things as the production of wine, descriptions of projects, and manufacturing a battery charger. Each chapter concludes with specific writing assignments. Many illustrations, graphs, and pictures are interspersed throughout the text. A brief bibliography of technical writing texts concludes this volume. This text is appropriate for basic technical writing courses and can be used selectively because of its scope and numerous writing assignments.

84 Collignon, Joseph P. *Patterns for Composition*. Beverly Hills, Cal.: Glencoe, 1969. 300 pp. $4.95 (P)

The author states in his preface that this text is "a program in planned imitation of the *sounds* of style and organization. You will do nothing more than imitate the sound of good sentences . . . the sound of good

paragraphs . . . the sound of good essays." The text
demands active and frequent participation by the student.
After every explanation there appear exercises for the
student, and review exercises are included periodically.
Unit one, The Sound of Good Prose, presents chapters
entitled Patterns for Sentence Variety and Sentences for
Rhythm; Introductory Pattern and Variations; Patterns for
Subordinating and Emphasizing; Creating Texture through
Patterns; Linking Patterns; and Patterns in Punctuation:
Dash, Colon, and Semicolon. Unit two, From Paragraph to
Theme, contains seven chapters entitled Organizing Units
of Thought; Working with Abstractions; Patterns in Logic
and Transition; From Literary Analysis to Literary Judgment; Writing a Book Review; The Personal Essay; and The
Library Paper. Unit three is entitled The Essay Examination while unit four is a section on building word power.
This text could be used in classes from high school to
college in which the aim is to center on the basic process
of writing, and it could, perhaps, be used as a remedial
college text.

85 Colwell, C. Carter and James H. Knox. *What's the Usage:*
    The Writer's Guide to English Grammar and Rhetoric.
    Reston, Va.: Reston Publishing, 1973. 340 pp. $7.95
    (P)

    This composition text attempts to include all the
information necessary for a composition course while
maintaining readability. The text is organized so the
student comes in contact with all the elements which go
into good writing, and he is reminded of them periodically.
The first unit is The Writer, an outline of how to write
a theme. The second part examines the parts of writing
--letters, words, sentences, and paragraphs. The third
part deals with arranging these parts. The fourth studies
the way they are connected in writing: prefixes and
suffixes, sentence structure, punctuation, and unity in
paragraph and essay. The fifth unit consists of a single
chapter on audience. The research paper is briefly discussed in the next chapter, followed by a chapter consisting of a sample paper with annotations. There are two
appendices, one on usage and the second a glossary of
terms. A variety of questions and short exercises are
placed throughout the chapters. The teacher's manual
contains answers to exercises and a few review tests.

86 Comprone, Joseph. *From Experience to Expression: A*
    College Rhetoric. Dubuque, Iowa: Wm. C. Brown, 1974.
    422 pp. $5.95 (P)

    This text is a college-level rhetoric "based upon the
principle that a writer works from self-discovery . . .
to public expression." The controlling idea of the book

is that by having students apply "rhetorical principles to readings, paintings, cartoons, and other contemporary cultural artifacts" rhetorical skills will develop from a desire to express an experience. The text is divided into five sections. Section one, The Roving Eye: An Overview of the Writing Process, gives a general introduction to experience as applied to writing and goes on to introduce such rhetorical skills as finding a thesis, selecting details, drawing inferences, constructing an argument, and describing. The material is supported by a number of exercises on writing, thinking, organizing, and so on. Section two, The Exploring Eye: Finding and Limiting Your Subject, deals with describing sensations and perceptions. Section three, The Controlling Eye: Finding Form in Experience, deals with such topics as showing and telling in exposition, describing concrete experiences, finding an organizing purpose, and narration Section four, The Generating Eye: Working from Sentences to Paragraphs, deals with methods of composing the paragraph; and the final section, From Eye to Thou: Self-Discovery to Public Expression, focuses on the writer's voice. The text closes with two appendices. The first discusses applying grammatical principles, and the second deals with keeping a journal. The author assumes each student will keep an informal journal.

87   Conlin, Mary Lou. *Concepts of Communication: Writing.* Boston: Houghton Mifflin, 1975. 364 pp. $7.50 (P); 105 pp. $4.95 (P); 134 pp. $4.95 (P)

This system consists of a series of three books which can be used separately or together. Each of these is a "discrete program of instruction, with its own objectives The instructor's manual provides diagnostic tests designe to assess student needs so that his attention can be directed to a particular module for instruction. The student writes a particular type of essay which is then read by the instructor who is supplied with a "fixed" and "defined" list of criteria for each form. All compositic forms are always evaluated according to the criteria for organization and content that each form requires. Three of the modules are contained within one volume. The first module, Writing Skills, starts with a brief overview (as do all others) which defines the principles briefly, explains the procedure of the module, and states the objects of the instruction and criteria of evaluation, then presents eight units, one each on words, sentences, punctuation, conventions, spelling, vocabulary and a set of writing tasks. Each unit is subdivided into tasks which offer instruction and are followed by a task worksheet--exercises and writing assignments. Module two covers the summary, defines the essay form, gives directions and steps for writing a summary, and provides

several essays to summarize. The third module deals with
paragraphs. The theme and essay test modules are published as separate volumes. The former module begins
with explanations then provides a series of essays and
excerpts, "grouped as mini-case-books related to a subject." The latter module offers a unit for practice and
instruction in the single-paragraph and the multiple-
paragraph response. This entire sequence can be used in
the classroom or in a writing lab.

88 Copperud, Roy H. *A Dictionary of Usage and Style: The
    Reference Guide for Professional Writers, Reporters,
    Editors, Teachers and Students*. New York: Hawthorn
    Books, 1964. 452 pp. $8.95 (H) $3.50 (P)

The author's intention is "to offer the reader information on which to base an intelligent choice of language,
to encourage precision, and to discourage excess." The
text is organized alphabetically and is cross-referenced.
A bibliography on style and usage appears in the back of
the text. All examples of usage problems and errors have
been abstracted from published materials.

89 Corbett, Edward P. J. *Classical Rhetoric for the Modern
    Student*. 2nd ed. New York: Oxford University Press,
    1971. 653 pp. $7.95 (H)

In his preface to the first edition the author states
that he "believes that the elaborate system of the
ancients, which taught the student how to find something
to say, how to select and organize his material, and how
to phrase it in the best possible way, is still useful
and effective. . . ." The introduction is an explanation
of classical rhetorical training. Chapter two, Discovery
of Arguments, discusses formulating a thesis, three modes
of persuasion, appeal to reason, definition, example,
emotional appeal, and many other areas. It also includes
several readings. Chapter three, Arrangement of Material,
discusses the parts of a discourse, statement of fact,
confirmation, refutation, introduction and conclusion,
and readings and analyses. Chapter four, Style, includes
grammatical competence, diction, sentence structure, and
a variety of figures of speech, plus many readings with
analyses. The last chapter is a survey of the history
of rhetoric. The primary audiences are college courses
in advanced composition and graduate classes in rhetoric.

90 Corbett, Edward P. J. *The Essay: Subjects and Stances*.
    Englewood Cliffs, N.J.: Prentice-Hall, 1974. 277 pp.
    $5.50 (P)

In his preface the author notes that "This collection
presents seventy-two essays by British and American

59

writers from the sixteenth to the twentieth century."
This text deals with the familiar essay and includes many
modern essays because, "although the familiar essay is
not so prominent a feature in the periodicals as it once
was, good examples of this delightful genre are still
being produced. It is divided into eight sections, each
of which contains several essays. Sections are entitled
The Art of the Essay, Discovering the Self, Discovering
other People, Observing Nature, Reporting Experiences,
Commenting on Contemporary Mores, Using Language, and
Reflection on the Meaning of Life. A chronological table
of contents is also provided. Most of the essays presented are short, each briefly introduced; and a bibliography of additional readings is included. This text is
intended as a supplementary reader for classes studying
the history and forms of the essay or as a source book
for general writing classes.

91   Corbett, Edward P. J. *The Little English Handbook:*
        Choices and Conventions. New York: John Wiley and
        Sons, 1973. 185 pp. $3.25 (P)

As indicated by the title, this text is a handbook
intended to be used as a quick reference for writing
problems. The author states that "It is assumed that the
user of this handbook has acquired at least a basic knowledge of formal grammar. . . ." The eight chapters are
as follows: Format of Manuscript, Grammar, Style, Paragraphing, Punctuation, Mechanics, Format of Research
Paper, and Forms for Letters. A glossary of grammatical
terms and a list of commonly misspelled words conclude
the text. Ninety percent of examples used to illustrate
principles are from student samples. All entries are
numbered so an instructor can note a number beside an
error in a composition; then the student can refer to it
in this text.

92   Corder, Jim W. *Finding a Voice.* Glenview, Ill.: Scott,
        Foresman, 1973. 796 pp. $7.50 (P)

The main purpose of this reader is to help one make his
voice worth hearing, and the method is to present readings which demonstrate how people have succeeded and
failed in this regard. The text includes a variety of
forms and genres encompassing many times, ideologies, and
assumptions. The introduction gives a definition of and
further explanation for finding a voice. It concludes
with general questions on a word's origin, structure,
style, purpose, and possible effect. Each of the three
major sections of the text is preceded by a brief introduction. Part one, Where Can We Live?, is broken down
into sections on where we belong, the scope of our

community, and how our earth can survive. Part two
focuses on learning: how to do it, the nature of educational institutions, and the rationale for learning. Part
three, With Whom Can We Live?, discusses the family situation, how we get along in the world, and how we choose
among competing social systems. The chapters often begin
with classical or ancient answers to the questions then
offer a chronological progression of answers right up to
contemporary writers. Genres included are speeches, prose
forms, and poetry. An alternate table of contents lists
the selections by genre. There are no questions following the selections nor are there topic suggestions. The
collection would be best used on the college level.

93 Corder, Jim W. *Rhetoric: A Text-Reader on Language and
    Its Use*. New York: Random House, 1965. 595 pp.
    $5.50 (P)

The author states in his preface that this text is
based on three primary beliefs: the student must study
the development and quality of his language to enhance
his prose style; he learns best by studying master prose
writers; and selections can be arranged in a sequence
which will facilitate learning. The text is divided into
two parts with an introduction before each. Part one,
On the Qualities of Language, contains selections which
discuss and illustrate language use. The essays are
arranged thematically in three groups. The first ones
describe significant stages in the history of language.
The second group deals with issues and controversies
arising from language study, (e.g., Dwight MacDonald's
"The String Untuned"). The essays in the third group
focus on style. Part two deals with the craft of prose
writing. The first four sections of this part center on
parts of essays: words, sentences, paragraphs, and
planning. The following four sections study methods of
exposition, narration, argumentation, and description.
Analyses follow most first selections. Discussion questions are included, and "A Writing Program" follows each
major division in the text. A bibliography of further
readings is included, also. The primary audience seems
to be those writing classes beyond the freshman year.

94 Cowan, Gregory and Elizabeth McPherson. *Plain English
    Please*. 2nd ed. New York: Random House, 1969.
    413 pp. $4.95 (P)

This second edition retains the same basic philosophy
and organization as the first; the book offers "some
everyday logic and some common sense advice on how to
organize and support ideas." The focus is on helping the
student establish purpose, planning, and sound content
in the belief that sound mechanics will follow logically.

Each chapter deals with a particular writing purpose.
Brief explanations of points are included in each chapter
comprising a sort of formula for each type of writing as
well as an examination of a sample theme. A list of
review questions on key words in the chapter, multiple
choice questions on vocabulary words, and several sets
of exercises follow. Separate chapters on giving directions, defining, comparison, classification, analysis,
objective reports, personal experience, persuasion, and
summary are included. The authors also add five
appendices on form, application letters, book reviews,
term paper writing, and comprehension questions. The
text has a workbook format and perforated pages. The
book is best suited for freshman English but could be use
on the advanced high school level. It presupposes the
basic fundamentals in usage and grammar.

95   Cox, Martha Heasley, ed. *A New Reading Approach to Col-
     lege Writing*. New York: Chandler, 1974.   350 pp.
     $5.50   (P)

     This text is a college-level reader to be used in con-
junction with a grammar text because it contains no discussion of basic grammar. The main concern of the editor
is "to supply provocative material which suggests worth-
while writing assignments as well as fostering increased
skill in analytical reading." Each section has an introductory discussion of basic rhetorical principles, a few
essays, and discussion questions. Sections are entitled
Idea and Purpose; Introduction and Conclusion; Words;
Sentences; Paragraphs; Example, Anecdote, and Other
Illustrations; Definition and Analysis; Comparison and
Contrast; Reasoning and Evidence; Review of Rhetorical
Principles; and For Further Study. This reader includes
such authors as Frederick Douglass, Walt Whitman, Ashley
Montagu, and Edith Hamilton. There are three appendices:
the first on content, the second on spelling, and the
third on choosing a topic (with over one hundred quotat-
tions to be used as suggested topics).

96   Cox, R. David and Stephen Lewis. *The Student Critic:
     Thinking and Writing about Literature*. Cambridge,
     Mass.: Winthrop, 1974.   211 pp. NPA (P)

     The authors state in their preface that this text is
offered "as a stepping stone toward understanding the
critical tools which should make your study of literature
more complete and hopefully more precise." The focus is
on meaning in literature and critical analysis. Hence,
the authors present separate formulas for the study of
genres with full knowledge that each formula is an end to
understanding literature rather than an end in itself.
The first major section presents chapters on the short

story, poetry, and drama. They begin with a sample; then
pertinent elements of these works are discussed in accordance with each formula. The formulas are as follows:
short story: response, exposition, plot and character,
other essential elements (style, movement, conflict,
climax), point of view, and theme; poetry: response,
language, structure, and theme. Each chapter includes a
model for the analysis of the genre--a structured diagram
or worksheet employing principles discussed. A section
about writing on the genre follows which provides instruction and a group of sample student essays. The second
major unit discusses secondary sources, particularly biographical, symbolic, and historical criticism. The
third section discusses writing and is divided into two
sections: a review of writing principles and writing
about literature. Again, several student essays serve as
examples. The final section, Reference, defines nine
major terms in detail (e.g., allegory, character, and
irony). The second subdivision details various poetic
forms, schools of literature, forms of drama, and types of
novels.

97 Crews, Frederick. *The Random House Handbook*. New York:
     Random House, 1974. 409 pp. $5.95 (H)

     This text begins with a general look at the essay and
subsequently narrows its field of attention. Section
one, A Writer's Work, defines the essay, discusses what
the reader might expect of an essay, and includes a brief
look at the various essay types--expository, descriptive,
narrative, and argumentative. The first section also
covers choosing topics and theses, making notes, outlining,
writing a first draft, revision, a checklist for the
writer, and a section on the form of the essay. The
third chapter, Being Reasonable, contains practical
advice about how to avoid "sloppy thought" in essay writing. The second section concentrates on style and contains a chapter on words--euphemisms, clichés, and jargon.
The next chapter works with sentence structure as well as
style and the sound of sentence elements. All of the
chapters contain some exercises, many of which call for
the student to correct errors or rewrite. Paragraphs are
discussed according to the goals of unity, continuity,
variety, and effective beginnings and endings. The third
section contains a lengthy review of grammar and usage.
Section four covers mechanics and spelling. The final
section of the text deals with writing the research paper,
and a sample paper is included. The text is designed for
freshman composition but could be used as a handbook for
more advanced classes.

98 Crosby, Harry H. and George F. Esty. *College Writing*.
     2nd ed. New York: Harper and Row, 1975. 329 pp.
     NPA (P)

The authors state in the preface that "it attempts, at
every opportunity, to stress the writing process rather
than the writing product. Students need to be able to
recognize good writing; hence samples of excellent writing of the past and present are included. More importantly, students need to know how excellent writing is
developed; accordingly, you will find numerous case
histories of how a student's ideas generated an outline,
a rough draft, a fair copy, and how an 'almost-submitted'
paper underwent rigorous last-minute revision." This
text is divided into five major units: Prewriting, Writi
(including sections on organization, development, and
style), Rewriting, Special Problems (the research report,
manuscript conventions, and technical reports and busines
communications), and a handbook of style. Every chapter
ends with projects which involve questions, rewriting or
analyzing selections provided, dividing the class into
committees which do outside work on some problem, or
writing individual themes. There are unedited student
themes provided for the students to criticize and edit.
This text is perhaps most appropriate in a freshman
English class.

99 Crosby, Harry H. and George F. Estey. *Just Rhetoric*.
    New York: Harper and Row, 1972. 274 pp. $5.95 (P)

This college-level composition text teaches rhetoric,
starting with "pre-rhetoric"--description, narration, and
report writing--to give the student a chance to write his
first papers on topics which interest him. It is divided
into nine main units: Observation: The Source of
Description, Narration and Report; Convention: A Source
of Structure; Perspective: You (point of view); Organization; Development; Style; and A Handbook of Grammar,
Spelling, Punctuation, and Manuscript Conventions. Each
chapter contains explanations of principles, short
examples from literature and journalism, and projects.
The projects include class discussion questions, exercises, and essay topics. The instructor's manual include
a short discussion of the objectives of each chapter,
expanded exercises for use in a writing laboratory, and
expansions of the writing topics in *Just Rhetoric*.

100 Damerst, William A. *Clear Technical Reports*. New York:
     Harcourt, Brace, Jovanovich, 1972. 338 pp. $6.80
     (P)

This book is divided into five parts. Part one is a
practical application of basic communication theory.
Chapter one of that part begins with an analogy between
radio transmission and reception and human communication;
then it reviews the importance of understanding the
reader's point of view. Chapter two examines the obstacl

to clear communication that are recognizable in the message to be transmitted. These obstacles may be created by the writer and include inaccuracy, incompletness, overwriting, lack of candor, lack of empathy, and omission of summary. Chapter three covers structures in technical writing, from the types of forms which might be used by companies through the order of development of a message. Outlining and paragraphing are both covered in this chapter as well. Chapter four deals with language, beginning with clauses and phrases, and continues through various types of sentences. The remainder of the chapter is devoted to style, mentioning gobbledy-geok and readability formulas such as Gunning's *Fog Index* and Damerst's *Clear Index*. Part two focuses on the basic principles and skills for designing and developing technical messages. Chapter five deals with research, interpretation of facts, bibliography and footnoting, and the dangers of illogical interpretation are itemized. Chapter six offers guidelines for handling the fundamental techniques of defining and describing the unknown and the unfamiliar. All types of definition are included. Chapter seven covers helpful adjuncts to technical writing--summaries, lists, and graphic aids. Parts three and four explain and illustrate application of the principles and skills discussed in the first two parts. Part three includes the writing of letters, memos and informal reports, formal reports, and proposals. Part four covers two special writing problems: articles and the job application. Part five, A Technical Writer's Handbook, includes sections on abbreviations, numbers, spelling, sentence unity and coherence, and diction. Also included is a list of grammatical terms to aid the student who has forgotten the names that are used in discussions of grammar and functions. Exercises for both discussion in class and writing assignments follow all chapters and the handbook.

101 Davis, O. B. *Workouts in Reading and Writing*. New York: Hayden, 1972. 129 pp. $3.75 (P)

The author in his preface states that "Between these covers I have tried to supply a verbal gymnasium, equipped for people who want some real workouts, who want to strengthen and tone up reading and writing muscles." The first part of this text is a series of short passages and poems followed by writing exercises designed to improve "mental coordination" and style. For example, a short passage from Hawthorne's "Ethan Brand" is quoted. Following this passage are four questions for the student to complete. Question three is "What are the various effects and implications of Hawthorne's use in this passage of the diabolic references (Hell, damnation, etc.)?" Part two is a series of drills which concentrate on particular

65

stylistic aspects: vocabulary, word choice, usage problems, for example. In part three, Literary Exercises, groups of questions on random works of literature are provided. The list includes twenty-six masterworks such as *The Great Gatsby* and *The Brothers Karamazov*. Clearly, the author intends this book to be used in conjunction with literary works such as these. Hence, this text is suitable for an introduction to literature course or can be used on its own in freshman composition.

102 Decker, Randall E. *Patterns of Exposition*. 4th ed.
   Boston: Little, Brown, 1974. 366 pp. $5.95 (P)

   This reader/rhetoric is divided into ten sections with a total of forty-three essays representing such authors as Samuel Johnson, D. H. Lawrence, Woody Allen, and Thomas Jefferson. Each section is briefly introduced; the essays, four per section, are each followed by questions on meaning and values, expository techniques, diction and vocabulary, and suggestions for writing and discussion. Three essays at the end of the text provide further reading and are not followed by exercises. Section titles are Illustrating Ideas by Use of Example; Analyzing a Subject by Classification; Explaining by Means of Comparison and Contrast; Using Analogy as an Expository Device; Explaining Through Process Analysis; Analyzing Cause and Effect Relationships; Using Definition to Help Explain; Reasoning by Use of Induction and Deduction; Explaining with the Help of Description; and Using Narration as an Expository Technique. A Guide to Terms is also included. This text could be used as a text for advanced composition classes, in freshman English courses as a supplementary text, or in any course which involves students who have mastered basic writing skills.

103 Deer, Irving, Harriet A. Deer, and James A. Gould. *Person to Person: Rhetoric, Reality, and Change*. New York: Holt, Rinehart and Winston, 1973. 397 pp. $5.95 (P)

   In their preface the authors state that "the teacher can and must, if he is to have any students, relate the most vital interests of his time to his special field of competence." To this end, the book includes essays which attempt to show the student how to cope with the written word--how to identify propaganda, for example. The essays cover a wide range of subjects, all of them dealing with some aspect of reality. This text is basically a reader with three major sections, each section preceded by a brief introduction. Section one, Hiding from Reality, includes essays by Henry Winthrop, Steven Kelman, *Mad Magazine*, and Richard D. Altick. Section two, The Consequences, includes selections by Henry Steele Commager, Eric Sevareid, and James Thurber. The final section,

Facing Reality, has pieces by Rollo May, Kingsley Amis, and Henry Nash Smith. Each of the readings is followed by a set of study questions. This text would be used primarily as a companion text or a source book for writing classes from the freshman to more advanced levels.

104   De Mordaunt, Walter J. *A Writer's Guide to Literature.* New York: McGraw-Hill, 1965. 397 pp. $4.95 (P)

The author states in the preface that "This book is designed to guide the college student through some of his problems in literary analysis and critical writing." More specifically, the text relates the techniques of literary investigation to the practical problems of organizing and developing a critical essay. The book moves from the simpler forms of interpretive writing to deeper analysis and discussion of the various kinds of literary critiques ending with discussion of background and evaluative studies. The text is divided into four units, the first on writing literary essays and exams (reading and analyzing; choosing a topic; planning for relevance; beginning, middle, and end; and sections on actually writing the essay using experience and interpretation). The first unit also contains chapters on types of paragraphs and essays and a number of exercises in which the student writes both short and long interpretive essays. The second unit is a checklist of grammar and mechanics with a correction key of editing symbols. The third unit is a glossary of literary terms; and the fourth unit, called Points of Departure, is a series of readings including essays on poetry, drama, the novel, the short story, and the essay form. These readings include excerpts from the preface to *Lyrical Ballads,* Johnson's "Preface to Shakespeare," Henry James's "The Art of Fiction," and the introduction to *Essays of Today* by R. H. Pritchard, among others. The author states in the preface that the chapters are self-contained and could be used in any order. He further says, "In all, the book aims to be the only companion text needed for a course in composition or literature in which papers or examinations are important teaching devices."

105   Dent, J. C. *Thought in English Prose.* Indianapolis: Odyssey, 1930. 149 pp. $2.00 (H)

This text is a rhetoric/reader of classical essays with an introduction by Warner Taylor. It was designed originally for freshman English but now seems more applicable to advanced considerations of style and rhetoric. It is an anthology of essays "designed to offer an antidote for fuzziness." The essays are presented to be intensely scrutinized for form and content. There are twenty-seven essays representing such authors as W. Somerset

Maugham, Thomas Babington Macaulay, Addison, Paine, Edmund Burke, and others. Each selection has numerous questions involving in-depth study of all facets of the essays, including some writing assignments. The book's total focus is on formal English prose.

106 DiPippo, Albert E. *Rhetoric*. Beverly Hills, Ca.: Glencoe Press, 1971. 323 pp. $4.95 (P)

The author insists that composition must be taught systematically and classifies this text as a "rhetoric course out to establish the primacy of definition and classification as logical processes." The text attempts to provide the following: "a simplified and logical rhetoric, ample examples of all ideas discussed and writing projects that require the practical application of what the student has learned." Each chapter is divided into a number of sections covering a specific principle, illustrated substantially by examples, and providing writing projects based on discussions. The process involves, first, a discussion of the senses and their importance to the writer. Chapter two deals with writing preparation: experience, critical reading, choosing and limiting a subject, etc. Chapter three discusses outlining and paragraphing (unity, coherence, "from paragraph to essay," etc.). Chapters four through six deal with organization: by illustration (example, logical comparison, rhetorical comparison, testimony and authority) through analysis (process analysis, classification, cause and effect) and through persuasion (argumentation, induction, deduction, erroneous reasoning). Chapter seven deals with language: forms, prefixes, suffixes, roots, connotation and denotation, clichés, and the like. Finally, chapter eight discusses rhetoric from many angles--processes, kinds, techniques and others--and forms a short survey of rhetoric as an art and craft. Most of the examples are brief and illustrative, and sources vary widely. This book is geared to levels beyond the remedial stage, offering no traditional instruction in usage. It seems best suited for advanced composition and can be used selectively and need not be supplemented.

107 Drabeck, Bernard A., Helen E. Ellis, Virginia Low, and Hartley Pfeil. *Structures for Composition*. Boston: Houghton Mifflin, 1974. 329 pp. $5.59 (P)

The authors state in the preface that like other composition texts this book "attempts to help students solve the reading and writing problems they encounter . . . . Unlike most other rhetoric books, however, the focus here is on *structures* in composition." The text is divided into six units: Chronology: Directions or Process; Chronology: The Report; Classification/Division:

Definition; Classification/Division: Comparison; Argument: Development by Division of Reasons; and Persuasion: The Sequential Argument. Each of these six chapters
consists of three parts: an introduction to each assignment, step-by-step instructions on how to complete a
given assignment, and a collection of essays illustrating
each type of structure. There are essays, photographs,
poems for the students to use as illustrations and study
questions after each selection to point out aspects of
the selection which a student should notice for his own
writing. At the end of every chapter a preliminary worksheet and an evaluation guide are provided for the student to fill out concerning his own essay. There are
examples of student essays in every chapter, along with
essays by such writers as Margaret Mead, W. H. Auden,
Ramsey Clark, St. Paul, S. I. Hayakawa, and Robert Frost.
The authors state that "This book contains a course in
freshman composition." It could be used in beginning
composition courses at almost any level.

108 Durham, John and Paul Zall. *Plain Style*. New York:
McGraw-Hill, 1967. 216 pp. $4.50 (P)

This book is based on three essential premises: "(1)
all writing, even the most complex, derives from a few
simple patterns of thought; (2) nearly all students, even
those with the most primitive grasp of the written language, can learn these patterns and can apply them to
their own writing; and (3) learning the patterns helps
students toward eliminating sentence errors, fuzzy diction, and imprecise thought." The patterns are presented
individually with constructs meant to approximate the
step-by-step organization of programmed learning. Rules
of usage and writing are introduced periodically and
repeated for reinforcement. The authors have intentionally simplified the language to facilitate the student
working on his own. The text is comprised of four major
sections. The first, Idea Units, teaches how to develop
ideas in three different ways: argument, explanation,
and narration. The authors introduce these as the fundamentals of all essay writing. The second part, Short
Essays, teaches how to use paragraphs in essays, offering
the three fundamental types again with some variations.
Part three covers planning and reading for research
papers. The final section is a reference/review of
grammar, punctuation, and spelling. Each chapter has
writing assignments consisting of one or more writing
rules, a definition of the type of writing involved, one
or more models, an analysis of the model, an assignment,
a list of topics, and a checklist to help with self-
criticism. The authors intend the book to be applicable
to all writers past the ninth grade level. Perhaps the
text is most suitable for a class in which students lack

the fundamentals of essay writing and need a concrete, formula approach.

109 Eastman, Arthur M., et al. *The Norton Reader: An Anthology of Expository Prose*. 3rd ed. shorter. New York: W. W. Norton, 1973. $3.95 (P)

The editors state in their preface that "the essays i the Reader are gathered into sections titled according t major fields of human concern--Education, Mind, Literature and the Arts, etc. The ordering remains unchanged --unobtrusive, we think, minimal, yet reflective of the individual's enlarging experience." The editors have also supplied an Index of Essays Illustrative of Rhetorical Modes and Devices and a section entitled Notes on Composition for those instructors who prefer to organize their courses rhetorically rather than by topic division This third edition contains an increase in material by women and black authors, and a totally new Signs of the Times section which contains selections by such contemporary authors as Adrienne Rich, Eldridge Cleaver and Anthony Burgess. Other topic listings include Personal Report, Politics and Government, History, Science and Religion. Study questions follow approximately half of the selections. This edition contains forty new selections. An instructor's guide with outlines for discussions of content and rhetoric and questions for writing is available. A longer edition with further topic headings is also available ($5.95 P).

110 Eastman, Richard M. *Style: Writing as the Discovery of Outlook*. New York: Oxford University Press, 1970. 280 pp. $3.50 (P)

The premise of this book is "that style is outlook an that outlook is discovery through the activity of writing itself." Hence, the writing method is the way one comes to know, and writing techniques are ways to expand one's power of discovery; rewriting is a final thrust of discovery. The author suggests the text was planned for composition classes with better-than-average preparation and for advanced composition classes; he feels it can be used in creative writing classes for reference and in literature classes that have composition as an auxilary aim. It is designed to be flexible and accessible, lead ing from condensed description of basic concepts to increasingly detailed demonstration; thus the book can b used selectively. A brief preview chapter begins the text, introducing the four main topics briefly (style an outlook, style and audience, style and language, from style to the larger scale). A few examples and several exercises follow. Chapter one deals with the three ways of seeing things (assertion, induction, and deduction);

three ways of focusing (selection, placement, organization); and imitation of models. Chapter two deals with
aspects of audience (knowledge of, importance of, point
of view, level of formality) and gives substantial sections on sentimentality and irony. Chapter three discusses vocabulary (general, detailed, feeling, intensi-
fication); sentencing (basic placement, syntax, complex
structures); and rhythm and sound. The final chapter
covers levels of sophistication, such as ordering ideas,
contrast, expansion, paragraph coherence, development,
revision, and so on. The author offers a bibliography of
books on writing and appendices on documentation and
usage. All discussions of principles are brief, and the
text is heavily weighted in favor of exercises.

111 Ehrlich, Eugene and Daniel Murphy. *Basic Grammar for
     Writing*. New York: McGraw-Hill, 1967. 109 pp.
     $1.95 (P)

This is a self-teaching text for "the student who
wishes to refresh his memory of grammar." Those elements
of grammar that are most useful for effective writing are
focused upon. The book is designed to be covered at the
pace of one lesson a day with the student taking all
tests and exercises. It supplies basic preparation for
writing effective sentences. There is an initial test
at the beginning of the text; sections follow on the
sentence, modifiers, verbs, verb tense, agreement and
reference, punctuation, style, and the sentence in context. Instruction is brief and oriented toward
re-acquainting the student with terminology and fundamentals. One or two examples accompany each principle.
A final test concludes the text; answers to all exercises
are given at the back of the book. This book could be
used as a review text for the college freshman.

112 Ehrlich, Eugene and Daniel Murphy. *Concise Index to
     English*. New York: McGraw-Hill, 1974. 140 pp.
     $2.45 (P)

In their preface the authors state that *Concise Index
to English* presents alphabetically "certain principles,
precepts, practices, and prejudices in matters of syntax
and style." This text is primarily a handbook presented
in the format of a glossary of items that a writer might
wish to consult in the course of composing a paper. The
listing includes such items as abbreviations, adjectives,
the word *but,* dangling modifiers, principal parts of
verbs, the relative clause, and spelling. Each entry is
followed by a brief explanation with short examples.
The text, then, is designed as a reference tool rather
than a teaching text and would serve well in a course
requiring such a handbook.

113 Elbow, Peter. *Writing Without Teachers*. New York: Oxford University Press, 1973. 196 pp. $1.50 (P)

The author states in his preface that he does not describe either good or bad characteristics of writing as instructional techniques. "Instead I try for two things 1) to help you actually generate words better--more freely, lucidly, and powerfully: not make judgments about words but generate them better; 2) to help you improve your ability to make your *own* judgment about which parts of your own writing to keep and which parts to throw away." Chapters discuss writing as a free exercise, writing as a process of growth, writing as cooking ("the smallest unit of generative action, the smallest piece of anti-entropy whereby a person spends his energy to buy new perceptions and insights from himself"), and two discussions on teacherless writing. Also included is an *Appendix Essay:* The Doubting Game and the Believing Game--An Analysis of the Intellectual Enterprise, discussing critical thinking, and A Few Books to Help You with Correct Usage. The text is not intended as a teaching text, but it could be used as a supplementary text in college-level writing classes although there are no student exercises included.

114 Elgin, Suzette Haden. *Pouring Down Words*. Englewood Cliffs, N.J.: Prentice-Hall, 1975. NPA (P)

This text focuses on language rather than strictly on writing skills. In her preface the author states that one should be able to deal with language by 1) deciding whether to notice the language sequence or not, 2) identifying the sequence as a particular kind of language, 3) deciding what motives lie behind the sequence, 4) trying to understand it, and 5) evaluating it. Also, one must decide about responding with language. The purpose of the book, then, is "to help you learn how to fulfill the language function, both as a processor and as a producer. The first chapter discusses the nature of language, and chapter two serves as a practical tool for using the book as a whole--establishing basic strategies for interpreting and evaluating sequences of language. Chapters three through eight discuss the nature and structure of various types of language: prose nonfiction, folklore, prose fiction, political language, religious language, and poetry, respectively. The final two chapters deal with language and media and the diversity of language. An appendix of source paragraphs and a list of courses conclude the text. Exercises which usually involve substantial writing tasks complete all chapters but the second one. This text is suitable for more advanced courses in rhetoric, style, or language study.

115   Ellis, Barbara Lenmark. *How to Write Themes, Term Papers and College Autobiographies*. Woodbury, N.Y.: Barron's Educational Series, 1971. 141 pp. $1.95 (P)

This book is designed as "a quick and ready reference on organizing, on theme content, and on style." Section one discusses themes from outline to conclusion, descriptive and expository essays, style, paragraphing, and spelling. All units are simple, especially the one on style. They provide brief fundamentals and a few examples. Section two gives a step-by-step account of term paper preparation and mechanics. Also included is a guide to reference works. This section is designed for students confronted with research paper projects, but the section on the college application autobiography is aimed particularly at high school seniors. The last few pages are a sample bibliography. The book presents a capsule approach, perhaps geared below the college level. Its simplistic approach extends primarily from the fact that the student would use it on his own outside of class.

116   Ellsworthy, Blanche. *English Simplified*. rev. ed. Scranton: Chandler, 1971. 32 pp. $1.75 (P)

This pamphlet presents basic rules on punctuation, grammar, mechanics, spelling, usage, documentation, and an index. It is designed for reference only; no exercises are included.

117   Elsbree, Langdon and Frederick Bracher. *Heath's Brief Guide to Rhetoric*. 8th ed. Lexington, Mass.: D. C. Heath, 1972. 406 pp. $6.95 (H) $4.95 (P)

This text is basically the first section of *Heath's College Handbook of Composition* with these exceptions: the chapter on the development of the English language and the material on the research paper have been moved to the section on Diction in this shorter version.

118   Elsbree, Langdon and Frederick Bracher. *Heath's Brief Handbook of Usage*. 8th ed. Lexington, Mass.: D. C. Heath, 1972. 396 pp. $3.95 (P)

This text is basically the second part of *Heath's College Handbook of Composition* with these exceptions: the sections on sentence unity, sentence coherence, and the chapter on diction in the first part of the *Handbook of Composition* are included under Grammar and Usage, the first unit in this text, and the short section on the development of English is omitted.

119   Elsbree, Langdon and Frederick Bracher. *Heath's College Handbook of Composition*. 8th ed. Lexington, Mass.: D. C. Heath, 1972. 644 pp. $6.95 (H)

This text is a general reference work for all phases of writing. The authors' intention is that the explanations be clear and unambiguous and that the examples illustrate the points at issue. The text is divided into two major units, the first on rhetoric and the second on grammar and usage. The unit on rhetoric has chapters entitled The Composition as a Whole, The Paragraph, Good Sentence and Diction. Each chapter is divided into sections dealing with different aspects of the subject, and these sections contain exercises for the student to complete. There are sections on organizing and outlining, logic, coherence and development, unity in paragraphs and sen-tences, sentence emphasis, and uses of the dictionary, among others. The rhetoric section ends with a glossary of words commonly misused. The second unit of the text is a handbook of grammar and usage. It begins with a short chapter on the development of English then goes on to chapters on the analysis of the sentence (including parts of speech, types of sentences, fragments, and comma splice errors as well as a section defining grammatical terms), grammatical usage (with sections on agreement, case, adjectives and adverbs, and tense and mood of verbs), punctuation, spelling, mechanics, and the research paper. Each section has explanation and examples to illustrate principles and a set of exercises. Most examples are from student papers. This text is aimed at students in freshman English and could be used as a supplement to a writing or literature course.

120   Emery, Donald W. and John M. Kierzek. *English Funda-*
        mentals. 5th ed. form B. New York: Macmillan,
        1971. 254 pp. $3.50 (P)

This text was first published in 1933, and this fifth edition represents the most extensive revision to date. The primary purpose of the text is the teaching of funda mentals, and the authors feel that the student who masters this text will have little trouble with freshman composition. The text begins with several diagnostic tests followed by thirty-three sections covering every aspect of fundamental English from parts of speech to sentence building. Twenty progress tests are given, and six achievement texts conclude the text. Each section begins with a brief, simple explanation of a principle. Almost all of the exercises are arranged in the order of increasing complexity, and they are easily corrected with an answer key. The authors diagram many sentences used as examples, and the exercises are on tear-out sheets. The book is suitable as a handbook text or could be used as a supplement. Forms A and C are also available.

121   Eschholz, Paul A., Alfred F. Rosa, and Virginia P. Clark
        eds. *Language Awareness.* New York: St. Martin's

Press, 1974. 270 pp. $3.95 (P)

This reader includes essays--by such authors as George Orwell, H. L. Mencken, Ossie Davis, and Stuart Chase--which focus on various aspects of language. Essays range from Orwell's "Politics and the English Language" to Alfred Rosa and Paul Eschholz's "Bunkerisms: Archie's Suppository Remarks in 'All in the Family.'" The text is divided into five sections: Perspectives, Language and Occupation, Prisoners of Language, Influencing Language, and Prospects. Each selection is briefly introduced and followed by from four to seven exercises for discussion and review. Extensive exercises and assignments for writing are given at the end of each section. This reader is primarily designed for standard English composition classes as a supplemental reader; it could be used in more advanced classes as well.

122 Estrin, Herman A. and Donald V. Mehus. *The American Language in the 1970's.* San Francisco: Boyd and Fraser, 1974. 353 pp. $5.95 (P)

The main premise of this reader is that during the last decade many new words, phrases, and expressions have come into use, especially slang and jargon. The authors hope "to help the individual student--through his becoming more aware of many aspects of the current American language--to improve his own ability to write good, clear, expository compositions on a variety of subjects." The text includes many articles from contemporary writers and publications (i.e., *Time* and *Saturday Review*). Several essays are included in each chapter, and chapter headings include The Development of American English; Dictionaries and Usage; Slang, Graffiti, and Euphemisms; The Language of Government and Politics; The Language of the Blacks; The Language of Women's Liberation; The Language of Science and Space; Academia and Its Jargon; The Arts and the Mass Media; Censorship and Pornography; Other Forms of Communication; Modern Living and Behavior; and The Future of English. This text would be suitable for standard or advanced composition classes.

123 Everett, Edwin M., Marie Dumas, and Charles Wall. *Correct Writing.* Form D. Lexington, Mass.: D. C. Heath, 1961. 384 pp. $4.95 (P)

This grammar workbook/handbook focuses, for the most part, on basic grammar and sentence structure. Chapters cover conventional grammar and usage principles (parts of speech, clauses, modifiers, and subordination, etc.), punctuation, mechanics, dictionary use, diction, vocabulary, spelling, and theme writing (fifteen pages). The normal construction of each chapter is to present briefly the definitions, rules, and concepts of the heading.

Following these are numerous exercises for the student to complete--118 in all. These generally involve underlining, filling in the blank, and punctuating although chapters on paragraphs and themes require actual writing A diagnostic test begins the text, and an achievement test ends it. An answer key is available for the exercises, and the text comes in Forms A, B, C, and D. This book could be used on the high school as well as the college level. It could be the sole text for a remedial college English course or a handbook for standard composition classes.

124 Fear, David E. *Technical Writing*. New York: Random House, 1973. 254 pp. $4.95 (P)

The author states in his preface that "This book has been written primarily for students in junior college technical-industrial programs, but it should also be useful as a basic technical writing text for students in technical institutes and for engineering students who do not intend to become involved in mid-or high-level management. No attempt is made to treat the writing problem faced by established scientists, engineers, or businessmen." The book begins with a survey of the various types of communications required of technical employees and lists the basic principles of technical communication: clarity, conciseness, and consideration of specific audience. Chapter two, Basic Techniques, introduces the basic patterns of technical writing: explanatory patterns, technical description, technical process writing, instructional process writing, definition, and outline forms. This chapter also includes some brief notes on style and mechanics but does not offer an in-depth review of grammar and usage. Chapter three deals with technical letter writing from physical form through style. Models of various types of letters are given. Informal reports such as minor project reports, special event reports, progress reports and prepared form reports are covered in chapter four. Again, models of reports are given. Chapter five deals with the formal report by discussing each of its component parts and giving several model reports. Chapter six covers the use of illustrations: informal and formal tables, bar and line graphs, organizational and flow charts, pictures and drawings. Chapter seven looks at the importance of oral reporting. Appendices review basic library usage and bibliography and supply a model report. Each topic throughout the text is followed by simple suggestions for class exercise

125 Fishman, Burton J., ed. *Viewpoints*. New York: St. Martin's Press, 1972. 210 pp. $4.50 (P)

This college level reader for composition courses

offers a variety of essays for use as examples in writing classes. The editor includes no commentary to explain types of essays or suggest writing topics. The book consists of twenty-two essays of varying length, subject matter, and style. The first group of essays concerns political-ethical topics, including alienation in America, feminism, Hiroshima, and Indians. The essays cover style, first politically then artistically, in terms of the novel and movies among other things. Other essays discuss the problems of education and the environment. Essayists include Peter Schrag, LeRoi Jones, John Corry, Nicholas von Hoffman, Pauline Kael, and Paul R. Erlich.

126   Fiske, Edward B. *The Contemporary Religious Experience.* Indianapolis: Bobbs-Merrill, 1967. 63 pp. $1.00 (P)

This book is part of *The Bobbs-Merrill Series in Composition and Rhetoric.* See listing under Johnson, Falk S. for the complete annotation.

127   Flachmann, Kim and Henry A. Bamman. *Time In: A Guide to Communication Skills.* Palo Alto, Ca.: Field Educational Publications, 1973. 384 pp. $5.50 (P)

In the introduction the authors state that "The primary goal of this communications text is to offer your students a variety of material that will be genuinely interesting to them with the hope that their own emotional and intellectual reactions to the selections, photographs, discussions, and projects will be of help in defining their minds, their social selves, and their basic needs." The text is divided into three main units: Then, Now, and When which are designed to take the student from his past to his future. There are questions before the readings to guide the student into the material. Vocabulary lists are given, and questions for comprehension follow the selections. Some of these questions could be used for class discussion. Assignments following the readings encourage the student to write themes, verse, fiction, musical pieces, drama, or whatever type of writing he has just read. A short glossary of literary terms is also supplied. Selections include such authors as Piri Thomas, Rainer Maria Rilke, James Dickey, James Thurber, Buffy Sainte-Marie, Erich Fromm, Ring Lardner, and Rod Serling. The book contains photographs, drawings, quotations, limericks, posters, advertisements, and photo-essays to represent types of communication and to stimulate the student. This text is designed for use in a lower-level composition course.

128 Flanigan, Lloyd A. and Sylvia A. Holladay. *Developing
Style: An Extension of Personality*. Boston: Holbrook
Press, 1972. 518 pp. $6.95 (P)

The authors state in their preface that this book
"demonstrates, in simple terms, various styles to the
novice writer." Part one, Style: A Way of Life and An
Angle of Vision, discusses approaches to style and
includes sample essays of formal, informal, and colloquial
style. Part two, Elements of Style, includes the following: 1) various points of view--six types are included,
2) mood and tone, 3) diction, and 4) language patterns.
Essays which demonstrate these principles are included.
Part three, Method and Style, discusses description,
narration, exposition, and argument and presents fifteen
essays and stories as examples. Part four, Fiction and
Criticism, includes examples of the short story and the
critical essay and gives a short story for analysis.
Parts one through four are introduced by brief explanations. Parts one through three have exercise material on
style and content and suggestions for writing. Part five,
Selections for Analysis of Style: Angles of Vision,
includes twenty selections by authors such as Langston
Hughes, Rupert Brooke, E. B. White, and Marshall McLuhan.
There are no questions or exercises for this section.
This text is suitable as a reading text in composition,
especially for advanced writing classes.

129 Fleming, Harold. *English Grammar: Forms and Structures*.
San Francisco: Boyd and Fraser, 1971. 378 pp.
$5.50 (P)

This transformational grammar workbook includes com-
paratively little text and a great many exercises. It
deals with fundamental grammar and relies heavily on the
tree diagram or sentence tree patterns which the book
teaches along with fundamental rules. Section one,
Sentence Patterns, introduces the reader to this method
of diagramming and develops the tree diagram of each
type of sentence pattern as well as diagramming sentence
errors. Section two, Word Forms and Sentence Structures,
includes classifying words as content or structure words,
classifying nouns by position, and so on. Verb forms and
irregular verbs are also covered in this chapter. Section three deals with modification; section four is a
detailed survey of grammatical transformations; section
five covers punctuation. All sections except section
four include a proficiency test, and all chapters conclud
with an assignment for an in-class theme. This text is
suitable for any writing class in which a transformationa
grammar review is necessary.

130 Flesch, Rudolf. *The Art of Readable Writing*. 25th
       anniversary edition, revised and enlarged. New York:
       Harper and Row, 1974. 291 pp. NPA (H)

This is a revised edition of a text which first
appeared in 1949. The illustrations and examples are not
updated, though the author states in his preface that he
has added postscripts to those chapters which need
updating or further explanation. This is a text which
deals with "scientific rhetoric," a handbook based on an
analytical study of the English language as it is used
today, and it could be used in a course in any discipline
in which the instructor wishes the students to write
clear, simple prose on any subject, including scientific
reports. The author uses formulas to test the readability of prose writing. "Some readers, I am afraid,
will expect a magic formula for good writing and will be
disappointed with my simple yardstick. Others, with a
passion for accuracy, will wallow in the little rules and
computations but lose sight of the principles of plain
English. What I hope for are readers who won't take the
formula too seriously and won't expect from it more than
a rough estimate." The chapters are discussions on a
broad variety of rhetorical principles such as the shaping
of ideas, creativity in prose, being factual, etc. There
are charts on the front and back covers from which the
student can compute the "Human Interest" of his writing
from the percent of "Personal Sentences" and can compute
the "Reading Ease" of his prose from the "Words per
Sentence" and the "Syllables per 100 Words." This text
is perhaps most applicable to more advanced rhetoric
studies. It includes no exercises.

131 Flesch, Rudolf. *Say What You Mean*. New York: Harper
       and Row, 1972. 163 pp. $6.95 (H)

This text attempts to explain how to put down on paper
exactly what you mean to say and thus is basically a book
on style that approaches the problem in a practical
manner. The primary audience is the person, not necessarily
the student, who wants to improve his writing and who does
not "need more grammar, punctuation and usage." The
author centers on effective communication; chapter two,
Talk on Paper, for example, attacks the problem of levels
and types of language. The third chapter, Get the Facts,
discusses being specific and accurately reporting facts
in communications. The remaining chapters discuss using
short sentences and short words, appropriate reactions to
letters, and how to explain, report, and apologize in
business communications. The book is suitable as a
supplementary text for a course in practical or business
writing.

132 Ford, Nick Aaron, ed. *Language in Uniform: A Reader on Propaganda*. Indianapolis: Odyssey, 1967. 212 pp. $2.00 (P)

The editor states in his preface that "The purpose of *Language in Uniform* is to acquaint students with the most common varieties of propagandistic writings and to help them toward understanding how to analyze and evaluate suc writings." The text is divided into five main sections: an introduction which has four selections discussing the nature of propaganda, and chapters entitled Political and Economic Discussion, Racial and Religious Considerations, In Pursuit of Educational Goals, and Effective Advertising: The Art of Hidden Persuasion. Brief biographical notes about the authors represented are included as well as a selected bibliography. Questions for study and discussion, a list of vocabulary words, and a writing assignment follow each selection. Writers included in this text are Walter Lippmann, Jonathan Swift, Daniel Webster, Adolph Hitler, John Milton, and J. D. Ratcliff, among others.

133 Francis, Nelle and J. Warren Smith. *Patterns for Prose Writing: From Notes to Themes*. Glenview, Ill.: Scott, Foresman, 1969. 330 pp. $5.50 (P)

The authors of this text assert that the practice of "good writing grows out of the analysis of excellent writing and the correct method of preparatory note-taking." The text is founded on the premise that if the student understands the basic patterns of successful writing he will be able to improve his writing. The book is broken down into four major sections: Description, Exposition, Argumentation, and Narration, designed to bring the student along from the paragraph to the completed theme. Model patterns are introduced for each type of writing. For example, in the section on description the patterns of space order, time order, order of climax, and accumulation of detail are treated. The principles are briefly explained then followed by samples which instruct the student in recognizing the pattern. Questions on technique are given followed by a step-by-step method of applying the principle from notes to theme. Pattern one of each section has an example of student writing. The section on exposition includes material on examples, analogy, use of comparison and contrast, definition, classification, cause and effect, and process. The section on argumentation includes material on induction and deduction, and the narration section offers segments on simple narration, character development, slice-of-life, and the stream of consciousne technique. Excerpts vary in length and complexity and include a wide range of authors. An appendix offers instruction on outlining. The text is designed for the beginning college student confronted with the problem of organized writing assignments.

134 Frank, Joseph. *You*. New York: Harcourt, Brace, Jovano-
      vich, 1972. 281 pp. $4.95 (P)

You, according to the author, assumes that each student has something to say and the he can say it in many voices. "No one is incapable of learning to write, and there is no necessarily correct style or prescribed voice . . . every selection, every question, every picture, tries to get you to think, talk, and write about the subject you know best: yourself." Each chapter contains many different types' of selections for the student to respond to-- pictures, paintings, stories, essays, and so on. The first section, You and Your Senses, contains material designed to make the student aware of each of his five senses. Part two, Your Sense of You, discusses a person's relationship to himself, to others, and to the whole universe. Basically this text is a source book with no formal student exercises although some questions are included for the student to think about or respond to. The intention of the book is to raise consciousness and awareness in the student. As a source book, this text is aimed at the college freshman but could be used on the high school level.

135 Freedman, Morris and Paul B. Davis. *Contemporary Contro-
      versy*. 2nd ed. New York: Macmillan, 1973. 516 pp.
      $4.95 (P)

The authors of this reader state in their preface that "We have found that in reading, writing, and discussion, students respond more intensely and perform more capably when stimulated and engaged by the controversial. This anthology is designed to provide such stimulation and engagement." Each of the fourteen sections include essays, reports, and articles about some current topic. The sections are entitled Channeling Opinion; The Public's Right to Know: The Pentagon Papers and the Supreme Court; Bearing Arms: Liberty or License; Method and Madness; Drug Addiction: Family Illness or Social Crime?; Christ and the Body; Population Control Begins at Home; Sex and the School Child; Soul Language and Standard English; What Difference Does It All Make?; Studies in Black and White; Women as Professors; The Death Sentence; and When Does Life End? Authors include J. Edgar Hoover, William Blake, LeRoi Jones, Richard Nixon, and writers for the Washington *Post*. At the end of each section are questions, assignments, and additional reading. The questions and assignments are intended to stimulate dis- cussion and/or writing. As a source book this text is primarily aimed at the college-level student.

136 Fuhr, Rita and Cyra McFadden. *Description: Using the Mind's Eye*. New York: Harper and Row, 1974. 38 pp. NPA (P)

This pamphlet is part of the *Harper Studies in Languag and Literature* listed in this bibliography under Shrodes, Caroline, editor.

137 Gallo, Joseph D. and Henry W. Rink. *Shaping College Writing: Paragraph and Essay*. 2nd ed. New York: Harcourt, Brace, Jovanovich, 1973. 133 pp. $3.50 (P)

The authors state in the preface that "the paragraph seems to us to be the best medium for introducing the student to pattern, structure, and arrangement in prose writing without immediately overwhelming him with the complexities of the full-length essay." On the whole this text deals with the paragraph although there is one chapter on multi-paragraph papers. There are seven chapters: The Topic Sentence, Unity, Coherence, Support, Organization, The Form of the One-Paragraph Essay, and The Form of the Essay. The text of the chapters is usually brief with many short examples to illustrate the points made. Exercises comprise more than half of this text. The exercises call for the student to practice principles given in the chapters and are varied in nature. The student classifies sentences provided, rewrites sentences and paragraphs, and writes sentences and paragraphs of his own on topics provided. The chapter on organization supplies a topic outline to be filled in and lists of sentences for the student to order into an outline. The authors further state in their preface that "We feel our book is adaptable to any basic composition course in which emphasis is placed on the principles of structure and concrete support as means of teaching the student to write."

138 Garcia, Anthony and Robert Myers. *Analogies: A Visual Approach to Writing*. New York: McGraw-Hill, 1974. 280 pp. $5.95 (P)

This text aims at convincing students "that writing is fun and easier than they thought." The authors affirm that the arts of communication are directly related to sensory awareness. Hence, the text begins with lessons and group experiences which provide the student with fresh perspectives from which to write. The next step is to explore connections between ways of viewing the world and language. The authors stress that verbal expression is "an urge as common as walking or eating" and that the unconscious is "the true source of all [the student's] thought." Focusing on the written art form, the authors attempt to demonstrate "the significance for life and sanity of all art forms." Many visual examples are given. Part one is divided into seven sections. The first investigates the relationship between signs, symbols, and words by offering widely diversified exercises designed to heighten sensory awareness. The student reacts to photographs, symbols, and so on. The second chapter deals with the element of self-confidence. Chapter three takes a look at the creative process, attempting to make the student aware of his unconscious and its role in original expression. Chapter four examines the created thing by discussing the importance or organic unity. Chapters five, six, and seven relate the image and the word with discussions of the sentence as "the first perceivable image unit in writing" and of the paragraph as a unit comprised of collective image units and continuity. The basic analogy used in these discussions is the student as movie camera. Part two deals with more specific rhetorical issues. Chapters deal with generality and concreteness, how to write a more detailed sentence, methods of para- graphing, rules of punctuation, and a set of "mini exercises" on a variety of writing aspects. The authors note that most of the lessons and exercises are designed for execution and evaluation in small groups, but the instructor can work with the entire class in most cases. This text can be used on the freshman level.

139 Gefvert, Constance, Richard Raspa, and Amy Richards. *Keys to American English*. New York: Harcourt, Brace, Jovanovich, 1975. 389 pp. NPA (P)

This text is more specific in its intended audience than many. The authors state in the preface that the book is intended "for beginning freshman English classes with students who need work in the basic grammatical structures of 'standard' English. . . . The students we are addressing, then, are those who traditionally are overlooked in freshman English texts and even in 'remedial' texts, that is, those students whose spoken, or 'commun- ity,' dialects vary more widely from the written forms of standard English than do the dialects of other freshmen." The book has an introduction which reviews the various origins of our language and looks at the factors which contribute to dialectical speech. The body of the text contains five sections: Verbs, Nouns and Pronouns, Adjectives and Adverbs, Questions and Negatives, and Sentence Patterns. The grammatical material is simple and traditional, and a number of exercises are included for each chapter in these sections. The authors do not attempt to replace a community dialect with what they call "standard dialect"; rather they present standard English as another dialect form. "Here, then, is the general plan of the book. In each part we first present a single feature that differs in some community dialects from the standard dialect. Next we have a series of exercises that we call Recognition Drills; the purpose of these is to give you practice in recognizing which sentences are written in a community dialect and which in the standard dialect. Next we have exercises we call Pattern Practice that give you intensive drill in using the standard forms. Finally, we have Conversion Drills in which we ask you to convert, or translate, from the community dialects into the standard dialect."

140   Gibb, Carson. *Exposition and Literature*. New York: Macmillan, 1971. 260 pp. $3.95 (P)

The author states in his preface that part one of this book has a dual purpose: "to set forth the principles of exposition and to show their use in writing about literature." Part one is divided into eight sections. The first five chapters discuss the topic of exposition with material on the theory of exposition, its substance (detail and illustration, comparison, analogy, cause and effect, definition, division, and deduction) unity, and order. The emphasis is on what to do, not on what not to do. The author has taken pains to be brief and simple. All principles are illustrated with student themes. The latter chapters of part one cover sentences and diction, including an appendix on constructing and punctuating. Part two aims at helping the student to understand literature, especially poetry. It consists of an essay on the characteristics and demands of poetry and includes material on images, figurative language, and syntax. The essay is intended to dispell misunderstandings of poetry. The book concludes with a glossary of literary terms. The chapters in part one include exercises which demand written responses and address specific points made in individual chapters. This book is designed as a text for introductory courses in literature and composition and as a supplementary text for any course in which the students will write about literature.

141   Gibson, Walker. *Euphemism*. New York: Harper and Row, 1974. 28 pp. NPA (P)

This pamphlet is a part of the *Harper Studies in Language and Literature* listed in this bibliography under Shrodes, Caroline, editor.

142   Gibson, Walker. *Persona: A Style Study for Readers and Writers*. New York: Random House, 1969. 90 pp. NPA (P)

This book centers its attention on the stylist's created persona in prose writing. The approach concentrates on the fact that "the message or utterance is seen as modified by the created personality put forth in the act of communicating." In the first three chapters the author attempts to identify personae in three familiar types of writing: the essay, newspaper writing, and a modern novel (Bellow's *Herzog*). A number of passages are included at the end of each chapter, preceded by some suggestions for practice in creating one's own persona in writing. The last three chapters deal more explicitly with the writing process. Chapter four focuses on choice in tone--the relation of persona to reader. Chapter five discusses choices in attitude--the relation of persona to subject, and the final chapter provides examples of how writers express themselves through role-playing and voice. These chapters also have Applications which demand writing. This text is best suited for an advanced composition course, particularly one dealing with fine points of style and tactic. The book could also be used in a creative writing class.

143 Gibson, Walker. *Seeing and Writing: Fifteen Exercises in Composing Experience*. 2nd ed. New York: David McKay, 1974. 198 pp. NPA (P)

In his preface the author assumes that "if young writers are encouraged to look hard at their own experience they will see something there and say something about it of interest to their teachers." The book attempts to place "the student in positions where he must see his experience from shifting points of view" and to help the writer become conscious of style. The first four chapters explore acts of "seeing" one's everyday experiences. Chapter one suggests a description of a college campus then juxtaposes it with a description of a campus taken from Ralph Ellison's *Invisible Man*. Chapter two raises the question of visual ambiguity and employs illustrations from *Scientific American*. Chapters three and four also deal with concepts of perception. Chapters five through eight raise the problem of "how I see myself as a student," with passages that offer the student new terms for perceiving himself. The later chapters focus on the writer as student-historian and student-scientist. The chapters involve description, historical metaphor, impressionistic reporting, and so on. In the final chapter the student is asked to reassess his activity as a composer of essays in light of the philosophical implications in modern physics. Each chapter has a brief passage preceding the directions for writing which explains terms and points of view. The author suggests using one chapter per week, supplementing the book with instruction in rhetoric, library use, or extra reading. This book can be used on many levels and is suitable for freshman composition.

144 Gilbert, Marilyn B. *Clear Writing*. New York: John
Wiley and Sons, 1972. 336 pp. $2.95 (P)

This text is primarily intended as a self-teaching
guide although it could be utilized in the classroom.
The book assumes that the student has a subject and can
write a first draft. "This book teaches you how to turn
that first draft--no matter how crude it may be--into
clear, effective English." The book teaches techniques
of copyediting as well as rewriting. Each chapter begins
with preview exercises which enable the student to judge
what he already knows before proceeding to the instructional material of the chapter. An appendix contains
practice exercises for each chapter, and exercise
material is incorporated into the chapters themselves.
Chapter one, Reading for Sense, deals with paragraphing
and misplaced sentences. Chapter two covers sentences,
clauses, and word choice. Chapter three discusses linking ideas; chapter four deals with placing emphasis by
stylistic methods. Chapter five is entitled Simplifying
Descriptions. Rules on mechanics are scattered throughout the material as the situation calls for their use.
Chapter six is devoted completely to methods of listing.
Chapter seven covers consistency, which in this particula
text refers to agreement (subject/verb, pronoun). Chapte
eight discusses shifts in viewpoint or time; chapter nine
deals with brevity; chapter ten covers being specific.
Chapter eleven includes mechanics of grammar which have
not been dealt with elsewhere. The appendices to the
book include practice exercises, A Concise Guide to Clear
Writing, a chart of copyediting symbols, grammatical
rules presented in chart form, and further information on
capitalization and numbers.

145 Gillespie, Sheena and Linda Stanley. *Someone likes Me:
Images for Writing*. 2nd ed. Cambridge, Mass.:
Winthrop, 1975. 332 pp. NPA (P)

This text pursues the inductive approach to the development of writing style by using essay models to suggest
various writing techniques. Thematic and rhetorical
units are integrated to illustrate essential writing
principles. Each of the six chapters presents a thematic
matrix--People, Places, Events and Experiences, Emotions,
Choices, and Philosophies. Each chapter focuses upon one
or two of the following writing techniques: choosing an
effective topic and selecting vocabulary and tone, organizing a paper and describing a place, developing the
paragraph and recreating an event, analyzing causes and
effects and achieving coherence, contrasting and comparin
alternatives, and analyzing a complex idea. Each chapter
presents four essays, two short stories, and three poems.
The authors note that the choice for the readings was

based on relating personal experience (all essays are in the first person), the subject students are primarily interested in writing about. There is a gradual movement from the purely personal and subjective experience to the objective and critical evaluation of ideas. Two sets of questions follow each reading, one set on meaning and the other investigating method. The rhetorical sections are broken down into three subdivisions: one points out how the essay writer develops technique; another states rhetorical principles used; and a final division indicates ways of implementing learned techniques. Essay topics, both autobiographical and critical, are suggested. Essays by Tom Wicker, Tom Wolfe, Bertrand Russell and Norman Podhoretz; poems by Adrienne Rich, Ted Hughes, Robert Bly, and Richard Eberhart; and stories by Albert Camus, Bernard Malamud, William Saroyan, and John Updike are included. Most of the selections are from modern American authors.

146   Glorfeld, Louis E., David A. Lauerman, and Norman C. Stageberg. *A Concise Guide for Writers*. 3rd ed. New York: Holt, Rinehart and Winston, 1974. 171 pp. $3.75 (P)

The authors state four purposes for this book: 1) to show college freshmen how to plan and begin a theme; 2) to help them overcome common faults; 3) to teach standard methods of developing thought in paragraphs and devices for a smooth, readable style; and 4) to show them how to cope with essay exams. The concept is to focus on important errors rather than present a handbook approach. Chapter one offers hints on getting started and outlining. Chapter two is a systematic approach to writing faults (subject/verb agreement, ambiguity, colon usage, misplaced modifiers, redundancy). Each section has a brief explanation accompanied by examples from student writing. Two revision exercises follow each section. Chapter three covers thought development and coherence, writing the essay exam, and outlining the long theme. The authors suggest the text can be used as a remedial reference or supplementary text.

147   Gordon, Edward J. *Writing About Imaginative Literature*. New York: Harcourt, Brace, Jovanovich, 1973. 196 pp. $3.95 (P)

The author states in his preface that "If the student is to write intelligently about any literary selection, he must first know how to read that selection with understanding. As he reads, he must ask the kinds of questions that a good literary critic asks." This text is divided into three major sections: The Short Story, Poetry, and

Drama. Each section begins with a selection, followed by an analysis. For example, The Short Story begins with de Maupassant's "The Piece of String" and a subsequent analysis. Discussions on point of view, plot, setting, characterization, and theme are given, and each is followed by exercise questions. Practical discussions about writing include material on topic selection, note taking, thesis statement, titles, development, conclusions, revision, and a sample essay. The section on poetry presents fifteen poems followed by analyses. Discussions of diction, imagery, comparison, symbol, sound, meter, free verse, blank verse, organization of a poem, and tempo are followed by exercises and discussions on writing about poetry. The section on drama includes three plays followed by analyses and exercises. An appendix covers the use of quotations.

148   Gorrell, Robert M. and Charlton Laird. *Modern English Handbook*. 5th ed. Englewood Cliffs, N.J.: Prentice-Hall, 1972. 675 pp. $7.50 (H)

Based on the principle that writing is hard work but becomes easier and better with serious study, this text offers both linguistic and rhetorical instruction. It begins with choosing, limiting, and specifying the topic. Chapters one through eleven deal with basic characteristics of essay writing: unity, development, coherence, organization, logic, and detail, for example. Chapters twelve through seventeen deal with all aspects of sentencing, and chapter eighteen focuses on emphasis in writing. Nineteen and twenty cover vocabulary and word usage. Following sections deal with style (tone and point of view), exam writing and impromptu writing, writing about literature, the investigative paper, and punctuation and mechanics. This text could be used in any composition course. Although there are no classic essays as examples, there are many illustrative examples and sets of discussion problems, writing exercises, and essay topics. The book could also be used for reference.

149   Gorrell, Robert M., Ronald Freeman, and Charlton Laird. *Modern English Reader*. Englewood Cliffs, N.J.: Prentice-Hall, 1970. 555 pp. $5.25 (P)

This text is organized to be a companion reader to the *Modern English Handbook* by the same authors. It could be used independently. Each section begins with a brief description of rhetorical principles, followed by several essays illustrating those principles. Study exercises follow, with one lengthy question addressed to each essay. The exercises are geared more to analytical study of the essays than to providing writing topics. The instructional sections are brief but clear; the essays vary widely in both type and length.

150 Gorrell, Robert M. and Charlton Laird. *Writing Modern English*. Englewood Cliffs, N.J.: Prentice-Hall, 1973. 278 pp. $5.25 (P)

This book attempts to cultivate "the habit of expression" and to stimulate "the search for something to express." It is based on four principles: 1) to write well, an author must have something to say and abundant detail to say it with; 2) good writing develops more from practicing what to do than from being told what not to do; 3) studying the way a language works helps a writer use the language well; 4) use of language cannot be reduced to a set of rules, and writing must be judged on whether or not it does what it purports to do. These principles are applied to formal aspects of composition: rhetoric, grammar, diction, and mechanics. The first sections emphasize that writing is a continuing process of pre-writing, writing, and rewriting. These sections also cover topics, unity, development, organization, and coherence. Section eight concerns paragraph patterns; other chapters deal with definition, induction, and logic. There are several sections on sentencing and a few on word choice and style. Writing on literature and objective writing are also covered. The book closes with extensive chapters on mechanics and punctuation and a glossary of usage and terms. The exercises are mainly guides for practice in writing techniques and are on perforated pages. Much writing practice is provided. The book moves from the fundamentals of writing to higher levels of sophistication and is designed for a standard college composition course.

151 Gowen, James A. *English Review Manual: A Program for Self-Instruction*. New York: McGraw-Hill, 1965. 412 pp. $6.95 (H) $4.95 (P)

This programmed text is designed to be used in an advanced high school class or a college-level composition class, either as the main text or as a supplement for usage problems. An instructor's manual and test booklets are available upon request. Chapters one through fifteen deal with basic grammar and style: basic sentence parts, major parts of speech, sentence patterns, phrases, compound and complex sentences, tense, voice, mood, subject/verb agreement, pronouns, modifiers, mixed and illogical constructions, and wordiness. Chapters sixteen through twenty-four cover punctuation. Chapter twenty-five deals with capitalization. The text is programmed to move step-by-step with frequent reviews. It could be used by a class or for independent review. A second edition (1970) was unavailable for examination.

152 Gowen, James A. *Progress in Writing: A Learning Program*. New York: McGraw-Hill, 1973. 191 pp. $4.50 (P)

This programmed textbook could be used in high school or college composition classes in which the student is taught the traditional fundamentals of writing good themes. The author states in his preface that "good writing is not the result of correctness. Rather, it is the result of effective word choice, skillful sentence building, sound paragraph organization, and finally, meaningful and coherent arrangement of all parts." This text is divided into four parts: Words, Sentences (focus clauses, nouns, adjective and verb clusters, absolute phrases), Paragraphs (general and particular statements, topic sentences, development and coherence), and The Whole Essay (topic, thesis, snowballing, outlining, and writing the essay). Each chapter contains short explanatory statements or examples and calls for some relative simple responses on the students' part. More complex material is gradually introduced. Each chapter reviews a major concept. Since this is a programmed text, there are no formal theme topics offered.

153 Gove, Philip B. *The Role of the Dictionary*. Indianapol Bobbs-Merrill, 1967. 63 pp. $1.00 (P)

This book is part of *The Bobbs-Merrill Series in Composition and Rhetoric*. See listing under Johnson, Falk S. for the complete annotation.

154 Graham, Sheila Y. *Harbrace College Workbook*. form 7A. New York: Harcourt, Brace, Jovanovich, 1972. 180 pp $3.50 (P) form 7B. $3.50 (P)

This workbook is designed to be used with the *Harbrac College Handbook* (see Hodges, John C.); however, since explanations of the grammar and usage rules which the exercises cover are included, it could be used in any composition course which requires a number of exercises. The organization of this workbook parallels that of the *Harbrace Handbook* through the first four units: Grammar Punctuation, Spelling and Diction, and Effective Sentences. The exercises are on tear-out pages. A form fo an individual spelling list is included so the student may record those words which give him particular problem The exercises in form A deal with ecology; the exercises in form B deal with male-female relationships. The book includes a list of commonly misspelled words, a list of correction symbols, and a diagram of the organization of the workbook.

155 Grant, Louis T. *Communitas of College and Community*. New York: D. Van Nostrand, 1972. 410 pp. $5.25 (P

Communitas is a reader which "aims to acquaint the student with excellence in writing" by asking him to explore the "individual's role in the many communities to which he belongs." In as much as this text does center on a broad, underlying theme, it attempts to unify the approach to writing. Included are poems, photographs, radical essays, and conservative essays. The essays are arranged in eight sections ranging from One's-Self I Sing: The "I" That Precedes All Communities to In the Midst of Irrational Things: The Ecology Community. The essays included are also listed in a traditional manner in the Rhetorical Table of Contents. The author's primary audience is the college student taking a standard composition course. This book could be used as a source book as well.

156   Graves, Harold F. and Lyne S. Hoffman. *Report Writing*.
      4th ed. Englewood Cliffs, N.J.: Prentice-Hall, 1965.
      $9.95 (H)

This textbook is designed for a college-level technical writing student. The information is presented in order of increasing complexity beginning with the letter and moving up to the report and manuscript preparation. Chapter one, The Demand for Reports, justifies the need for lucid presentation of technical material. Chapter two, Letter and Memorandum, includes the letter of inquiry, the letter of instructions and how to answer such letters, the letter report, and notes on form and style. Chapter three, The Style of a Good Report, teaches the principles of unity, clarity, economy, accuracy and then discusses the problems involved in writing a good sentence and a good paragraph. Chapter four covers collecting data from all sources (reading, experiment, interview, etc.). Chapters five, six, and seven deal with actually planning and writing a report. Chapter five, Planning the Report, discusses both long and short reports, progress reports, periodic reports, investigative reports, and proposals and recommendations. Chapter six analyzes the parts of a report, and chapter seven deals with format and manuscript preparation. Following chapter seven, the authors include six specimen reports, offering a variety of examples. Each chapter concludes with a summary of material presented and a selection of assignments and exercises. The final major section of the text is a detailed handbook on the mechanics of grammar and preferred usage. The book closes with an appendix on the letter of application and a bibliography of abstracts and indices useful in technical fields.

157   Gray, Dwight E. *So You Have to Write a Technical Report: Elements of Technical Report Writing*. Washington, D.C.: Information Resources Press, 1970. 117 pp. NPA (P)

This book is a guide to report writing for the working technician and is concerned primarily with formal research reports. Most of the fundamental principles that relate to the preparation of these documents apply to the less formal categories as well. The reader will have no difficulty modifying suggested procedures for the less elaborate kinds of technical reports. The first two chapters of the book deal briefly with prewriting activities. The report is analyzed and broken down into its logical sections, and the problems of organization and outlining are dealt with. The next six chapters deal directly with writing the various component parts of a technical report. These parts are discussed in the order in which the author feels they should be written, not necessarily in the order in which they will appear in the final presentation of the report. The order which Gray recommends is as follows:

1. Introduction
2. Body of the Report
3. Conclusions and Recommendations
4. Appendices, Bibliography, and Table of Contents
5. Abstract
6. Title and Title Page.

No inclusive example of the formal report is given, although examples of bibliographical form and title forms are included. Chapter nine concentrates on the characteristics which insure an effective technical report: completeness, clarity, conciseness, veracity, restraint, and general appearance. The final chapter gives a capsule summary of all of the preceding chapters. The book gives no review of grammar or punctuation but does include an appendix bibliography of basic texts on style and usage. This text is not specifically designed for classroom use.

158 Greenberg, Florence Bonzer and Ann P. Heffley. *Tradition and Dissent: A Rhetoric/Reader*. 2nd ed. Indianapolis: Bobbs-Merrill, 1971. 584 pp. $3.95 (P)

This text is divided into two sections: The Rhetoric and The Reader. The first section in The Rhetoric attempts to start the student at a point at which he can succeed; the method involves observing and writing about the student's own environment in simple descriptions of haiku. The chapters have readings, photographs, lithographs, and prints of paintings as examples. There are writing assignments at the end of each chapter, some of which direct the student to the library for more information. The second part of the first section is entitled The Persuasive Essay and discusses such concepts as the controlling idea, development, introductions, conclusions

transitions, and types of proof such as definition and
evidence. Each of these chapters also ends with writing
assignments in which the student uses the principles in
the chapter to write essays with his own topics. There
are also exercises called "practice" at the end of the
chapters which have the student do more objective practicing of the principles. The second section of the
text, The Reader, has essays from a variety of authors on
different subjects, many of them contemporary. There are
study questions before each example and writing assignments after each chapter. Photographs, cartoons, essays,
poems, and stories are included. Some of the chapter
headings of the readings are Education in Transition,
Conscience in Conflict with Authority, Human Relations,
and War and Mankind. The artists included are Bertrand
Russell, Jessamyn West, Claude Brown, Charles M. Schulz,
Christopher Marlowe, and Henry Thoreau, among others.

159 Grieder, Theodore and Josephine Grieder. *A Student's
     First Aid to Writing*. Totowa, N.J.: Littlefield,
     Adams, 1972. 165 pp. $2.95 (P)

The authors explain in the preface that they have used
traditional terminology because it is the terminology
most students know. The first twelve chapters deal with
basic grammatical and mechanical problems, starting with
punctuation. The text goes on to cover types of dependent clauses, sentence fragments, further problems in
punctuation, case, sentence structure, usage problems,
mechanics, spelling, and finally a chapter on the whole
composition. Each chapter consists of two to five pages
of explanations with examples, followed by a set of
exercises with answers in the back of the book. After
every four chapters there are review exercises to cover
all the previous material. The exercises are on tear-out
pages. The first exercises are fairly "objective," but
later exercises involve rewriting sentences or paragraphs
provided. The final chapter ends with an exercise in
which the student writes introductory and concluding
paragraphs of his own and describes to the instructor a
method of group composition for the more advanced students. There is a topic index at the end which refers
students to chapters and page numbers according to their
particular problems. This workbook would be appropriate
in courses which are designed to teach fundamental
English rules or in remedial college English courses for
the student who needs review in the basic rules.

160 Griffin, Jacqueline P. and G. Howard Poteet. *Sentence
     Strategies: Writing for College*. New York: Harcourt,
     Brace, Jovanovich, 1971. 290 pp. NPA (P)

This text consists almost entirely of exercises on
perforated pages. The only explanations are short

paragraphs before each group of exercises. There is little emphasis on definition of terms; parts of speech are taught through position in sentences. Many of the exercises involve rewriting sentences and are not totally objective. The authors state in the preface, "Although we reject the traditional (Latin-based) parts-of-speech approach to English because it erroneously assumes that English, like Latin, is an inflected language, we do include lessons on the two highly inflected words in English, the verb and the personal pronoun." The text begins by having the student change statements into questions then identify subjects and verbs, discuss agreement, use time sequence, complements, and sentence structure. The student is to expand subjects and complements by using modifiers, expand by clauses or appositives, structure the complete subject, and combine short sentences through linking words, includers, or clauses. This is a college-level text for students who need practice writing sentences, and it could also be used in a high school.

161 Griggs, Irwin and Robert Llewellyn. *Basic Writer and Reader*. new alt. form. New York: D. van Nostrand, 1972. 516 pp. $5.95 (P)

The authors state in their preface that this text is "a combined handbook, workbook, and reader that will serve as the chief textbook in basic courses in English composition." The text is divided into two parts: The Basic Writer and The Basic Reader. The first part center on grammar--parts of speech, sentence structure, diction, punctuation, mechanics, and spelling as well as selecting the essay topic, outlining, dictionary use, and paragraphing. After most of the twenty-six chapters in this first part student exercises are given, many of which require the student to point out what is wrong with a sentence and then revise it. In most of these exercises the first ten sentences illustrate all the principles involved. Part two is divided into five chapters: Specimens of Writing, Early Years Remembered, Education, Character, and Living in Our Time. Each of these. chapter contains essays and stories that illustrate particular aspects of writing. Under Specimens of Writing, for example, readings illustrate concreteness, observation, definition, process, and so forth. Most of the readings are followed by student exercises which include sections entitled Content, Style and Organization, Words, and Suggestions for Themes. Authors represented range from Mark Twain and H. L. Mencken to Euell Gibbons.

162 Guerard, Albert J., Maclin B. Guerard, John Hawkes, and Claire Rosenfield, eds. *The Personal Voice: A Contemporary Prose Reader*. shorter ed. Philadelphia

J. B. Lippincott, 1968. 365 pp. $4.50 (P)

This college-level reader provides a variety of written material for the student to respond to. The text is divided into four major units: The Journey Within (including "a number of autobiographical, self-analytic essays" from such authors as W. B. Yeats, James Agee, and Yvor Winters); Intellectual Adventures (with essays involving "the natural and behavioral sciences" including such writers as Loren Eiseley, Ruth Benedict and E. M. Forster); American Problems (with essays which the authors feel are "personal" by such people as Norman Mailer and George F. Kennan); and Imagination, Fantasy, Dream (including selections from Herman Melville, William Faulkner, Jorge Luis Borges, and Bernard Malamud). Each unit begins with an introduction which discusses the various essays included and gives some reading guidelines. There is a short sketch about the author before each selection. Discussion and thought questions on the selections are given at the back of the book. In the preface the editors say that "The primary purpose of this book is to encourage the reading and writing of good prose, together with the qualities of mind and spirit on which good prose depends. . . . Our basic assumption is that reading and writing are highly personal acts and should engage the whole person."

163   Guth, Hans P. *Words and Ideas: A Handbook for College Writing.* 4th ed. Belmont, Ca.: Wadsworth, 1975. 496 pp. NPA (P)

"*Words and Ideas* is a rhetoric-handbook for courses in college composition." The book is organized under three main headings. Part one, A Writing Program, introduces the student to different kinds of writing situations applied to the theme as a whole. "The assignments in the Writing Program move naturally from emphasis on *substance* to emphasis on *structure* and from there to emphasis on *style*." The sequence begins with a preview of the whole theme. Early chapters stress perception, observation, experience, and material applying to the substance of writing. The middle chapters (Opinion, Definition, Argument) shift the emphasis to methods by which the writer shapes his material. Later chapters (Persuasion, Tone and Style) direct the writer's attention to his audience. The final chapters of the Writing Program deal specifically with the research paper and writing about literature. Part two, The Writer's Tools, consists of chapters entitled Paragraphs, Words, and Sentences. The chapter on words is lengthy and ranges in topic from word history and meaning through expressive and direct language. The chapter on sentences covers sentence construction as well as stylistic variety in sentences and sentence weaknesses. Part three, A Reference Handbook, focuses on "the basic requirements of literacy" and contains standard material in all aspects of grammar and usage as well as a wealth of exercises for the student. All of the informative material of the text is accompanied by exercises which may be used for class discussion or assignments.

164   Hairston, Maxine. *A Contemporary Rhetoric*. Boston: Houghton Mifflin, 1974. 351 pp. $6.50 (H)

This text aims at the students' interests and capabilities by stressing critical reasoning and writing and by attempting to create realistic writing situations. Major premises of the text are understanding audience and purpose. The ultimate aim is for the student to write clear, precise prose rather than highly stylized prose. The initial chapter gives a general outline on writing; then chapter two discusses the components of rhetoric. Other chapters are entitled Where Rhetoric Starts--and Stops, Controlling the Explanatory Power of Words, Exploring the Persuasive Power of Words, Modes of Argument (definition, cause and effect, for example), Three Modes of Reasoning (induction, deduction, Rogerian approach), Fallacies and Propaganda, and Writing About Literature. An appendix provides sample passages for rhetorical analysis, some sample student themes, tips on reading expository prose, a glossary of usage, and a brief handbook of grammar. Each chapter has exercises based on principles discussed, most of which demand writing. Suggested writing assignments are given. Formal readings are not included in the individual chapters, but selected examples are. This text is directed to freshman English classes but could be used in more advanced classes as well.

165   Hall, Donald. *Writing Well*. Boston: Little, Brown, 1973. 324 pp. $5.95 (P)

This text is a composition book and generally deals with questions of style. The first major unit deals with general questions on writing such as why one wishes to write at all and how to revise. Examples are given from some professional writers. There are exercises which involve student writing of short and long themes at the end of every unit. The second unit, Words, deals first with what words are then with types of words such as verbs, nouns, modifiers and originality in word choice. Exercises come after each section in this unit. The third unit is on sentences and deals with style, variety, and unity. Again, there are exercises after each section. The fourth unit deals with paragraphs and includes information on focus, length, unity and coherence, types of paragraphs, methods of development, topic sentences, and

transition. The fifth unit, The Paper, first goes
through the basic steps to approaching a paper then
describes with examples four types of papers: exposition,
argument and persuasion, description, and narrative. The
fifth unit also deals with dialogue and quotation, autobiography, fiction, research, and writing about writing.
There is a glossary of literary terms and commonly misused
expressions included before the subject index. Exercises
contain short work on principles described in each section and suggested theme topics or short writing assignments. A brief list of common editing and revision
symbols is given on the back cover. Examples come from
James Agee, James Dickey, Robert Frost, Germain Greer,
and Ezra Pound, among others. This writing text is
appropriate for use in a freshman composition course.

166   Hamalian, Leo and Edmond L. Volpe. *Grammar in Context.*
       form B. New York: G. B. Putman's Sons, 1962. 278
       pp. $2.75 (P)

This grammar workbook would be appropriate for use in
a college level remedial English class, in a writing
laboratory, or in a high school grammar class. It is
designed so the students learn grammar in the context of
essays by professional writers. At the beginning of each
chapter a short essay by a writer such as James Thurber
is given. After the essay there are writing suggestions
for the student. Following the essay suggestions the
authors include a chapter on some part of speech. "Each
part of speech in its manifest functions is considered
fully in its own chapter." Throughout the chapter short
"Test Yourself" exercises which could be used orally in
class are included. At the end of each chapter there are
a number of longer objective exercises on tear-out pages.
There are chapters entitled The Verb, The Noun, The
Pronoun, The Adjective, The Adverb, Prepositions and
Prepositional Phrases, Verbals and Verbal Phrases, Conjunctions and Clauses, The Sentence (with sections on
variety, emphasis, conciseness, awkwardness, and parallel
structure), Punctuation, and Diction (including sections
on concrete and abstract words, vagueness, denotation and
connotation, the trite phrase, pompous writing, and
spelling). A subject index and a list of correction
symbols can be found at the back of the book.

167   Hamilton, Harlan H. *New Preface to Writing: Series One,
       Two, or Three.* Indianapolis: Odyssey, 1957. $1.95
       (P)

The purpose of this book, according to the author, is
"to reduce the study of English grammar to its practical
essentials" and "to develop those habits of expression
which must become almost second nature before a student

learns to write freely and effectively." As its title indicates, the book should serve as a preface to composition. Six diagnostic tests begin the text, followed by a brief drill in dictionary usage. The six major divisions follow--the sentence, parts of speech, punctuation and mechanics, spelling, word choice, and "getting started"--each divided into subsections which are subsequently followed by exercises. The lessons are concise and definition oriented. The exercises are basically multiple choice or fill in the blank; there are no writing assignments. This text is designed for teaching basics to freshmen in college.

168   Hamon, Esther M. *Rhetorical Tactics*. New York: John Wiley and Sons, 1972. 174 pp. $4.25 (P)

This composition text, appropriate for advanced high school or lower-level college writing classes, teaches writing as persuasion using classical rhetorical methods. The first chapter introduces the concept of rhetoric, and following chapters slowly build to the essay. Chapters include The Nature of Words; The Sentence; The Paragraph; The Proposition; The Appeals (persuasion); The Topics; Three Kinds of Rhetorical Discourse; The Whole Composition: Each Part of the Plan for the Whole; The Entire Composition: Joining All the Parts Together; Style; and Reading. Each chapter includes textual explanation of the principles involved, discussions, questions, brief examples, and many exercises scattered throughout the text to make the student use the ideas presented. There is no discussion of punctuation, spelling, usage, or grammar as the author believes these problems tend to disappear if the student is trying to persuade the reader of his own ideas. Classical terms of rhetoric are used and explained, and contemporary examples are employed to illustrate them.

169   Hancock, Sheila and Ed Hancock. *Connections: Ideas for Writing*. New York: Harcourt, Brace, Jovanovich, 1974. 312 pp. NPA (P)

This composition text/reader gives suggestions and discussions for both prewriting activities and composition itself. Each chapter presents "a different pair of opposed but complementary concepts" by offering the student pictures, quotations, poetry, short stories, and expository pieces. Each chapter also includes rhetorical modes and a writing strategy with hints for revision, a student essay, and student exercises. The text is divided into eight sections. Section one, Opposition and Balance, deals with prewriting and good writing and contains class exercises and writing exercises as well as a group of readings for the student to respond to.

Section two, Youth and Age, offers readings revolving around this general theme and also discusses free writing. Section three, Anxiety and Tranquility, gives selections including poetry by T. S. Eliot, Yeats, and LeRoi Jones, an essay from *Time*, and a selection from *Invisible Man*. Section four presents the concept of Primitivism and Civilization; section five includes selections dealing with Consciousness and Reverie; six with Female and Male; seven with Individual and Mass; and eight with Known and Unknown. The inclusion of drawings, pictures, poetry, quotations, and prose, together with exercises and suggestions for class discussion, make this text useful for standard composition classes or as a source book for more advanced classes. The material on prewriting and the sample student essays also make this book appropriate for classes where it can be assumed the students have little experience with composition skills.

170 Hardison, O. B. *Practical Rhetoric*. New York: Appleton-Century-Crofts, 1966. 350 pp. $5.50 (P)

The author states in the preface that "The guiding principle of *Practical Rhetoric* is indicated by the first word of its title. Its purpose is to teach writing, not the history of rhetoric, the fundamentals of logic or the theory of general semantics. . . . In general, the movement of the text is from fundamentals (organization, paragraphing, basic elements of style) to specialized techniques (methods of development, advanced principles of style, deductive logic, the term paper and rhetorical criticism)." There are fourteen chapters: Organization; The Paragraph; Style; Development by Detail; Development by Example; Argumentation (I): Induction, Comparison and Contrast, Definition; Style (II); Introductions and Conclusions, Argumentation (II): Deduction; Style (III), The Research Paper; and Rhetoric and Criticism. Examples are scattered throughout the text to illustrate points made; some of the examples are from the classics, but there are others from newspapers, popular magazines, government publications, textbooks, and research reports. After each chapter a list of terms to be studied, exercises, and theme topics are given. Topics suggested for writings are for both paragraphs and themes. A glossary of terms is provided at the end. This textbook does not attempt to teach grammar; it is a text of fundamentals for good writing after basic grammatical skills have been mastered. The author points out in the preface that most composition courses are divided into a semester on rhetoric and a semester on the term paper or writing about literature. "Practical Rhetoric is intended to serve as the basic text for the first semester or quarter of this sequence. It can also be used in the second semester or

quarter in conjunction with supplementary materials--
'sourcebooks' and library assignments intended to teach
research techniques, or readings intended to enhance
appreciation of literature and teach principles of literary criticism."

171 Harmon, Gary L. and Ruth F. Dickinson. *Write Now!:*
     Substance, Strategy, Style. New York: Holt, Rinehart
     and Winston, 1972. 276 pp. $4.95 (P)

The text is based on the concept that writing is "one
of the best ways for an individual to expand and communicate his own personality and public identity" and is
designed to inform and interest students who already have
the basic skills. The authors feel they have attempted
to make the book flexible enough to adapt to various
degrees of sophistication in writing, and much of the
book can be handled by the student without outside instru-
tion. The authors suggest referring students to selected
sections to address particular problems. There are
twelve main chapters. In the first three chapters general discussions on thinking about writing, writing the
college paper, and consideration of audience are presente
Following chapters deal with more formal and stylistic
matters including paragraphing, sentence strategies,
grammar and usage problems, and word choice. Chapter
eight discusses essay forms--formal, personal, critical,
and research--with an example of each. Chapter nine dea
with critical thinking in writing, and the following two
chapters cover research writing and library use listing
descriptions of many major library references. The fina
chapter presents procedures for evaluating your own writing. Indices of authors and subjects follow. Most
chapters are brief but contain many explanations, illustrations, exercises, and points on writing, and most hav
a Learning Aids section which provides practice and
review of discussed principles. This text is particular
applicable to freshman composition and emphasizes writing
the essay as a whole.

172 Hart, Monte M. and Benson R. Schulman. *From Experience:*
     A Basic Rhetoric and Reader. Dubuque, Iowa: Wm. C.
     Brown, 1972. 345 pp. $5.50 (P)

This text has a workbook format with perforated pages
and is based upon the premise that "written expression
proceeds best from the individual's desire and *need* to
record his own experiences and ideas." The authors
point out its intended flexibility and that it might als
be followed systematically to its conclusion. The inten
tion is for the student to lose his fear of writing and
develop an enjoyment for it. Part one begins with a
detailed discussion of the methods, objectives, contents

and special features followed by chapters on understanding
writing and the writer's purpose. Part two deals with the
elements of narration with individual chapters on types of
sentences, re-creating experience through narration,
various types of points of view, dialogue, sense impressions, mood sequence, and the distinction between narration and exposition. Part three deals with the elements
of exposition with chapters covering purposes and techniques, paragraph development and several on the essay
(introduction, topical development, organization, rational
development, conclusions, and the outline). A final part
on combining skills concludes the text. Each chapter
contains readings to illustrate points followed by extensive questions on style, comprehension of content, and
vocabulary. Evaluation sheets--prescriptive charts which
establish content requirements and credit earned for each
aspect accomplished--conclude each chapter. A supplementary text for grammar is suggested. This text is
particularly aimed and suited for individualized instruction but could be used in conventional classes, particularly those on basic writing skills.

173 Hartnett, Carolyn. *Ideas in Motion: A Program for
     Learning Basic Composition*. Pacific Palisades, Ca.:
     Goodyear, 1973. 243 pp. $5.95 (P)

This text is aimed at cultivating skills for writing
short reports in various disciplines. It is, in effect,
a course in itself and is designed for a specific type
of classroom structure (lab and tutoring). Each unit
has a pre-test to diagnose problems. The first section
on the book is on classification--a multiplicity of
exercises on how to classify thoughts. The method for
all sections is self-explanatory. Unit two--definition
--discusses using the right word, and unit three deals
with mechanics. The following sections cover descriptive writing, comparison and contrast, cause and effect,
and argumentation. Each section has exercises and
questions with an answer key given in the back of the
book. In the introduction the author gives a list of
journal topics and suggests a daily ten minute writing
exercise to be done concurrently with the other assignments. Illustrations and cartoons are used in the
chapters. Each major section is followed by a "check-
test" which reviews essential principles.

174 Hartwell, Patrick. *Analysis: From Detail to Discovery*.
     New York: Harper and Row, 1974. 39 pp. NPA (P)

This pamplet is a part of the *Harper Studies in
Language and Literature* listed in this bibliography under
Shrodes, Caroline, editor.

175 Harwell, George C. *Technical Communication*. New York:
     Macmillan, 1960. 332 pp. $7.50 (H)

    The author states that "This textbook was written with
the engineering student primarily in mind." He feels,
however, it will serve just as well for students in a
variety of other fields from medicine to forestry. The
text has six general divisions. Chapters one, two and
three discuss preliminary matters: the qualities of good
writing (with particular reference to technical subject
matter); the organization of material (by such methods as
order of occurrence, order of descending importance, order
of ascending importance, etc.); and the use of exposition
by such methods as explication, description, definition,
and narration. Chapter four takes up business letters of
all types. Chapters five, six, and seven are the core of
the book: an extended treatment of reports. The formal
report is explained before the informal because the
latter is treated as a simplified form of the longer
type. Various types of reports are considered and attention is given to form as well as to content. Chapters
eight and nine deal with other forms of communication in
technical fields--the magazine article and public speaking. Chapter ten covers illustrative material. Each
chapter contains a basic selection of exercises and
assignments. The book concludes with a handbook of
general principles of composition and a glossary of
usage. An appendix gives abbreviations for scientific
and engineering terms as compiled by the American Standards Association.

176 Hawley, Robert C. and Isabel L. Hawley. *Writing for the*
     Fun of It: An Experience-Based Approach to Composi-
     tion. Amherst, Mass.: Educational Research Associate
     Press, 1974. 109 pp. $2.95 (P)

    This text assumes a non-competitive classroom struc-
ture in which the students work together and evaluation
is a group process. In the foreword the author states
that "Without doubt the largest single consideration
which prevents people from enjoying writing is the fear
that their writing will be judged (negatively) on the
basis of the way it is expressed rather than received as
a message being communicated, whether well or badly.
Correctness and effectiveness of expression are, of
course, proper subjects for study--but *after* the need
for them has been established through the production of
significant writing." The text is divided into three
main units: Teaching Writing--discussion on gathering,
organizing, and presenting information and on the "nuts
and bolts" aspects of the organization of the course, A
Compendium of Activities--class projects, a list with
short explanations of some poetry forms which can be

effective in beginning writing attempts, and extended
projects for the class, and Further Considerations--a
short chapter on mechanics, a discussion on coordinating
writing with literature, a discussion of evaluation
complete with a number of forms for self and group
evaluation, and list of additional sources. This text
would probably be most appropriate on the high school
level.

177 Hayakawa, S. I. *Language in Thought and Action*. 3rd ed.
New York: Harcourt, Brace, Jovanovich, 1972. 289 pp.
$7.95 (P)

This text approaches writing from a semantic perspec-
tive. Book one, The Functions of Language, contains
chapters on Language and Survival; Symbols; Reports,
Inferences, Judgments, Contexts; The Double Task of
Language; The Language of Social Cohesion; The Language
of Social Control; The Language of Effective Communication; and Art and Tension. Book two, Language and
Thought, has chapters entitled How We Know What We Know;
The Little Man Who Wasn't There; Classification; The
Two-Valued Orientation; The Multi-Valued Orientation;
Poetry and Advertising; The Dime in the Jukebox; Rats
and Men; and Toward Order Within and Without. Each of
the chapters is followed by a section entitled Applications which is intended to stimulate the student and to
allow him to put into practice some of the principles
discussed. This text is not aimed at the freshman level;
it is perhaps more appropriate for students who have
mastered basic composition and have an interest in
semantics.

178 Hays, Robert. *Principles of Technical Writing*. Reading,
Mass.: Addison-Wesley, 1965. 324 pp. $9.95 (H)

According to the author, this text "shows a step-by-
step, realistic and practical approach to technical
writing. The book concentrates on the beginning writer,
and helps to train even those without a flair for
expression to write clear reports. It will furnish
primary material for a one-quarter or one-semester course
in report writing or technical writing." The book opens
with three chapters on material preliminary to report
writing--types of reports, the need for reports, the
audience involved, and the background of the report.
Chapters four through six deal with gathering, recording,
and evaluating and analyzing data. Chapter seven discusses the planning and preparation involved in report
writing including material on various ways of putting a
report together and several types of possible outline
methods. Chapter eight is entitled Duplication Methods,
Format, and Physical Makeup. Chapter nine, Writing the

Rough Draft, includes information on style and sentence structure as well as further material on format. Chapter ten discusses types of visual aids and their inclusion. Chapters eleven and twelve return to material on editing the rough draft and preparing the final draft. The last chapter discusses the technicalities of submitting the completed report: preserving the master file copy, safeguarding confidential material, and distribution. A series of appendices form a handbook of grammar and usage and give examples of editing and outlining. Each chapter contains questions and exercises which are designed to be sequential and cumulative in testing the reader's grasp of content.

179   Heatherington, Madelon E. *Outside-In*. Glenview, Ill.: Scott, Foresman, 1971. 113 pp. $2.95 (P)

This text deals primarily with the non-fiction expository essay. The author states in the preface that "Concentrating on the personal essay and avoiding hard-line dictates about composition, the book has three interrelated aims: first, to state some general principles about what goes into any kind of good writing, particularly non-fiction; second, to explain the reasons behind these principles; and third, to explain the pragmatism of cause and effect in regard to composition." The book is divided into eight major units: How Versus What and Assorted Assumptions, Outside-In and Other Nonmagical Principles, Narratives, Explanation, Analysis, Persuasion, Paragraphs, and Sentences. There are two appendices: the first on Induction, Deduction, and Some Fallacies, the second A Short Bibliography of Paperbound References. The principle of *Outside-In* is basically that one organizes before writing. There are no exercises, discussion questions, or paper topics in this text; the book is designed as a basic guide in an introductory composition course.

180   Heywood, Jean E. *A Question of Choice*. Belmont, Ca.: Dickenson, 1970. 358 pp. $4.95 (P)

The author states in her preface that the text is based on the concept that "ideas can be expressed in any style that suits the purpose and the occasion." The text is a book of readings designed to broaden the student's choices of expression. The readings have been selected because they illustrate what can be done with language. The idea is for the student to make contact with language in action thereby heightening his awareness of words and his feeling for English syntax. There are sixteen chapters, all including from two to six relatively brief reading selections. No chapter titles indicate the rationale for the groupings, but they are collected with

a common point of illustration in mind. For example,
chapter one has selections dealing with place descriptions, and chapter two deals with character descriptions.
The authors are established writers such as John Steinbeck, Charles Dickens, E. B. White, S. I. Hayakawa, and
Henry David Thoreau. Each selection is followed by a
detailed Study Guide which points out features of language
and rhetorical techniques. These guides are usually as
long as the selection itself. Each set of guides concludes with writing assignments which can be used
selectively. This text puts its emphasis on stylistic
technique rather than on basic techniques of composition
and is therefore most appropriate for advanced writing
classes.

181   Hildick, Wallace. *Thirteen Types of Narrative*. New
      York: Clarkson N. Potter, 1970. 136 pp. $3.95
      (H) $1.95   (P)

This book teaches different types of narrative by
offering the same story in many different forms. It is
divided into fourteen chapters; each of the first thirteen
discusses a different type of narrative structure. The
fourteenth chapter is a conclusion which tries to draw
together the ideas presented in the text. Structures
dealt with are a series of first-person narratives, the
documentary style, the epistolary method, the play, first-
person past (as if written), first-person past (as if
spoken), third person past, and others. Literary
examples are also used, and there are no exercises or
suggestions for writing. This text could be used either
in a literary criticism class in which the instructor
wished to teach the students to recognize the various
types of narrative or as a source book in a creative
writing composition class.

182   Hildick, Wallace. *Word for Word: The Rewriting of
      Fiction*. W. W. Norton, 1965. 127 pp. $1.95   (P)

This book is an abridged version of *Word for Word: A
Study of Author's Alterations,* originally published by
Faber and Faber. There are six chapters, each of which
deals with a major writer. The chapter on George Eliot
contains excerpts from *Middlemarch*; the one on D. H.
Lawrence contains excerpts from "The White Peacock,"
"Odour of Chrysanthemums," and "The Rainbow." Samuel
Butler is represented by examples from *The Way of All
Flesh*; Thomas Hardy is represented by excerpts from *Tess
of the D'Urbervilles*. Selections from *The Portrait of a
Lady* by Henry James and *Mrs. Dalloway* by Virginia Woolf
are included, also. Each chapter begins with a prefatory
note which describes the manuscript the author is working
from, and each passage has a short note introducing it in

the context of the rest of the work. Besides these notes
the chapters consist of typed copies of edited manuscript
with revisions marked typographically. After the introduction the author gives a short explanation of his syste
of modifications as they translate from the typed copy to
the manuscript. The introduction discusses types of
revisions which are made in manuscripts with examples of
each type. The text would be appropriate for a creative
writing course or a stylistics course in which the
instructor wished to stress revision.

183 Hodges, John C., and Mary E. Whitten. *Harbrace College
Handbook*. 7th ed. New York: Harcourt, Brace,
Jovanovich, 1972. 532 pp. $5.95 (P)

This text is divided into six major units with a
glossary of grammatical terms at the end. The first unit
is on grammar and contains chapters on sentence sense,
sentence fragments, comma splices and fused sentences,
adjectives and adverbs, case, agreement, and tense and
mood. The second unit discusses mechanics and contains
chapters on manuscript form, capitals, italics, and
abbreviations and numbers. The third unit is on punctuation, including chapters on the various punctuation mark
and their usage. The fourth unit focuses on spelling and
diction. The fifth unit covers effective sentences, and
chapters deal with unity and logical thinking, subordination, coherence, parallelism, point of view, pronoun
reference, emphasis, and variety. The sixth unit covers
the larger elements of writing and contains chapters on
the paragraph, planning and writing the whole composition
the library paper, and letters. Each chapter not only
has information on the subject involved; exercises for
the student to complete are scattered throughout. A
sample research paper complete with comments on facing
pages is provided. Separate rules are listed within
chapters according to a number and letter system which is
duplicated in the index and allows the student to find a
rule either through its page number or through its relation to other rules in the same chapter. There are
diagrams of the organization of the handbook on the
inside of the front and back covers so the student can
find rules according to major headings. A list of symbol
found in the text and commonly found on edited papers is
also included. This text is designed as a supplementary
text for any college-level composition course.

184 Hogins, James Burl. *People and Words: A Visual Rhetoric
and Resource Book for Writing*. Chicago: Science
Research Associates, 1972. 232 pp. $4.95 (P)

The author states that "I did not want to start by
asking the student to scrap all his notions and beliefs
and to mistrust his own experiences, but I did want to

dwell on how we use language and how we construct our verbal walls and how we can communicate *naturally* and thereby see our own beliefs and experiences as the basis for beginning a study of language." This text uses photographs, drawings, and cartoons along with written explanations. The book contains seven chapters: College Writing; Types of Prose Writing; Organization; Methods of Development; Words, Sentences, Style, Notes; and Research and Writing. A glossary defining terms in rhetoric, usage, and mechanics is included at the end as well as a bibliography of further texts on the subject of language use. Exercises for practice are scattered throughout each chapter which involve writing theme length assignments and sometimes conducting research outside of class. The chapter on types of prose writing includes considerations of argumentation, exposition, description, and narration along with less formal types of writing. The chapter on methods of development includes analysis, clarification, exemplification, definition, and comparison/contrast. A short section discussing propaganda is included in the chapter on notes. Explanations in this text are brief; visual aids are plentiful.

185 Hogins, James Burl. *Probing Common Ground: Sources for Writing*. Englewood Cliffs, N.J.: Prentice-Hall, 1974. 284 pp. $5.95 (P)

This text is divided into two distinct parts. Part one (chapters one through five) "describes an orderly progression from the beginning to the finishing touches of acceptable college writing" showing the student how to look for material inside and outside himself, deal with varying lengths of assignments, organize, develop, and support, and give special emphasis to the language he uses. Part two (chapters six through ten) concentrates on outside stimuli which help students break out of ordinary ways of perceiving things. One chapter deals with pictures as writing stimuli, another on the use of advertising and cartoons. The next two chapters consider what makes people memorable and writing about situations in which actual or imaginary characters are involved in specific incidents. The last chapter provides questions based on writing and observation principles dealt with in prior chapters. Each chapter includes introductory discussions on principles, suggestions for topics, a poem, two essays, a student paper, and a short story. The suggestions relate the literature to introductory matter. The author suggests that parts one and two can be studied separately or in conjunction. This text is most applicable for a course in basic composition.

186   Hogins, James Burl and Gerald A. Bryant, Jr. *Juxtaposi-*
       tion, Encore! Chicago: Science Research Associates,
       1975. 286 pp. $6.95 (P)

       This publication is a source book based on the premise
that "By examining several objects in juxtaposition, the
creative mind often arrives at new insights. . . ."
Using photographs, cartoons, news articles, advertisements, poems and diagrams--many entries are in full
color--the authors seek to stimulate and capture the
attention of the student. The text is divided into eight
sections ranging from "Hot Issues" to "The Arts." The
selections are almost exclusively contemporary. As a
source book, this collection could be used as a supplement in almost any composition course. A lengthy
instructor's guide which contains suggested assignments
is available.

187   Hogins, James Burl and Thomas Lillard. *The Structure of*
       Writing. Lexington, Mass.: D. C. Heath, 1972. 308
       pp. $7.95 (H)

       This text has a diversified format. Part one discusses
the problems of writing, focusing on patterns of thinking
and the thrust of argument. The book attempts to develop
new attitudes toward language. A brief discussion of
style ensues: formal, informal, and colloquial styles,
and definitions of tone, sentence structure, and diction
A section on the emotive resources of the language -
focuses on figurative language and defines figures of
speech in brief discussions. Also, the text deals with
manipulation of effect through word choice. Part two
gives a discussion on the history, nature, and use of
the dictionary, goes into types of definition, and discusses misleading definition. Part three is an elementary
study in logic complete with systematic charts and
examples. Part four concerns the rhetoric of college
writing--organizing, structuring the paragraph, casting
the sentence, and word choice. Each section is brief and
heavily weighted with practice exercises. Part five deal
with types of college writing--the personal essay, the
argumentative term paper, the advocatory essay, the
summary, analysis, and the essay test. The basic principles of the initial chapters are presented here in
slight variation. The authors conclude with four
appendices: a brief history of the English language, an
extended discussion on library use, a presentation of
manuscript form, and several sample papers by college
students.

188   Hogins, James Burl and Robert Earl Yarber. *Annotated*
       Cycle 7: Essays, Short Stories, Poems for Freshman
       English. Chicago: Science Research Associates, 1973.
       493 pp. $7.95 (P)

This book is a reader for freshman-level composition courses which "attempts to provide both classic and contemporary models of good writing and thinking, to offer a number of viewpoints on a variety of topics, and to present poems and short stories that will provoke discussion and writing." The essay selections are annotated with rhetorical terms. Figurative language, description, definition, and exemplification are marked along with other rhetorical devices as they appear in the essays. The selections are arranged according to theme: The Inner Person; Oppressed Peoples; Language, Education, and Media; Creators and Creations; Spaceship in Trouble (ecology); Society: Some Alternatives; and Values. A glossary of rhetorical terms and a guide to rhetoric are included. There are discussion topics and vocabulary lists at the end of the selections. The instructor's guide provides multiple-choice tests for each essay and for some of the poems and short stories. Authors represented in this reader include James Baldwin, Carl Jung, Gloria Steinem, Ben Jonson, Jorge Luis Borges, and Ernest Hemingway.

189 Hogins, James Burl and Robert Earl Yarber. *Models for Writing*. Chicago: Science Research Associates, 1975. 466 pp. NPA (P)

This text is a rhetorical edition of *Phase Blue, Revised*. It contains the same selections as *Phase Blue, Revised*, but they are arranged according to rhetorical type. The sections are entitled Argumentation, Exposition, Description, Narration, Analysis, Classification, Exemplification, Definition, Comparison and Contrast, and Other Rhetorical Features. Each listing under the sections in the table of contents includes other essays in the text which also contain features of the rhetorical type dealt with in that section. A short introduction begins each section and includes essay topics on ideas suggested in the assignment and by the readings. Discussion questions and vocabulary lists follow each selection. Some of the selections are annotated as they are in *Phase Blue, Revised*. The text ends with a glossary of rhetorical terms. This reader would be appropriate for freshman composition courses.

190 Hogins, James Burl and Robert E. Yarber. *Phase Blue: A Systems Approach to College English*. annotated ed. Chicago: Science Research Associates, 1970. 526 pp. $5.95 (P)

This reader offers "for the first time, a systems approach to freshman English--one that provides several points of access to the study of reading, writing and rhetoric." There are six complementary components which can accompany this text: stimulus tapes, critique tapes,

overhead projector transparencies, student book,
instructor's guide, and a classroom assessment program.
This anthology may be used independently, however, and
there are sixty-four selections grouped under ten head-
ings: The 70's: In Pursuit of Dreams; Visions of the
Future; Dialog between the Generations; The Student and
His Language; Violence in America; Religion and Philosophy
Evaluations; America: A Self-Analysis; The Black Rage;
The Arts; and Developing a Life Style. The essays are
generally brief and include such writers as Richard
Nixon, Art Buchwald, Aldous Huxley, and Marshall McLuhan.
Each essay is followed by discussions of theme and
rhetoric, writing assignments, library exploration, and
vocabulary. There is a Guide to Rhetoric which lists
rhetorical devices and principles and where they appear
in the essays. This annotated version has rhetorical
abbreviations and markings on each essay. This text
could be used in a freshman composition course to develop
reading, writing, discussion, and critical skills.

191   Hogins, James Burl and Robert E. Yarber. *Phase Blue*.
      rev. annotated ed. Chicago: Science Research
      Associates, 1974. 453 pp. $5.95 (P)

   This college level reader is based on the same principles as the original *Phase Blue* but has different
thematic chapter headings and selections. An introductory
section of readings suggests the changing nature of
humanity. The nine following units have selections on
varied topical themes: The Student, Society, Women's
Liberation, Minority Cultures, Ecology, The Future,
Sports, Media and the Arts, and Language and Prose.
These readings are annotated to point out particularly
good examples of rhetorical devices such as alliteration,
diction, sarcasm, transition, and others. Selections are
by such authors as William F. Buckley, Jr., Ray Bradbury,
Samuel Clemens, and Malcolm X. Each selection ends with
a number of questions for study and discussion and a
list of vocabulary words. A guide to rhetoric which lists
rhetorical devices and principles and where they appear
in the selections is also included. The text *Phase Blue,
Too* is designed to accompany this reader.

192   Hogins, James Burl and Robert E. Yarber. *Phase Blue,
      Too*. rev. ed. Chicago: Science Research Associates,
      1974. 187 pp. $3.95 (P)

   This text is designed to accompany *Phase Blue*, rev.
ed. *Phase Blue, Too* contains a writing program, educational objectives, tests (with answers), a guide to usage
and punctuation, and a glossary of rhetorical terms. In
the first section, Writing and Rhetoric Program, differen
rhetorical devices are explained, and exercises for

practice are given. The second section, Objectives, is designed to give the student some idea of what he should get out of assignments in *Phase Blue*. The third section, Self-Evaluation Program, consists of tests on selections in *Phase Blue* and an answer key. The text ends with a guide to usage and punctuation and a glossary of rhetorical terms.

193   Hogins, James Burl and Robert E. Yarber. *Reading Writing and Rhetoric*. rev. ed. Chicago: Science Research Associates, 1972. 594 pp. $6.95 (P)

The authors' aims are "to provide, for the instructor, teachable essays that can be used as the basis for classroom discussion and writing assignments; and to provide, for the student, all the help we can to make learning easier and more rewarding." Generally, the selections are taken from recent works and deal with contemporary topics. Section headings include The Freshman and His Language; The American Scene; Personal Values; The Voices of Science; The Antic Muse; Religion and Philosophy: Diverse Views; The Lively Arts; and Other Peoples, Other Places. Each essay is preceded by a brief note and followed by discussion questions, theme topics, library problems, and a glossary of difficult words. The book also provides a Glossary of Rhetorical Terms and a Guide to Rhetoric which uses paragraphs in the text as examples of rhetorical types or to illustrate a term such as figurative language. A Teacher's Manual includes further theme topics and tests. The text could be used in college or pre-college composition courses.

194   Hood, Richard F., ed. *Précis Writing Practice: Exercise to Improve Reading Comprehension and to Strengthen Communication Skills*. Cambridge, Mass.: Educators Publishing Service, 1967. 82 pp. NPA (P)

As the title indicates, the sole focus of this brief text is précis writing. The ten chapters are entitled Précis Writing Defined, The Value of Précis Writing, Précis Writing--An Aid to Reading Comprehension, Précis Writing--Practical Training to Strengthen Communication Skills, How to Make a Précis--Suggested Procedures, Guidelines for Précis Writing, Student Précis Writing-- Several Examples, Narrative Passages for Précis Writing, Poetry for Précis Writing Practice, and Student Poems for Précis Writing Practice. The general structure of this text is a brief introduction by the editor followed by a passage from a work of literature, questions, and exercises. This text is aimed at students from the high school level through the first year of college.

195 Hook, J. N. and Robert L. Stevens. *Competence in English A Programmed Handbook*. New York: Harcourt, Brace, Jovanovich, 1967. 399 pp. $5.95 (H)

This programmed handbook is designed for "students who have not yet mastered certain fundamentals of syntax, diction, mechanics, and usage." The authors have set up the text so that the student is largely responsible for his own learning. Each of the four major sections is broken down into a number of shorter units on specific problems. The basic section of each of the smaller units is "a programmed exercise designed to build, inductively, a grasp of a specific concept or a small group of closely related concepts." The exercises are simple, and the correct answers for the exercises are given beside each question. Following the programmed exercise is a brief commentary on whatever principle has been taught. Review exercises are the final element of each unit. These exercises may be used for practice or turned in as assignments. The book also contains an extensive diagnostic test and a final mastery test.

196 Hopper, Vincent F. *1001 Pitfalls in English Grammar Spelling and Usage,* rev. ed. Woodbury, N.Y.: Barron's Educational Series, 1970. 346 pp. $2.95 (P)

The author states in the foreword that "This book has been prepared to give both native-born and foreign students a solid sense of security in their mastery of the English language." There are no exercises or theme topics; the student with a particular problem can look it up and find the desired information. A large part of the text consists of conjugations of irregular verbs. Other matters included are mechanics of abbreviations, conjunctions, contractions, the negative, numbers, prepositions, punctuation, sentence parts, suffixes and word order and idiomatic usage. This reference work could be used in a writing laboratory or as a guide to basic problems in beginning composition classes.

197 Hopper, Vincent F. and Cedric Gale. *Practice for Effective Writing*. rev. ed. Woodbury, N.Y.: Barron's Educational Series, 1971. 160 pp. $1.95 (P)

The author states that this text is "A graduated series of practical exercises leading to mastery of basic writing techniques." This text consists totally of exercises; no informative material is included. It is specifically designed as a companion volume to *Essentials of English* by the same author (see following annotation). An index at the beginning of the book correlates exercises with sections in *Essentials of English*; some of the exercises could be used as tests. The pages tear out, and no answers are provided in the student workbook.

This workbook might be used with any text on the basics
of English but is not designed to be used alone. The
exercises are graduated so that a teacher need use only
those appropriate to the level of the class.

198 Hopper, Vincent F., Cedric Gale, and Ronald C. Foote.
     Essentials of English. rev. ed. Woodbury, N.Y.:
     Barron's Educational Series, 1973. 240 pp. $2.25
     (P)

This handbook is divided into seven units: The Word
(defining parts of speech and discussing some elements of
usage); The Sentence and Its Parts; Sentence Errors
(fragments, comma faults, the fused sentence); Logic and
Clarity (agreement, case, modifiers, split constructions,
faulty comparison, omission of necessary words); Emphasis,
Consistency, and Appropriateness; Punctuation; The Paragraph (development, unity, topic sentences, coherence,
transition); and The Writer's Approach to His Subject
(selecting a subject, planning, tone, organization, and
manuscript form). A glossary of frequently misused words
and phrases appears after the last unit. Following the
glossary there is a list of conjugations and principal
parts of irregular verbs. This is a book of information;
there are no exercises or theme topics. The authors
suggest that the instructor who wishes the student to
practice these principles use *Practice for Effective
Writing,* a companion volume, and Mersand's *Spelling Your
Way to Success* for practice in spelling problems. The
discussion on preparing the manuscript includes information on footnote and bibliography form. The text is
organized to move from the simplest part of a theme--the
word--to writing the whole theme. This book is designed
for introductory college composition courses.

199 Howard, C. Jeriel, Eileen Lundy, and Celine Werner.
     Reprise: A Review of Basic Writing Skills. Pacific
     Palisades, Ca.: Goodyear, 1975. 221 pp. NPA (P)

This text is a remedial workbook (with perforated
pages) for students enrolled in freshman English. It is
suited to any student who needs intensive instruction
and drill and practice in basic English. The units
include discussions of the sentence, subject/verb agreement, verb tenses, pronouns, and paragraph writing. The
text begins with recognizing complete sentences and moves
from there to discuss other aspects of basic English.
Only those elements really necessary for clear writing
are presented. Parts of speech, for example, are not
discussed in and for themselves but only as they apply
to other basic principles taught. Each section of the
five units begins with a pre-test and ends with a post-
test. There is no independent discussion of punctuation
and mechanics.

200 Howard, C. Jeriel and Richard Francis Tracz. *--30--: A*
      Journalistic Approach to Freshman Composition. Pacifi
      Palisades, Ca.: Goodyear, 1973. 174 pp. $4.95 (P)

This text is divided into two units. Shaping the
General News Story deals with general principles of
writing and has chapters on advertising, language,
audience, organization, and accuracy. The second unit,
Shaping the Specialized News Story, has chapters on the
editorial, the feature story, the sport story, women's
news, and the entertainment review. Each chapter has
explanations of the general principles involved and
examples taken from newspapers or magazines. Assignments
for student work are given throughout the chapters, some
of which involve writing an original essay while others
involve rewriting a news story. The authors suggest some
sort of class newspaper as a project to get the students'
work in print.

201 Howe, Irving. *Student Activism.* Indianapolis: Bobbs-
      Merrill, 1967. 64 pp. $1.00 (P)

This book is part of the *Bobbs-Merrill Series in
Composition and Rhetoric.* See listing under Johnson,
Falk S. for the complete annotation.

202 Howe, James. *The Making of Style.* Philadelphia:
      Chilton Book Co., 1972. 216 pp. $5.95 (P)

The text, as the author states in his preface, is
designed to help the student teach himself. It is meant
to give the writer "a point of view toward writing in
general, and can serve as a reference book to forms of
expression." The author feels that details about good
writing, particularly evaluation and technical explanations of how language works, must be provided by one's
instructor. It is, in effect, "a book of principles"
and was conceived to be used in conjunction with contemporary magazines. The emphasis is on trial and error,
experience, and getting the writer to think in terms of
audience. The first four sections of the text--covering
argumentation, description, the news story, and
narration--serve as introductions to the principal skills
of expository writing for advanced students. All chapter
are essentially explanatory and contain few lengthy
examples or illustrations. The remaining chapters cover
a broad spectrum of specialized writing types: informational articles, satire, riddles, personal essays
(formal and informal), letters, and allegory. There are
no writing assignments suggested nor are there complete
readings.

303 Huffman, Harry and Syrell Rogovin. *Programmed College
      English.* New York: McGraw-Hill, 1968. 554 pp.

$8.50 (P)

The authors state in their preface that this text is "specifically designed for one-term collegiate courses in which the students' primary objectives" are to understand fully basic sentence patterns and their use and to increase proficiency in principles of contemporary standard English usage and style. The text is divided into eleven sections, and each section is broken down into a number of smaller programmed units. Each unit is immediately followed by a non-programmed worksheet with tear-out pages on which the student can apply the concepts presented. At times the student must compose his own sentences for these workbook sections. An instructor's manual and key provide facsimile keys to the worksheets. The eleven sections which make up the text are entitled The Sentence--Its Essential Parts and Basic Patterns; Verbs; Adapting Basic Sentence Patterns to Achieve Special Effects; Nouns; Pronouns; Noun Clusters; Sentence Functions and Constructions; Verbals; Principles of Pronoun-Antecedent Agreement; Interrogative and Relative Pronouns, Clauses; and Common English-Usage Problems. A section on mechanics is included as well as an appendix of commonly used determiners, irregular verbs, linking verbs, prepositions, and so on. This text is designed for students who need work with basic skills and could be used as a remedial text or in a writing laboratory.

204   Hughes, Richard E. and P. Albert Duhamel. *Principles of Rhetoric*. Englewood Cliffs, N.J.: Prentice-Hall, 1966. 247 pp. $4.95 (P)

This book "is a thorough revision of the text of the earlier book, *Rhetoric: Principles and Usage*. . . . The goal of this book is still the same--efficient and persuasive writing; the path is less circuitous." The text is designed for college-level composition courses and teaches composition through an Aristotelian approach to rhetoric. It is divided into three main categories: Organization (principles of effective organization, description, narration, and exposition); Invention (argument, induction and deduction, the topics, and persuasion); and Style (the analysis of style and the function of details, rhetorical qualities of words, the rhetoric of the sentence). Each chapter under the main categories is further divided into the basic principles of rhetoric, with explanations and examples. No exercises, discussion questions, or topic suggestions are given. There is a section on the rhetorical quality of words (usage) which contains short definitions of figures of speech.

205   Hurley, John. *A Practical Rhetoric*. Dubueque, Iowa: Wm. C. Brown, 1971. 166 pp. $2.95 (P)

The text begins with a chapter which discusses the topic sentence and its function within a paragraph. Chapter two presents a discussion of telling how to do something. Chapter three deals with the Tell-Why Method, establishing a thesis statement, and developing support for the thesis. The fourth chapter, The Tell-What Method, examines what elements of stories or works of art elicit what responses. Following chapters are entitled The Binding Sentence, Previewing an Essay, Developing Material, Using an Outline to Arrange Material, Opening Paragraphs, The Finished Essay, The Argumentative Essay, Process Analysis, Comparison and Contrast, and Manipulative Grammar (a chapter dealing with problems in grammar and usage). Each of the chapters gives examples and readings and contains some exercises for the student. Writing assignments are given periodically.

206   Hurtik, Emil. *Insight: A Rhetoric Reader*. 2nd ed. Philadelphia: J. B. Lippincott, 1973. 572 pp. NPA (P)

This college-level rhetoric contains the standard divisions of narrative, description, comparison and contrast, analogy, definition, classification, analysis and process, reports and abstracts, arguments and persuasion. Reviews, letters and miscellany are also included. The book includes a "Thematic Table of Contents" which organizes each essay into a particular grouping: Humor and Satire, Men vs. Women, Art and Culture, for example. The readings are largely contemporary, but some older or classic selections occasionally appear. Each essay is followed by questions on vocabulary, rhetoric, theme, and by topics for written assignments. Perhaps this reader should be accompanied by a text dealing strictly with composition unless it is assumed the students have a firm grasp of such matters. An answer key is provided for the instructor.

207   Hurtik, Emil and Thomas Lillard. *In Phase: Sentence, Structure, Style*. Philadelphia: J.B. Lippincott, 1973. 259 pp. $4.60 (P)

The authors state in their preface that "The purpose of *In Phase* is twofold: to provide the freshman student with a review of English grammar and to help him apply his grammatical knowledge to his writing." This workbook is divided into two major sections: A Grammar Review and Writing Exercises. In the grammar review there are chapters on identifying the parts of speech, examining the simple sentence, using clauses to build sentences, using phrases to improve sentences, avoiding errors that obscure meaning, avoiding errors that distract the reader, solving verb problems, achieving sentence variety and punctuation and related topics. Each chapter in this section has explanations of the terms and principles being taught along with objective exercises on tear-out pages. The second section has chapters covering the same basic material as the first eight chapters, but the student is asked to apply these grammar principles to writing sentences. The student both rewrites sentences provided and writes his own sentences. Exercises and tests are also included. Two appendices follow the second section, one on spelling and the other a glossary of usage. An answer key and additional exercises are provided in a teacher's manual, but the student is not provided with the answers in his text.

208 Hutchinson, Helene D. *Horizons: Readings and Communication Activities for Vocational-Technical Students.* Beverly Hills, Ca.: Glencoe, 1975. 324 pp. NPA (P)

The text is a "multi-genre collection of readings for the vocational-technical student." The purpose of the book is to broaden the student's personal perspective first then to affect him as a technician. The text is divided into seven chapters. The first deals with Practicalities and contains selections covering job-hunting, job availability, letters of application, resumés, follow-up letters, memo writing, telephone technique, and other practical matters. Chapter two has selections which discuss the concept of consumerism, the twelve selling words, cash and credit, and the wording of warranties and guarantees. Chapter three presents brief selections dealing with contemporary problems and trends in various areas of business. Chapter four deals with leisure and how we spend it. Chapter five, Creativity, Process, and Design, gives several selections from contemporary periodicals. The last two chapters focus on the self and human relations and the importance of communication. Many types of selections are represented: the essay, the article, the short story, poetry, tests and questionnaires, directions, advertisements, photographs, and drawings. Each selection is brief and is followed by exercises. Some examine the implications of language; others are questions for discussion, and still others offer exercises in role playing and writing, both technical and creative.

209 Hutchinson, Helene D. *Mixed Bag: Artifacts from the Contemporary Culture.* Glenview, Ill.: Scott, Foresman, 1970. 318 pp. $8.50 (H)

The author states that the "purpose of this book is to excite and elicit emotional response by bringing into the classroom the colors and forms of the outside world."

The book integrates advertisements, slogans, cartoons, photographs, painting, graffiti, and song lyrics with poems, essays, and stories to encourage intellectual reaction from students. There is no editorial intrusion either by instruction or exercises. The author wishes to introduce the student to provocative materials which will lead to ideas for writing and discussion. The author has selected the materials for their emotional appeal. There are six sections: Family, Violence, Race, Death, Religion, and Tigers. Serious and humorous aspects are juxtaposed.

210   Irmscher, William F. *The Holt Guide to English: A Contemporary Handbook of Rhetoric, Language, and Literature.* New York: Holt, Rinehart and Winston, 1972. 646 pp. $6.95 (H)

This text is designed to be "complete and flexible" and to serve both reference and teaching purposes. The author lists a number of objectives in his preface: he attempts to point out what the writer should strive for rather than what he should avoid, to address rhetorical considerations in a fresh way, to provide backgrounds for dealing with literature critically, to give adequate information for research papers, to give broad grammatical coverage, to treat usage rules flexibly, to provide brief historical information, to define terms understandably, to supply a full reference guide to manuscript form, to present a workable approach to spelling problems and to provide a helpful glossary of terms. The text is divided into thirty-three parts, beginning with discussions on the elements of rhetoric. Individual chapters deal with the role of rhetoric, the writer's role, audience, generating a topic, structure, logic, paragraphing, sentencing, style, and revision. A segment on writing about literature follows including sections on all genres and methods of approaching them critically. A chapter on reference papers follows. There is a section on the origins, growth, and change of the English language with chapters on heritage, sources of words, changing meanings and values of words, grammar, usage, a glossary of usage, and dictionaries. The final major section, a review of grammar usage and terminology, concludes with a glossary of linguistic, literary, and rhetorical terms. The text utilizes examples but does not include exercises or suggested topics; these can be found in the teacher's manual. The book is designed for the beginning writer.

211   Irmscher, William F. *The Nature of Literature: Writing on Literary Topics.* New York: Holt, Rinehart and Winston, 1975. 190 pp. NPA (P)

The author states his aims as brevity, completeness, and readability. The text is intended "as a catalyst to be added to a course, not a recipe book to be followed step by step," and it can be used to provide an overview to a course prior to readings or as a reference tool to return to in addressing particular problems in writing about literature. The text confronts the problem of dealing critically with the nature, forms, and meaning of literature. The author eschews a genre approach to the subject in favor of one which defines and discusses seven major components of literature--character, action, setting, form, language, style, and meaning--in separate chapters. The initial chapter discusses the nature of literature--what criticism is and is not, meaning, the fictional universe, influences of literature, and the basic elements of the three genres. The discussions are generally brief. Chapters two through eight cover those seven components of literature in brief subsections. For example, the chapter on language discusses metaphorical language, symbol, imagery, stylized language, irony, humor, and satire. The final chapter discusses various approaches, both specific and general, for writing on literature. Nine student essays are also included. A glossary of literary and rhetorical terms concludes the text. Each chapter has ten suggestions for writing at its end.

212   Irmscher, William F. *Ways of Writing*. New York: McGraw-Hill, 1969.   259 pp. $6.50   (H) $4.50   (P)

"This text is essentially an informal, nontechnical book about writing--a rhetoric that doesn't use the word." Irmscher also states in his preface that in this age of neo-romanticism in education "it becomes urgent to appeal to the personal initiative and sensibilities of students, not to substitute the mechanical conformity and prohibitions that are characteristic of many approaches to writing." This college-level composition text is divided into eight main chapters: The Nature of Composition; Thinking, Talking and Writing; Content; The Shape of Content; Diction; Telling; Style; and Mechanics. There are three appendices, one on outlining, one on punctuation in the 19th century, and one on footnote and bibliographical forms. Each chapter consists of explanations, short examples from literature, discussion questions, and exercises. The exercises sometimes involve writing a paragraph or short theme, but they generally consist of short answer questions. This text would, perhaps, be most appropriate for a freshman composition course.

213   Jackson, Dixie S., ed. *Who Needs Nature?* New York: John Wiley and Sons, 1973.   234 pp. $4.25   (P)

This collection is one of a series of topical readers under the general title *Perception in Communication*. These books present expository prose, verse, fiction, drama, and nonverbal media to the student of composition. The editor feels "Experience demonstrates that a student tends to write better when a timely, substantial subject engages his interest, or when the subject is elaborated and reviewed in a variety of modes of communication." Other volumes in the series (general editor, Charles Sanders) include *The Voices of War; Male and Female; Identity; Alienation: Minority Groups; The American Movie Goddess*.

214 Jacobs, Suzanne E. and Roderick A. Jacobs. *The College Writer's Handbook*. Lexington, Mass.: Xerox College Publishing, 1973. 225 pp. $3.95 (P)

This text is designed to help college students with term papers and exams as well as regular composition writing. It attempts to focus on trouble areas in student writing. The text is designed as a reference, but parts can be used as a teaching text. The book emphasizes two basic points: writing assignments must stress what the student knows, and the student must say things that are important to him. Chapter one offers discussions of basic criticisms the writer will encounter vagueness, repetition, generality, etc., giving examples of each. Chapter two deals with organizing and developing a topic, choosing a unifying idea, outlining, and development of various rhetorical methods. Exercises and examples are interspersed throughout. Chapter three is on checking organization, and four gives sample approaches and suggestions for brief papers. Chapter five gives rules for a research paper; six deals with grammar, attacking basic problems only as they apply to writing. Chapter seven deals with word choice; eight covers mechanics.

215 Johnson, Falk S., James Kreuzer, Franklin Norvish, general eds. *The Bobbs-Merrill Series in Composition and Rhetoric*. Indianapolis: Bobbs-Merrill.

This series consists of eighteen short (approximately 64 pp. each) texts devoted to some aspect of composition and rhetoric. Each is independent of the other, and instructors could choose any number of these texts to form an anthology suitable to the particular course. Each text begins with an overview of the topic involved then provides a number of selections by both classical and contemporary authors. Each selection is followed by Suggestions for Discussion and Writing. Prices range from $1.00 to $1.50. An alphabetical, by author, list of individual texts follows: Maurianne Adams,

Autobiography (1968); P. M. Banks and V. M. Burke, *Black Americans: Images in Conflict* (1970); Monroe C. Beardsley, *Literature and Esthetics* (1968); Monroe C. Beardsley, *Modes of Argument* (1967); Virginia M. Burke, *The Paragraph in Context* (1969); Edward B. Fiske, *The Contemporary Religious Experience* (1967); Philip B. Grove, *The Role of the Dictionary* (1967); Irving Stone, *Student Activism* (1967); Kenneth R. Johnson and W. T. Lhamon, Jr., *The Rhetoric of Conflict* (1969); D. G. Kehl, *Literary Style of the Old Bible and the New* (1970); Richard Larson, *Rhetoric* (1968); Leonard Lief, *The New Conservatives* (1967); M. B. McNamee, *Essays by the Masters* (1968); Emmanuel G. Mesthene, *Technology and Social Change* (1967); John Nist, *Style in English* (1969); Andrew Sarris, *The Film* (1968); Owen Thomas, *The Structure of Language* (1967); Stanley Weintraub, *Biography and Truth* (1967).

216 Johnson, Willoughby and Thomas M. Davis. *College Reading and College Writing*. rev. ed. Glenview, Ill.: Scott, Foresman, 1971. 550 pp. $6.50 (P)

The authors state that they tried to avoid collecting readings that reflected only their own interests. This anthology focuses on essays directly relevant to student experience, essays related to the student's past, present, and future. The authors have also attempted to select writings which may be directly approached and analyzed as examples of effective organization and clear expression. The text is divided into eight chapters: 1) The American Character--essays which discuss habits of Americans, how Americans have been perceived by others, patriotism, American types, and other concepts. 2) What Happened at Home--essays which focus on domestic or everyday experiences. 3) The World Science Has Created--selections which deal with the impact of science and technology on society and ways of thinking. 4) Poetry and Fiction. 5) Problems of Writing--essays which examine the basics of language, the condition of language, the pros and cons of standardized language. 6) On Campus and Off--essays which are directed primarily at civil rights questions, race relations, and others. 7) On Men and Women. 8) Facing Tomorrow Today--essays on such social problems as population control. Each selection is followed by study questions which deal with the writer's ideas, rhetorical methods, structures, tones, and points of view. Theme subjects also follow each essay. The authors note that these topics are purposely too broad for brief themes. The introduction to the text provides some basic instruction on rhetorical principles.

121

217 Johnston, Kenneth R. and W. T. Lhamon, Jr. *The Rhetoric of Conflict*. Indianapolis: Bobbs-Merrill, 1969. 64 pp. $1.00 (P)

This book is part of the *Bobbs-Merrill Series in Composition and Rhetoric*. See listing under Johnson, Falk S. for the complete annotation.

218 Jones, W. Paul. *Writing Scientific Papers and Reports*. 6th ed. Dubuque, Iowa: Wm. C. Brown, 1971. 361 pp. $5.50 (P)

This text is intended for upperclassmen in technical or scientific study who have discovered the importance o skill in the use of language. The book opens with background material on scientific writing as opposed to other modes of expression and a chapter on organization which includes material on all types of outlines and methods of organization such as chronology, space arrang ment, partition, classification, cause and effect, and so on. The second section, Scientific Papers, covers the major methods of presenting scientific information. There are chapters on definition, classification, analysis, comparison, description of mechanisms, processes, sets of directions, organizations, layouts, writing the abstract, the book review, and the popular-science article. Each chapter contains an introductory list of the contents, examples, exercises, and a bibliography of suggested readings. There is a separate section on proposal and report writing which includes th structure of both the long and the short report. The final two chapters of the book deal with style in scientific writing, sentence structure, and diction.

219 Kakonis, Tom E. and James C. Wilcox, eds. *Forms of Rhetoric: Ordering Experience*. New York: McGraw-Hill, 1969. 253 pp. $4.50 (P)

This text consists of nineteen essays by various writers, each of whom addresses himself to the skills of rhetoric. Short examples from literature are quoted within these essays; and the text is divided into three major parts: Organization, The Modes of Discourse (exposition, argumentation, description, and narration), and Style. Writers contributing to this text include John E. Jordan ("Rhetoric and Knowledge: Getting a Subject"), Monroe C. Beardsley ("Classification"), and Edward P. J. Corbett ("The Study of Style"), among others. The section on outlines has an outline form for the student to fill in. A test of reading comprehension is included in which the student reads a number of different opinions about the points of rhetoric then answers questions on the content of these opinions.

220 Kane, Thomas S. and Leonard J. Peters. *Writing Prose: Techniques and Purposes*. 3rd ed. New York: Oxford University Press, 1969. 449 pp. $3.95 (P)

This text is based on the assumption "that the close study of good models is an indispensable aid to both teaching and learning, that one learns to write by imitation--an imitation of the basic patterns, forms, and structures that lie behind the infinite variety of all English prose." In the preface the authors emphasize that this book focuses upon techniques rather than ideas. Section headings include Exposition, Definition, Judgment, Argument, Description of Character, Narration, Beginnings and Closings, Essays, and Style. Groups of essays illustrate these points while each chapter ends with discussion questions and theme topics. The chapter entitled Essays includes longer essays, and the chapter entitled Style includes a sophisticated discussion of style. There is a glossary of terms at the end. This text is a college-level reader for basic or advanced composition courses.

221 Kaplan, Robert B., ed. *Reading and Rhetoric*. Indianapolis: Odyssey, 1963. 124 pp. $1.45 (P)

This text was designed with the international or foreign student in mind. The author states that he has tried to avoid two pitfalls common to many other readers: condescending or oversimplified presentation which often insults the intelligent international student and selections about contemporary American culture which present the international student with cultural assumptions he cannot grasp. The selections in this text are designed according to rhetorical patterns so that the book can be coordinated with a composition course. Selections are designed to introduce the student to basic facts and cultural assumptions of American civilization. Exercises following the selections are designed to increase vocabulary, to stimulate interest in structure and content, and to provide topics and models for assignments. The text is divided into nine sections: description, definition, classification, process, characterization, formal analysis, comparison and contrast, logic and informal argument, and formal argument. An appendix offers a brief history of the English language. The descriptions of principles are concise, and there are from two to four selections in each section. Some of the authors included are Mark Twain, Charles Dickens, Cardinal Newman, and Benjamin Franklin.

222 Kehl, D. G. *Literary Style of the Old Bible and the New*. Indianapolis: Bobbs-Merrill, 1970. 64 pp. $1.00 (P)

This book is part of the *Bobbs-Merrill Series in Composition and Rhetoric*. See listing under Johnson, Falk S. for the complete annotation.

223   Kermode, Frank and Richard Poirier, eds. *The Oxford Reader: Varieties of Contemporary Discourse.* shorter ed. New York: Oxford University Press, 1971. 612 pp. $4.95 (P)

In their preface the editors state that this text is "special because it refuses to be specialized"; there is no central focus imposed. The editors state the pieces assembled are "alive now in what they express and will remain alive because of the way they are written." Selections are by such writers as George Plimpton, George Orwell, Ernest Hemingway, and Tom Wolfe. The text is introduced by a prologue and is followed by eight sections and an epilogue. Section titles are Images of Childhood, School and Youth, Persons, Communities, Language, Performances, Investigations, and Science and Technology. The text is designed strictly as a reader; it includes no rhetorical divisions and no exercises. Thus, it is primarily designed as a supplementary text for either standard freshman composition courses or more advanced writing courses.

224   Kerrigan, William J. *Writing to the Point: Six Basic Steps.* New York: Harcourt, Brace, Jovanovich, 1974. 200 pp. NPA (P)

The text presupposes that the student has the need to start from scratch. The text, as the author notes, is a course in itself and "supplies the principles, exlanations, examples, assignments, and even answers to student objections." It is structured and teaches highly structured writing. Step one, then, is to write a sentence, with a number of reminders concerning the nature and function of a sentence. Step two concerns expanding the sentence to several sentences. The third step concerns further expansion--writing four or five sentences about the sentences in the previous step. Step four involves making the sentences written in the previous step as specific and concrete as possible. The following section gives procedure for correcting a paper in an effort to raise the student's awareness of his own mistakes. The next section, A Breathing Space, is a lengthy illustration of the procedures explained thus far. The author then restates the basic premises of step four--that one must remember the need for specific detail. Two sections in step five follow--transitions and linking paragraphs. The final step is making "sure every sentence in your theme is connected with, and make clear reference to, the preceding sentence." This step

124

also includes discussions on types of thematic writing: analysis, contrast, and argumentation. The language is informal, a sort of running dialogue with the student, interspersed with questions and observations. Formal assignments are given periodically.

225 Kinsella, Paul L. *The Techniques of Writing*. 2nd ed. New York: Harcourt, Brace, Jovanovich, 1975. 337 pp. NPA (P)

This text has a workbook format, "gives priority to the problems that harass a large percentage of college freshmen," and emphasizes "writing as a branch of language closely related to speaking rather than as a highly technical and special form of communication." The author also has designed the text to treat a few principles thoroughly rather than many superficially. There is a strong emphasis on organization. The first four chapters treat theme organization, introductions and conclusions, paragraphing, and logic. The next four cover language: deadwood, inflated diction, weak words, and clichés. The following three deal with various problems in sentence structure, and the final chapters focus upon correct usage, agreement, punctuation, and spelling. Each chapter has a concise explanation of a principle then numerous exercises of a wide variety, some requiring actual writing. Each set of exercises is on perforated sheets. The text is suitable for freshman composition or a language usage class; it could be used as the sole text or as a supplement, depending on the design of the course.

226 Knapper, Arno F. and Loda I. Newcomb. *A Style Manual for Written Communication*. Columbus, Ohio: Grid, 1974. 202 pp. NPA (P)

In their introduction the authors state that they "have attempted to give a straight-forward presentation of correct, acceptable usage and style without lengthy discussions of semantics, word derivations, and pros and cons of acceptable usage and style." They also state they "stood decidedly in favor of traditionally correct English usage." The first chapter is devoted to letter mechanics and discusses, with examples, letter styles, letter forms, and correct folding techniques. Chapter two centers on report mechanics and discusses outlines, pagination, format, headings, footnotes, and bibliography. The third chapter discusses how to construct tables while chapter four deals with proofreading. Chapter five briefly discusses parallelism and pronouns as well as problems in grammar. Chapter six presents matters of punctuation. Remaining chapters discuss abbreviations, capitalization, number style, word division, troublesome words, trite expressions, and idiomatic prepositions.

This text is written in the format of a handbook and doe
not contain any exercises for student drill and practice
It is designed basically as a supplementary text for
classes in written communication and could be used for
this purpose on all levels--high school through college.

227 Knott, John R. and Reeve Parker, eds. *The Triumph of*
     Style: Modes of Nonfiction. New York: Houghton
     Mifflin, 1969. 423 pp. $5.95 (P)

In the general introduction the editors point out tha
many beginning English college courses emphasize poetry
and fiction until the student may believe these are the
only varieties of "creative" writing. This anthology
presents examples of non-fiction writing to balance thin,
out. The major sections are entitled Lives (biography),
Places, Reportage, Journals, Reviews, Letters, and Satir
There is an introduction to each section which discusses
stylistic diversity and technique. There are no discuss
questions or theme topics after the selections. There a
some "classic" essays and articles, such as Swift's
"Modest Proposal" and a passage from Boswell's *London
Journal*, but most of the selections are modern.

228 Knox, William A. *Turning on to Writing.* New York:
     Harper and Row, 1974. 27 pp. NPA (P)

This pamplet is part of the *Harper Studies in Language*
and Literature listed in this bibliography under Shrodes
Caroline, editor.

229 Kreuzer, James R. and Lee Cogan. *Studies in Prose Writ-*
     ing. 3rd ed. New York: Holt, Rinehart and Winston,
     1974. 453 pp. $5.50 (P)

This book is designed so that individual aspects of
writing can be addressed in single class units. The
fundamental principles are presented from the largest to
the smallest--organization of the whole, the paragraph,
the sentence, and diction. Each major section is subdivided. The organization section is broken down into
sections on the concept of organization, the guiding
purpose, limiting the topic, point of view, unity, order
ing ideas, coherence, logic, emphasis, subordination,
beginning and ending, correctness, and relevance. Subdivisions of the paragraph section include topic sentence
methods of paragraph development, unity, coherence,
adequacy, variety, and paragraphs in combination. Sectio
three, on the sentence, consists of parts or types of
sentences, variety in structure, length, parallelism,
balance, subordination, and rhythm. The final section
discusses clichés, jargon, concreteness, active verbs,
levels of diction, connotation and denotation, imagery,
figurative language, and tone. Each section includes

readings which illustrate the various rhetorical principles and presents contemporary as well as "literary" models. All sample selections are broken down by number for easy reference to particular paragraphs or sentences. A brief statement of explanation of the principle follows the models; then questions are posed to penetrate the problem. Exercises for classroom use and theme assignments follow. The authors also suggest alternate selections for study.

230 Kunz, Linda Ann and Robert R. Viscount. *Write Me a Ream: A Course in Controlled Composition.* New York: Teacher's College Press, 1973. 62 pp. $1.50 (P)

This text consists solely of passages presented with each sentence numbered. At the end of the passage instructions are given for the student to modify the passage. For example, a passage entitled "Aquarians," adapted from *Celebrity Birthdays* by Simon Jay, is presented. The first instruction is "Rewrite the entire passage changing the words an *Aquarian* to *Aquarians* wherever they appear. This means that you will be writing about many Aquarians in general instead of just one. Your first sentence will be: *Aquarians are born between January 20 and February 19.*" The premise of this text is that the student learns to write by actually writing and that this text provides the opportunity to write a great deal under controlled conditions. The student does not write his own sentences; he rewrites sentences presented in the selection.

231 Kytle, Ray. *Clear Thinking for Composition.* 2nd ed. New York: Random House, 1973. 112 pp. $2.95 (P)

The author points out in the preface that this text is liberally biased in order to provide some controversy for the classroom. The text is divided into three main sections: Logical Thinking, Blocks to Logical Thinking, and Subjects Requiring Special Knowledge. The text relies heavily on teaching the student objective, logical thought. It gives instruction on how to analyze a subject, how to cover those forces and reasoning habits which interfere with disinterested and logically valid analysis, and finally how to examine the type of subject that requires information before you can address it. Each chapter opens with a dialogue which is then analyzed for its application to writing skills. The text has many examples of errors in logic and many suggested topics interspersed throughout. This is a college-level composition text which could be used in introductory courses on the freshman level.

232 Kytle, Ray. *The Comp Box.* New York: Aspen Communications, 1972. NPA

127

As the title suggests, this text comes in a box.
Inside are six folders, each containing source material
for writing in a particular area: Liberation, Man's
Inhumanity to Man, Life Styles, Mass Media, Minorities
in America, and Miscellany. Each area contains cartoons
poems, essays, photographs, news articles, and stories
printed on 8 1/2 x 11 paper, unbound and not paginated.
The Comp Box is strictly a collection of source material
designed to stimulate the student to write by providing
him an abundance of material to react to. An author's
guide suggests to the teacher various ways the text coul
be utilized in class and states that it "is compatible
with the philosophy and methods of the open classroom.
It allows for a multiplicity of projects in the context
of a writing workshop approach to college composition."

233 Kytle, Ray. *Composition: Discovery and Communication.*
     New York: Random House, 1970. 292 pp. $3.95 (P)

     The author states that "The Premise . . . is that the
production of an expository-argumentative essay involves
a process. The two major aspects of this process are
analysis, the stage of discovery, and composition, the
stage of communication." In pursuit of this end, the
author divides the text into six sections: Preliminarie
to Composition, a discussion of analysis; Composition,
focusing on the paragraph--introductory, body paragraph,
and conclusions; Polishing Composition; Springboards to
Composition--five examples of writing for the student to
read, one each by Ken W. Purdy, John Collier, Dashiell
Hammett, Alberto Moravia, and Brenden Gill (theme topics
are included); Clear Thinking for Composition, discussin
a variety of related ideas; and The Research Paper.
There are brief exercises and study questions scattered
throughout the text, but this is a book mainly devoted
to explanations and examples. This composition text
could be used in high school or standard college composition courses.

234 Kytle, Ray. *Concepts in Context: Aspects of the Writer*
     Craft. New York: John Wiley and Sons, 1974. 194 pp
     $3.50 (P)

     This text is a college-level reader for composition
courses. In each section "a rhetorical concept is
introduced and explained. . . . Next, a piece of writing
is discussed in terms of the preceding explanation.
Third, the student . . . [analyzes] an illustrative
example. Fourth . . . the student is asked to consider
the concept in the total context of . . . complete works
Finally, the student applies the . . . consideration . .
through varied writing options." Section headings
include Audience, Purpose and Tone, Beginnings, Types of

Composition, Patterns of Development and Organization, Aspects of the Paragraph, and Perspectives on the Sentence. There is a brief index of terms at the end. The writing options are not actually topics but more generally "choose a subject you are knowledgeable about" and use the rhetorical patterns in the chapter to illustrate it. The readings are generally contemporary, aimed at "youth" topics, and vary greatly in form and length.

235 La Casce, Steward and Terry Belanger. *The Art of Persuasion: How to Write Effectively About Almost Anything.* New York: Charles Scribner's Sons, 1972. 113 pp. NPA (P)

This is a college-level text for a composition class with an emphasis on rhetoric. The chapters are entitled Proof Structure (presenting an argument with proof), Beginnings and Endings, The Appeal to Reason, The Appeal to Emotion, The Ethical Appeal, and Style. Each chapter contains explanations of rhetorical concepts and examples generally in paragraphs taken from literature, scholarship, journalism, oratory, etc. There are no exercises or suggestions for theme topics. Each rhetorical concept (e.g., comparison) has a number of examples and explanations of problems inherent in using that particular method. Words used in a classic rhetoric (*exordium,* for example) are incorporated into the explanation. The text is not written for students who read with difficulty.

236 Larson, Richard. *Rhetoric.* Indianapolis: Bobbs-Merrill, 1968. 64 pp. $1.25 (P)

This book is part of *The Bobbs-Merrill Series in Composition and Rhetoric.* See listing under Johnson, Falk S. for the complete annotation.

237 Laster, Ann A. and Nell Ann Pickett. *Writing for Occupational Education.* San Francisco: Canfield Press, 1974. 320 pp. $5.95 (P)

These two women have also written *Writing and Reading in Technical English,* which is listed in this bibliography under Pickett, Nell Ann. *Writing for Occupational Education* contains the same material contained in part one of *Writing and Reading in Technical English.*

238 Leary, William G., James Steel Smith, and Richard C. Blakeslee. *Thought and Statement.* 3rd ed. New York: Harcourt, Brace, Jovanovich, 1969. 458 pp. $5.95 (H)

This reader is designed to help the student learn composition by presenting readings which will interest the reader, thereby making him read more closely, think

more exactly, and write more coherently. The readings
are designed to give the students "a systematic inquiry
into their own thought processes." Part one, Thought:
Problems of Straight Thinking, gives readings on Observation, Inference, Assumptions, and Pitfalls. Part two,
Statement: Problems of Language, offers readings on
Definition, Reports, Persuasion, and Fictions. The readings included are for the most part by well-known
figures, from S. I. Hayakawa to Shakespeare to Freud.
Each reading is followed by a series of exercises mainly
aimed at analyzing the selection. The book is oriented
toward standard college composition classes. It includes
no technical sections on the mechanics of grammar or
composition.

239   Lefevre, Helen E. and Carl A. Lefevre. *Writing by Pat-
      terns*. New York: Alfred A. Knopf, 1965. 277 pp.
      $3.95   (P)

      This workbook has the student imitate and learn basic
sentence patterns. Explanations are influenced by concepts of transformational grammar, but the student does
not produce complete transformations himself. The
authors state in the preface that "we see that the basic
building block of effective writing is the whole sentence
not the individual words. While incapacitated readers
may indeed 'read words'--single words, word by word--
capable readers, and writers alike, think in terms of
unitary meaning-bearing sentence patterns." This text
attempts to get the student to see sentences in this
light. Unit headings are Common Sentence Patterns; Pattern Transformations and Inversions; Structure Words;
Word Clauses and Word-Form Changes; Expansion of Word
Groups (including noun groups, verb groups, adjective
and adverb groups, and sentence patterns with pattern
adjuncts); Substitutions; Programmed Review of Common
Sentence Patterns, Expansions, and Substitutions; Working with Compound Predicates and Compound Sentences;
Practicing Patterns that May Present Punctuation Problems
and Developing Variety and Interest in Sentence Structure
As the text progresses the student writes more and more
of his own sentences. The final exercises in the book
contain practice in analyzing paragraphs by writing
summary sentences, writing sentences imitating more
complicated models, and finally writing original paragraphs. Exercises are on tear-out pages. This workbook
could be used in a high school or college composition
class in conjunction with a more advanced text of readings or in a writing skills lab.

240   Leggett, Glenn, C. David Mead, and William Charvat.
      Prentice-Hall Handbook for Writers. 6th ed. Engle-
      wood Cliffs, N.J.: Prentice-Hall, 1974. 516 pp.
      (H)

The authors state in their preface that this book "is both a reference work for the individual writer and a text for class use. As a summary of grammatical usage and elementary rhetoric, it provides the essentials of clear writing." Sections one through five are entitled Sentence Sense, Case, Tense and Mood, Adjectives and Adverbs, and Diagraming Grammatical Relationships. Basic Sentence Faults, sections six through fourteen, has individual sections entitled Sentence Fragment, Comma Splice or Run-together or Fused Sentence, Faulty Agreement, Faulty Reference of Pronouns, Shifts in Point of View and Mixed Constructions, Misplaced Parts, Dangling Constructions, Omissions and Incomplete and Illogical Comparisons, and Awkwardness and Obscurity. Sections fifteen through eighteen, Manuscript Mechanics, centers on manuscript form, numbers, abbreviations, and syllabication. Punctuation, sections nineteen to twenty-six, and Word Punctuation, sections twenty-seven to thirty, follow; then Larger Elements, sections thirty-one and thirty-two, discusses and the composition as a whole and effective paragraphing. Following larger units are entitled Effective Sentences, Logic, Words, The Library and the Research Paper, Writing Summaries and Examinations, and An Index to Grammatical Terms. Exercises appear after each discussion, usually ten questions per set. This handbook would be useful as a teaching text on all levels except, perhaps, the remedial.

241   Lester, James D. *Patterns: Readings for Composition*. Dubuque, Iowa: Wm. C. Brown, 1974. 399 pp. $5.50 (P)

In the address to the student Lester states that the purpose of this text is to acquaint the student with basic structures--"the dominant modes and patterns . . . that our language makes available to conscientious writers." The main focus is on expository prose, not fiction or argumentation. The text is divided into thirteen chapters with each of the first twelve including a writing pattern with its rhetorical aspects and the occasions which require that technique, several essays which illustrate the various patterns, study questions and discussion topics following individual essays, and suggested writing assignments at the end of each chapter. The final chapter gives essays for further reading. The essays are preceded by brief explanatory notes pointing out what to look for (e.g., "In this essay look for Stevenson's handling of impressionistic description"), and the questions are broken down into three sections: one on issues addressed by the author, another on the specific writing patterns used, and some final questions on language. Each chapter has a brief essay at the beginning which discusses the particular rhetorical pattern at issue. The chapters cover description, example, comparison and contrast, analogy, definition, classification, process analysis, cause and effect, induction, deduction, narration, and irony. Most of the essays are brief (under ten pages) and contemporary in nature (e.g., Art Buchwald, Margaret Mead, Richard Wright, Vance Packard, Tom Wolfe). Each paragraph is numbered for easy reference. The author includes a cross referenced glossary of rhetorical terminology with explanations and examples. There is a teacher's manual which contains quizzes on essay content, rhetorical quizzes, and notes and answers for the study questions. The text is designed especially for the beginning college writer.

242 Levin, Gerald. *Prose Models: An Inductive Approach to Writing.* 3rd ed. New York: Harcourt, Brace, Jovanovich, 1975. 434 pp. $5.50 (P)

The author states in his preface "that the book progresses from part to whole. It begins with such topics as emphasis, coordination and subordination of ideas, and climax in the paragraph and the sentence, and moves to their use in the whole essay." The text is divided into two parts, The Elements of the Essay and The Whole Essay. The first part is divided into sections on The Paragraph, The Sentence, and Diction. Each of these sections is subdivided into smaller units which contain several readings. The Paragraph contains essays under the headings Topic Sentence, Main and Subordinate Ideas, Unity, Transitions, Climax, Point of View, Definition, Division and Classification, Comparison and Contrast, Analogy, Example, Process Analysis, Cause and Effect, and Variety of Paragraph Development. Under The Sentence appear essays in the following divisions: Emphasis, Loose and Periodic Sentences, Parallelism, Balance, Antithesis, Length, and Climax. Under Diction are Varieties of Usage, Tone, Imagery, Figurative Language, Concreteness, and Faulty Diction. The second part is divided into two sections: the first, The Ordering of Ideas, contains essays under the topics of Thesis, Main and Subordinate Ideas, Beginning and Ending, Order of Ideas, and Style. The second, Logical Analysis, contains Definition, Division, Classification; Deductive Reasoning; Inductive Reasoning; Persuasion; and Interpretation of Evidence. The first essay under each of these smaller units is followed by a discussion of the idea of the unit as a whole. This essay and all others are followed by brief sets of questions for the student and by writing assignments. Authors represented are Charles Dickens, James Joyce, John Henry Newman, and Norman Mailer, among others. Approximately one hundred essays and pieces of fiction are included. The intended

audience is college level--from freshman composition
courses to advanced classes.

243 Levine, Norman. *Technical Writing*. New York: Harper
        and Row, 1974. 28 pp. NPA (P)

    This pamphlet is a part of the *Harper Studies in
Language and Literature* listed in this bibliography under
Shrodes, Caroline, editor.

244 Liedlich, Raymond D., ed. *Coming to Terms with Language:
        An Anthology*. New York: John Wiley and Sons, 1973.
        289 pp. $4.95 (P)

    This reader contains "thirty essays on language and
communication in their contemporary social contexts."
They deal with such topics as advertising, obscenity,
protest, and race. The text is divided into six sections:
A World of Words: Language and Reality; Hangups, Taboos,
Communication Gaps: The Use and Abuse of Language; Up
Against the Wall: Rhetoric and Revolution; Color Schemes:
Language and Race; The Silent Languages: Verbal and
Non-verbal Communication; and The Last Word: Language
and Culture. Each essay is briefly introduced, and its
central concerns are discussed. Following each essay are
five suggestions for discussion and writing. The primary
audience is the first year college student and this text
could be used as a supplement reader.

245 Lief, Leonard. *The New Conservatives*. Indianapolis:
        Bobbs-Merrill, 1967. 64 pp. $1.00 (P)

    This book is part of *The Bobbs-Merrill Series in
Composition and Rhetoric*. See listing under Johnson,
Falk S. for complete annotation.

246 Lindsey, Alfred J. and Arthur C. Donart. *The Student
        Speaks Out: A Rhetorical View of Typical Freshman
        Essays*. Dubuque, Iowa: Wm. C. Brown, 1972. 282 pp.
        $4.50 (P)

    The authors state in their preface that "We believe
that one of the primary purposes of a composition class
is to teach students how to deliver their important ideas
in a logical, rhetorical fashion." This text is divided
into five major sections, dealing with different aspects
or methods of organization in an essay: Logical
Development, Classification and Analysis, Comparison and
Contrast, Time and Special Order, and Thesis and Support.
There is also a topical table of contents including such
topics as Education, Generation Gap, Pollution, Abortion,
Campus Unrest, and Sports, among others. The text consists mainly of student essays under these classifications
which the authors analyze in some depth. They are
printed with marginal notes which detail points or offer

questions designed to make students aware of writing errors. Following the papers are short discussions called "therapy" in which the authors make general suggestions about the papers. There is a list of other essays at the end with room for notes in the margins. After these other essays an outline of the main points to consider in evaluating an essay and a glossary of common fallacies found in student papers (with examples) are given.

247 Lipscomb, Delores H., Judith I. Martin, and Alice J. Robinson. *The Mature Students' Guide to Reading and Composition: Book I.* Chicago: Aldine Publishing, 1975. 271 pp. $4.95 (P)

This text is designed for adults with basic problems in writing skills. The first five chapters are appropriate for non-reading adults since the emphasis is on basic phonetics with pictures to connect with sounds. The fifth chapter is a review of the first four and could be used as a diagnostic text at the beginning of the course; those students who can pass the fifth chapter need not start at the first. The first chapter is devoted entirely to phonetics; each chapter after the first has a section on phonetics, one on composition (in the second chapter this section introduces the concepts of nouns, verbs, and sentence signals like capitalization and end punctuation), and one on reading comprehension which usually involves reading a short section and answering questions about it or writing a similar piece. The text offers considerable material for in-class work, both oral and written. The content of the readings and writings are designed to be appropriate for the adult student. For example, in one of the exercises the student is asked to read a lease for renting an apartment then write on another piece of paper the major requirements for both renter and rentee in the lease. This text is the first of two designed for the adult student, and it "concentrates on skills and does not concern itself with usage rules at this early stage." The teacher's manual gives answers to the exercises in the text and offers the instructor additional material to use orally in class.

248 Lutz, William D. *The Age of Communication.* Pacific Palisades, Ca.: Goodyear, 1974. 431 pp. NPA (P)

This reader is based on the author's belief, as he states in his preface, that the term "rhetoric" can be broadly applied to the contemporary world: "There is a rhetoric of advertising just as there is a journalistic rhetoric." The text is divided into three sections: Advertising, The News Media, and Current Culture. The first part, Advertising, includes advertisements from newspapers, magazines, and other popular media, both in black and white and full color. Brief comments by the author introduce both this section and the other two. Topics for discussion and rhetoric questions related to the piece under consideration appear following all entries. Topics for discussion related to each section as a whole are at the end of each of the three sections. The second part of the section on advertising consists of essays about advertising such as "Advertising and International Orientation" by S. I. Hayakawa, "The Built-In Sexual Overtone" by Vance Packard, and "The Unseemly Economics of Opulence" by John Kenneth Galbraith, to name a few. The second section presents approximately twenty essays which center on the news media; authors represented include A. J. Liebling, Bill Moyers, Seymour Hersh, and Walter Cronkite. The third section, Current Culture, presents pieces on such topics as black movies, daytime television, James Bond, current radio offerings, and pop culture. This text is not aimed directly at any limited audience. It could be useful as a text on the advanced high school level, in two and four year colleges, and as a reader in classes in advertising, mass media, journalism, or communications.

249 Lutz, William and Harry Brent. *Rhetorical Considerations: Essays for Analysis*. Cambridge, Mass.: Winthrop, 1974. 571 pp. $5.95 (P)

This text is a standard reader addressed mainly to the college student who has had experience writing and who has mastered basic grammar. It can be used in conjunction with either a basic composition text or some type of handbook. It is divided into six sections according to subjects which range from The Inner Person to Science and the Future. In addition, the essays included are grouped according to rhetorical type: narration, example, and exposition, for example. At the conclusion of each essay topics for discussion appear which deal with the content of the essay, plus rhetorical considerations examining specific writing techniques employed in each essay. One could employ a modular approach.

250 Maca, Suanne and Dorothy Patterson. *Awareness: Exercises in Basic Composition Skills*. Lexington, Mass.: Xerox College Publishing, 1972. 192 pp. $3.95 (P)

The authors state that "This text is designed to lay foundations and then build on them; thus, chapter 1 is the only logical beginning." Chapter one is entitled Overview and is designed to loosen the student up, acquainting him with how to apply his thinking processes, imagination, past experiences, and observation skills in writing. Exercises concentrate on free, impressionistic writing. The second part of chapter one covers writing sentences, introducing the basics of sentence structure. Exercises applying all principles introduced follow, usually involving writing sentences. Chapter two deals with paragraphing quite analytically, breaking down basic parts and emphasizing coordination. Following chapters concern the topic sentence, supporting statements, and tone, interspersed with grammatical principles such as avoiding run-ons, fragments, etc. The second half of the book (chapters six through nine) "give you practice in writing as well as you can by offering topics that call for your comments about yourself and your environment." It is geared to making the student aware of procedures in writing and of the resources the writer has within himself. The topics introduced are pollution, prejudice, education, war, drugs, and society. Short articles and cartoons are offered for the student to respond to; then topics to think about and do are presented. The assignments are usually brief paragraphs. Usage principles are again interspersed. Chapter nine deals with writing a longer paper (though really short) discussing organization and basic patterns. Appendices give exceptions to spelling rules and basic rules of punctuation. The exercises are innovative, varied, and usually brief. They help to connect thinking and writing. The whole approach is geared to breaking the barriers of the beginning writer and is very elementary. Diagrams, illustrations, and writing exercises keep things moving. This text would be useful for high school and remedial college writing courses. It also could be used as a workbook.

251 McAuliffe, Conn, ed. *Counterpoint: Dialogue for the 70's.* Philadelphia: J. B. Lippincott, 1970. 462 pp. $5.25 (P)

The editor says that this text "is a response to the need, voiced by students and instructors alike, for a more relevant education." There are classic and contemporary authors included such as C. S. Lewis, John Steinbeck, James Thurber, D. H. Lawrence, Cesar Chavez, Judith Crist, and Erich Fromm. The essays are divided into seven units according to theme: Into the Seventies, Areas of Impact, Forces at Work, Quest for Communication, The Moral Vise, Goals and Gods, and The Nature of Man. However, there is an alternative table of contents listing the essays according to rhetorical types: Argument by Reason and Evidence, Analysis and Process, Description, Definition, Comparison and Contrast, Example, and Satire. The editor says in the preface that the essays have been selected so that the instructor may choose which ones he wishes to use. There are no introductions to the chapters; the text consists entirely of essays for reading and questions after each essay. The questions are divided into four sections: Developing Insight through 1) The Idea (questions on content), 2) The Form (questions on rhetoric and style), 3) The Word (questions on vocabulary and diction), and 4) The Written Response (assignments for student themes relating to the essays read). This college-level reader would be appropriate in either a freshman or advanced-level composition course.

252 McAuliffe, Conn. *Re·Action*. San Francisco, Ca.: Boyd and Fraser, 1971. 418 pp. $5.50 (P)

The author states in the preface that "The purpose of *RE·ACTION* is to encourage in the student these critical and analytical skills and to help him function with more certainty in a world convulsed by change. The emphasis of this text is upon the reaction of the individual--how he reacts to varying conditions, why he reacts in such a way . . . and the probable reaction he can expect from others." Major units are Reacting to the Need to Explore, Reacting to the Environment, Reacting to One's Fellow-Man, Reacting to the Family Unit Crisis, and Reacting to the Work-Leisure Seesaw. Each unit is divided into categories of thought, each with a number of selections from literature, journalism, the sports world, etc. At the end of each unit there are exercises which test vocabulary and reading comprehension and give practice writing the short essay. This is not a text which teaches the student how to write; it is simply a reader. Contributors include Robert Frost, Marshall McLuhan, Art Buchwald, Thor Heyerdahl, Joan Baez, Paul Dunbar, and Joe Namath, among many others. This text would probably be most appropriate in a more general high school English course, but it could be used in lower-level college composition courses.

253 McCrimmon, James M. *Writing With a Purpose*. 5th ed. Boston: Houghton Mifflin, 1972. 446 pp. $7.50 (H)

This text, initially published in 1950, has been revised with more concentrated exposition, newer student and professional models, a renewed emphasis for the necessity of the writer's awareness of his audience, a strong sense of student involvement through discussion of models and exercises, and a heavy emphasis on revision. Part one examines the practice of prewriting. Chapter one discusses purpose--writing as a decision-making process, considering your reader, how to choose a subject and narrow it, and the formulation of a thesis. Each explanatory section is brief and concentrated, and one never goes more than two pages without exercises, usually based on a sample paragraph or essay. Chapter two discusses the sources available to the writer, i.e., personal experience, reading, interpretation, etc. Chapter three discusses various patterns of organization (process, classification, comparison-contrast, and so forth), and chapter four goes into detail on the outline. Part two explores the topic of writing and rewriting with separate chapters on the paragraph (development, unity, coherence, introductions, conclusions, etc.), effective sentencing, and proper word choice. Chapter eight is a new addition to the text, defining "style comprehensively" as the way a writer works out the implications of his purpose." Part three turns attention to special assignments: essay exams, critical essays, library use, research papers, and persuasion. Samples abound, and the latter two sections are particularly comprehensive with the chapters on persuasion attempting "to unite the classical modes of persuasion with Kenneth Burke's theory of identification," with emphasis on the writer's obligation to make his position easy to share. Part four is a grammar and usage handbook, opening with a discussion of the point of having grammar conventions then going into intensive drills on sentence structure, diction, word order, forms of words, punctuation, mechanics, and ending with a glossary which lists those words and constructions which frequently cause trouble in composition, advising whether certain usages are acceptable in college writing. This section is very concentrated and focuses on problem usage rather than abstract rules; exercises accompany each principle. The book is for freshman composition and constitutes a course in itself.

254 McCrimmon, James M. *Writing with a Purpose*. short ed. Boston: Houghton Mifflin, 1973. 356 pp. $6.95 (H)

The author states that "This shorter form of *Writing with a Purpose* is issued at the urging of those instructors who wish to teach the material on rhetoric but do not use a handbook. The text is the same as that of the first three parts of the fifth edition, except that Chapter 10 has been considerably expanded to meet the needs of classes which make writing about literature a major part of the work in composition." See the preceding entry on *Writing with a Purpose* in this bibliography.

255 McCuen, Jo Ray and Anthony C. Winkler. *Readings for Writers*. New York: Harcourt, Brace, Jovanovich, 1974. 530 pp. NPA (P)

This text is a comprehensive writing anthology which includes eighty-six articles or excerpts, seventeen poems, thirteen short stories, and four speeches. Each chapter is structured in the following manner: a) a model selection (a short piece serving as a model of excellence for the chapter topic), b) a selection by an expert in style or rhetoric on the chapter topic, c) discussion selections which further treat the chapter topic, and d) example sections, a variety which demonstrates mastery of the principle. There are three main sections-- Prewriting: rhetoric, finding a voice, controlling idea, and organization; Writing: paragraphs, development, semantics, logic, and style; and Special Assignments: research papers, themes on literature, writing for the sciences, and writing reports. Each selection, except for the advice selections, is preceded by a headnote and followed by helpful lists of vocabulary words and questions on both content and form of the articles. There are suggested writing assignments for each as well (suggestions for research papers are integrated throughout the book). There is a helpful thematic table of contents of the articles with the following headings: Science, Language, Man and Woman, American Values, Education, Literature and the Arts, Philosophy and Religion, Thinking, Social Problems, and Portrait of the Individual. This text is suitable for any writing course which uses a reader as its basis.

256 McDonald, Daniel. *The Language of Argument*. 2nd ed. New York: Thomas Y. Crowell, 1975. 274 pp. $4.25 (P)

In his preface the author notes that "The purpose of this text is to teach students how to read argument and to provide materials around which they can write argumentative essays of their own." Part one, Forms of Argument, contains chapters on "Truth" and Argument, Induction, Deduction, Argument by Authority, Semantic Argument, Fallacies, Statistics, and Exercises for Review. Part two is entitled Argument for Analysis and contains twenty-two selections--essays, cartoons, advertisements, etc.--for the student to read and respond to. Part three is a chapter entitled How to Write Argument. An alternate table of contents is included which classifies the subjects discussed in this text: Physical Health, Psychological Health, Social Problems, Religion, and Areas of Speculation. Most of the selections are followed by discussion questions, and each section is provided with an introduction. This rhetoric/reader is designed as a supplementary text on beginning levels, but it could serve as the single text on more advanced levels of writing.

257 McKean, Keith F. and Charles Wheeler. *The World of Informative-Persuasive Prose*. New York: Holt, Rinehart and Winston, 1971. 338 pp. $5.95 (P)

The editors say in their preface that many readers contain writing so elevated in style the student cannot hope to effectively emulate them. "In contrast, we have tried to choose selections for *The World of Informative-Persuasive Prose* which provide a realistic cross-section of everyday prose of the kind most students are likely to read and to write." The selections come from journalistic sources, business, school newspapers, and student themes. The first unit deals with the preliminaries of writing and offers short examples from other sources. The readings are under such chapter headings as News Stories, Editorials, The Interview, The Review, The Argumentative Article, The Personal Essay, On-The-Job Writing, and School and College Writing, among others. Each chapter begins with an introduction which discusses the type of writing to be found in the chapter. After every selection there are questions which could be used for discussion in class or for writing assignments. At the end of every chapter there are short lists of writing assignments related to the type of writing found in the chapters. These assignments are explained so the student knows in what direction to head, for example, "Write your own review of a current film, play, television show, recital, or exhibit. Study the text examples to find ways to organize and develop your material." The last unit is on Common Problems in Writing and contains chapters on prewriting and rewriting. There is a short glossary of grammar and diction at the end. This textbook could be used in beginning composition courses on the advanced high school or beginning college levels.

258 McKowen, Clark. *Image: Reflections on Language.* New York: Macmillan, 1973. 383 pp. $6.95 (P)

This text is designed to give the student something to react to. There is no table of contents or index, and the text consists largely of a variety of short quotations, photographs, drawings, poems, essays, short stories, journal entries, and suggestions for student work (for example, "Draw a picture of *laziness*, but don't use people or animals."). The student would probably be keeping a journal while using this text as there are occasional references to journal keeping.

259 McMahan, Elizabeth. *A Crash Course in Composition.* New York: McGraw-Hill, 1973. 180 pp. NPA (P)

The author states in the preface that "This handbook is designed to help anyone who wants to learn to write clearly and effectively in the plain style." It is divided into two main parts and a short appendix of grammar. The first part, How to Put a Paper Together, includes sections on the preliminary stages of thinking and organizing, the actual writing, and Smart Reading and Straight Thinking, which discusses having an inquisitive attitude toward one's sources and some basics in logic. The second part is Further Advice for Those Who Need It, including sections on punctuation, agreement, modifiers and usage, and the research paper. At the end of the first section in the first unit there is a list of suggested topics for papers, and at the end of the second section there is a checklist for revising. In the second part of the text, which deals more with rules of mechanics and usage, there are exercises for the student to do scattered throughout the explanations, with answers for the exercises immediately following. They are designed to familiarize the student with the rules rather than to test him. The section on actual writing gives advice on sentencing, word usage, introductions, transitions, detail, wordiness, avoiding the passive voice, clichés, conclusions, revising, and proofreading. This text could be used in any lower-level college composition course.

260 McNamee, M. B. *Essays by the Masters.* Indianapolis: Bobbs-Merrill, 1968. 64 pp. $1.25 (P)

This book is part of *The Bobbs-Merrill Series in Composition and Rhetoric.* See listing under Johnson, Falk S. for the complete annotation.

261 McQuade, Donald and Robert Atwan. *Popular Writing in America: The Interaction of Style and Audience.* New York: Oxford University Press, 1974. 647 pp. $5.95 (P)

This book is based on the premise that "*any* form of writing can be made the subject of rewarding critical attention." The authors, therefore, have included selections entitled Advertising, Press, Magazine Articles, Best Sellers, and Classics, each of which is briefly introduced. Although this text is basically a reader, a rhetorical table of contents is provided which gives page numbers and titles for those selections which demonstrate various rhetorical devices: Varieties of Diction, Using Details, Description, Narration, Exposition (process, definition, classification, comparison and contrast, cause and effect), Argument and Persuasion, and Personal Experience. This text would serve as a source book for almost any writing course, and its size allows for selectivity so that the instructor can gear the readings to his particular class.

262 McQueen, William A. *A Short Guide to English Composition.* Belmont, Ca.: Wadsworth, 1972. 183 pp. $2.95 (P)

This text is a deliberately concise discussion of "the

basic information that a student needs when he writes or revises." Rarely used principles and elaborate distinctions are not treated. The author suggests that it can be used as a theme correction guide as well. It is divided into sections on grammar, sentence structure, clarity of thought, diction, punctuation, mechanics, spelling, outlines, paragraphs, and there is a list of terms. Terms are defined in each section with a brief example or two. A helpful list of terms is included at the end along with a list of possible theme topics. The author notes considerable revision from the first edition, including expanded sections on sentence structure, diction, and paragraphing. It is designed to be a quick reference text for students, and the instructor could assign chapters on sections out of sequence. The text is best suited for brushing up on the basic elements of English usage and terminology.

263 Macrorie, Ken. *Telling Writing*. Rochelle Park, N.J.: Hayden, 1970. 270 pp. $5.50 (P)

The author states that the purpose of this text is directed away from conventional writing, the child of the "New English Movement," which "constantly messes around in reality." It is designed to free the student to use his natural powers of language and perception. It "gives the student first, freedom, to find his voice and let his subjects find him; and second, discipline, to learn more professional craft to supplement his already considerable language skills." Chapters gradually try to liberate students from writing paranoia. They are brief and conversational and have many examples. The aim is to get each student to be honest, clear, and precise. Chapters are interspersed with innovative writing assignments. The approach is self-teaching oriented and could be used with a journal assignment as you go along. Different methods of writing like paraphrasing, dialogue, critical writing, and addressing a particular audience are discussed. The book should be used from beginning to end and is geared to freshman college composition classes.

264 Macrorie, Ken. *Writing to be Read*. Rochelle Park, N.J.: Hayden, 1968. 278 pp. $5.35 (P)

This text could be used in either high schools or colleges for basic composition courses. It "shows teachers how to train students to become helpful critics of each other's writing, and how to act as editors rather than correctors, leading a student through draft after draft of his writing until it becomes a work hard for the reader to put down." The text begins with practice in free writing (writing spontaneously and quickly on random thoughts) and has chapters entitled Tightening, Writing Case-Histories, Criticizing, Comparing, Controlling Sound, Writing Indirectly, and Observing Conventions, among others. Each chapter contains suggestions concerning how to write in a particular way or for a particular assignment, examples of such writings from other student writers as well as from literature, and writing assignments which follow the examples in the chapter. The text also discusses revising and includes assignments. Since the author assumes that the student will learn to write better if he is trying to communicate something he and his classmates consider important, the essay assignments are often quite personal. There is a short final chapter on Observing Conventions which discusses footnote form, punctuation surrounding titles of literature, and quotation marks; but the text is generally not designed to teach students specifically to write, say, a critical paper about literature.

265 Makely, William, ed. *City Life: Writing From Experience*. New York: St. Martin's Press, 1974. 277 pp. $4.50 (P)

The author states that this book is intended for students of writing who live in cities or attend school there, based on the beliefs that students write best on what they find most interesting or closest to them experientially and that examples of good writing used to further the student's development should be relevant to his experience. The author has included a variety of approaches, methods, and various points of view all centering on the city experience. There are six main headings: City Places, City People, City Experiences, The Way It Was, The Way It Is, and The Way It Will Be. Each chapter has a prefatory headnote followed by from three to five selections. Each selection is followed by sets of questions for discussion and writing. A unique aspect entitled Voices, consisting of quotations, advertisements, handbills, and poems intended to provoke the student's feelings about city life, separates each chapter. Random photographs and illustrations serve the same purpose. Thomas Wolfe, LeRoi Jones, Herbert Gold, and Kingsley Widmer are among the authors included in the collection. The text obviously appeals to a specific audience and can be used most beneficially on the freshman level. The text concludes with a list of topics for longer papers and a table of contents of selections by rhetorical type.

266 Malarkey, Stoddard, ed. *Style: Diagnosis and Prescriptions*. New York: Harcourt, Brace, Jovanovich, 1972. 264 pp. $3.95 (P)

This book is a compendium of essays on style divided into four major chapters. Chapter one, The Disease Described: Some Causes and Some Symptoms, offers ten essays on the problems of poor writing. The editor has taken great pains to avoid the overly scholarly and technical type of essay, focusing rather on those that read easily and present a common sense approach to writing principles. None of the essays are exceptionally long or complex; they range from approximately two to fifteen pages, and each is accompanied by a brief introduction. Selections include Willard Thorp's "The Well of English, Now Defined," Stuart Chase's "Gobbledygook," Russell Lynes's "Dirty Words," and Wallace Stegner's "Good-bye to All T--t." Chapter two, The Results of Contagion: Style and "The Real World," includes seven essays which address current trends in the language. George Orwell's "Politics and the English Language," John Kenneth Galbraith's "The Age of Wordface," and others by Ossie Davis, Arthur Schlesinger, de Tocqueville, etc., offer wide-ranging approaches. Chapter three, Some Remedies and Prescriptions, offers the traditional and contemporary, from Francis Bacon to Jacque Barzun. The final chapter is a series of six essays analyzing style, including studies of the language in *Catcher in the Rye, The Declaration of Independence,* Hemingway, Cooper, and others. The book closes with three noteworthy samples: *The Gettysberg Address, The Declaration of Independence,* and Kennedy's *Inaugural Address.* There are no exercises or drills outside the context of the essays themselves nor are there formal assignments suggested. The book is suitable for an advanced rhetoric course, especially if used in conjunction with a conventional composition text.

267 Malmstrom, Jean. *An Introduction to Modern English Grammar.* New York: Hayden, 1968. 216 pp. $6.60 (H) $4.90 (P)

The author defines grammar as "the machinery of language" and "employs modern methods of analysis to help you understand your knowledge of English grammar." The text begins with a foreword that offers reasons for studying language, focusing on the nature of language and practical uses of language study and emphasizing the necessity for preciseness. Chapter one opens with a lengthy excerpt from *Alice in Wonderland* illustrating nonsense language then poses five answers to the question "how can we choose language appropriate to the situation in which we use it?" The chapter continues by studying these dimensions of American English: young and old; spoken language vs. written language; standard-nonstandard formal, informal and technical types; and Northern, Midland, and Southern dialects. Numerous examples are given, some very long, from master writers like Twain,

Steinbeck, and Harper Lee. Chapter two examines how pre-school children learn grammar then considers how much and what aspects of grammar children actually do learn. The chapter also studies forms of words and how words work, offering a systematic study of nouns, pronouns, verbs, sentence patterns, adjective, and adverbs. Many exercises are interspersed with commentary as well as examples from Lawrence, Hemingway, Lewis Carrol, and others. Chapter three deals with transformation of sentences--by negatives, conjunctions, phrase usage, and adverbalization. Chapter four recognizes non-sentences in English, those word groups foreigners might use, then takes a look at how poets (Marvel, Yeats, Cummings, etc.) stretch and manipulate grammar to interesting extremes without producing non-sentences. Chapters five and six consider ambiguity and variety and are filled with many examples and exercises. Rules are not stressed--the approach is through usage and understanding of expression. The text is geared toward lower levels of college instruction and could be used in high school, especially as an alternative method of teaching grammar to the students who never learned through the old system.

268 Martin, Lee J. revised by Harry P. Kroitor. *The Five-Hundred-Word Theme*. 2nd ed. Englewood Cliffs, N.J.: Prentice-Hall, 1974. 214 pp. $3.75 (P)

In the preface the author states, "This book offers the freshman composition student the basic knowledge necessary to write a short theme of the type most often required in beginning composition courses." Avoiding burdening the student with "the trivia of mechanics," the author provides an orderly approach to the problem of organizing and writing. As the title indicates, the short theme is the focus because longer ones tend to be burdensome for the beginning writer. A highly structured approach employing writing diagrams is used, but the student should be able to step outside the mold after one semester. Part one--Focus, Discovery, Organization-- has chapters on seeing the whole paper, getting started, unity and coherence, paragraphing, and assembling the whole paper. Part two discusses Revision and Style, with chapters on diction and sentences. Exercises follow each established principle or step (at least one set per chapter), writing assignments conclude part one, and summary exercises conclude part two. Many excerpts from student essays are interspersed throughout the text.

269 Mattson, Marylu, Sophia Leshing, and Elaine Levi. *Help Yourself: A Guide to Writing and Rewriting*. Columbus, Ohio: Charles E. Merrill, 1972. 298 pp. $7.50 (P)

This text is designed to be used by the student alone; it is not an in-class textbook. The table of contents is matched up with editing marks so the student can use the book to explain problems in graded papers. The text starts with a discussion of sentence fragments and has chapters on subject-verb agreement, pronouns, voice, tense, modifiers, punctuation, parallellism, wordiness, and general style. The last chapter is entitled The Paper (organization, transition, etc.). There are short appendices on the parts of speech. The sections are organized into explanation, examples, exercises, quizzes, and tests with answers. There is a pre-test with answers for each chapter in the beginning so the student working alone can find out which sections he needs particular help with. This text would be particularly applicable to a writing lab in which the students work on their own.

270   Menzel, Donald H., Howard Mumford Jones, and Lyle G.
      Boyd. *Writing a Technical Paper*. New York: McGraw-
      Hill, 1961. 132 pp. $1.95 (P)

      "This book attempts to give practical help to the
scientist, the technician, the advanced student, the
technical writer reporting on the research of others.
. . ." The book is not aimed at the beginning student
and concentrates on helping the reader produce a paper
which might be accepted by a technical journal. The
first chapter deals with the original plan and outline;
the second with revision and reorganization. Chapter
three, Presenting the Data, covers the use and misuse of
technical symbols, tables, equations, and mathematical
English. The chapters on grammar and style review only
selective problems which the authors feel are common to
technical writing. There is a chapter on professional
jargon and a final chapter on preparing and submitting
the manuscript. The book is a concise "help" book but
not a complete study of technical writing. No exercises
or assignments are included.

271. Mesthene, Emmanuel G. *Technology and Social Change*.
      Indianapolis: Bobbs-Merrill, 1967. 64 pp. $1.00
      (P)

      This book is part of *The Bobbs-Merrill Series in
Composition and Rhetoric*. See listing under Johnson,
Falk S. for the complete annotation.

272   Meyer, Robert H. *Anatomy of a Theme*. Beverly Hills,
      Ca.: Glencoe, 1969. 115 pp. $2.95 (P)

      The purpose of this text is "to stimulate critical
thinking and thereby assist the student in writing clear,
articulate themes." It can be used as a major or

supplementary text and is divided into three sections:
The Essay, The Short Story, and Poetry. Each section
begins with a very brief introduction which explores the
fundamentals of each form (i.e., the short story:
conflict, character, theme, point of view, etc.). There
is a limited number of relatively brief readings by
master writers in each one followed by model student
themes, those same themes with corrections and editorial
comments, and rewritten themes. Questions and suggested
topics are also included, usually addressing the reading
or a similar subject. A final section deals with poems
for further study with suggested topics followed by a
short glossary of literary terms. The book's appeal is
especially toward dealing with how to criticize and
write on literature. The text presupposes grasps of
rhetorical and grammatical fundamentals and is particularly
appropriate to courses in which themes on literature
are the primary focus. Its brevity and succinctness
make it very workable for the teacher who does not plan
to spend considerable time instructing on writing.

273 Meyers, Walter E. *Handbook of Contemporary English*.
     New York: Harcourt, Brace, Jovanovich, 1974. 506
     pp. $5.95 (P)

This comprehensive handbook assumes that "students
have a natural interest in language, an interest that can
be increased if language is approached as a continent to
be explored, not a backyard of mistakes to be weeded
out." This text is designed both for college composition classes in which a detailed study of grammar is
included and for classes which need only a grammar reference. For the former, the systematic transformational
grammar approach is used. The text is divided into two
main sections: A Grammar of English and A Practical
Rhetoric. The grammar includes chapters on nouns and
noun phrases, modifiers, verbs and verb phrases, adver-
bials, pronouns, agreement, embedded sentences, subordination, conjunctions and compounds, and sentence variety.
The rhetoric section discusses choosing a topic, the
format of the paper, punctuation, diction and levels of
usage, research sources, etc., and assumes some knowledge
of basic composition skills. Exercises and examples are
interspersed throughout all chapters. This text is applicable
to both standard and advanced composition classes.

274 Miles, Robert. *First Principles of the Essay*. 2nd ed.
     New York: Harper and Row, 1975. 267 pp. NPA (P)

The author states that "The purpose of this text is
to present basic principles that will enable the student
to write clear, persuasive essays." Chapter one, The
Paragraph, includes subsections dealing with idea content,

defending and clarifying this content, establishing a
solid and complete argument, topic and subtopic sentences, arranging evidence, transitions, and offers paragraphs for analysis. Chapter two, The Essay, includes
subsections entitled The Essay-Idea, Planning the
Paragraph-Ideas, The Introduction, Continuity, The Conclusion, The Title, and Essays for Analysis. Chapter
three is a short chapter on research and documentation.
Chapter four, Prose Style, discusses the informal style,
exact and specific wording, shaping of sentences, and
conciseness. Chapter five offers information on books
useful to the student of writing, and chapter six is a
thirty-one page guide to usage dealing briefly with
grammar, syntax, diction, punctuation, and mechanics.
Each chapter offers illustrative examples and many
exercises. The text's primary audience would be students
on all levels who need instruction in basic composition
skills.

275   Miller, James E. *Word, Self, Reality: The Rhetoric of*
      Imagination. New York: Dodd, Mead, 1972. 224 pp.
      $3.95 (P)

The main thrust of this reader is to open up new
worlds to the student which he can write about and
reflect upon. Interspersed throughout are famous quotations which are integrated into the main idea presented
within the individual sections. Each subsection of each
individual chapter ends with two sections designed to
stimulate the student's thoughts and suggest ideas for
written assignments: Ideas and Experiments and Further
Points of Departure. The text is divided into two
major parts, each containing three large chapters
divided into smaller subsections. Under part one, Words
in the World, appear chapters entitled Language as
Creation; Writing, Thinking, and Feeling; and Writing
and Meaning. In part two, The World in Words, the fourth
chapter discusses writing as discovery, the fifth writing
as exploration while the last chapter covers the individual voice. Although termed a rhetoric, this text does
not divide the parts into the typical and traditional
rhetorical modes--comparison and contrast and definition,
for example. For students with a grasp of basic fundamentals of composition this text could serve as a source
book/reader and could be used as a companion text or as
the sole text for a particular course. It is not
designed for remedial college English classes, but it
would be appropriate for an advanced high school class
in composition.

276   Mills, Gordon H. and John A. Walter. *Technical Writing*.
      New York: Holt, Rinehart and Winston, 1970. 573 pp.
      NPA (H)

This book gives a more sophisticated view of technical writing than many. It presents a philosophical interest in "defining and sub-dividing the subject of technical writing" and "identifying what might be called its basic concepts." Section one deals with these Preliminary Problems. Chapters include introductory definitions of technical writing, The Five Basic Principles of Good Technical Writing, Style in Technical Writing, and a chapter entitled Outlines and Abstracts. Section two, Special Techniques of Technical Writing, emphasizes rhetorical techniques such as definition, description, classification and partition, and interpretation as applied to aspects of technical knowledge. Section three-- Transitions, Introductions, and Conclusions--presents a basic discussion of these principles as they apply to technical writing problems. Sections four, five, and six are dedicated to report writing. Section four covers the progress report, recommendation reports, proposals, forms of report organization, oral reports, and business letters. The chapters in this section, as in the others, are broken up with summaries and examples of the material covered as well as with suggestions for writing. Section five, Report Layout, includes material on the format of both formal and informal reports and a note on the relation of format to style. The more technical aspects of typescript standards are also discussed with examples. A separate chapter on all types of graphic aids is included as well as suggestions for their use in report writing. Section six deals with the library research report. This section includes a chapter on finding published information, including information in technical trade literature and a chapter on writing the library research report, which covers everything from selection of a subject through preparing and appraising a final copy. The book contains several appendices including a lengthy bibliography, a complete example of a professional technical report in several stages of preparation, examples of the types of instructions for report writing which one might be issued professionally, a study of the use of manuals, information on the decision-making process, and a list of the approved abbreviations of scientific and engineering terms. The text would be best utilized in a course for the upper-division technical writing student.

277 Mills, Helen and Wayne Harsh. *Commanding Sentences: A Chartered Course in Basic Writing Skills*. Glenview, Ill.: Scott, Foresman, 1974. 324 pp. $5.25 (P)

This text is designed for work in "individualized instruction in sentence writing," "instruction in a learning lab," "modular scheduling," and "lecture-discussion classes." It combines sentence patterns with mechanics. For example, the first section defines the

noun and verb and works on basic sentence patterns; the
second section uses more complicated sentence patterns
and discusses modifiers. Further sections deal with
coordination, subject-verb agreement, subordination,
mechanics, and style. The sections, which include explan
ation, examples, and exercises, are short and use a
modular approach. Answers to the exercises are in the
back along with a short index. An effort has been made,
through the use of charts and illustrations, to make the
pages more interesting. This text would be appropriate
for most high school basic composition classes as well
as remedial college writing.

278   Moore, L. Hugh and Karl F. Knight. *A Concise Handbook of
      English Composition.* Englewood Cliffs, N.J.:
      Prentice-Hall, 1972. 113 pp. $2.75 (P)

This book is not designed as a textbook but as a quick
reference tool. It has ten sections: Sentences, Paragraphs, Grammar, Punctuation, Spelling, Diction and Style
Library Papers, Mechanics of Manuscripts, Logic and
Clarity, and Glossary of Usage. Each section is subdivided into smaller units with examples. A chart of
correction symbols appears in the front of the book. The
authors suggest that because of its brevity, simplicity,
and easy-to-use format it can be used in courses other
than freshman composition.

279   Moore, Robert E. *The Bright Blue Plymouth Station Wagon.*
      San Francisco: Boyd and Fraser, 1972. 183 pp. NPA
      (P)

This text is a review of fundamentals for the writer
who may have forgotten them. The first half of the book
is made up of "short and simple" lessons, each with
corresponding exercises and tests in the back (part two).
The author suggests that the student read the lesson,
find the exercises for that lesson and tear them out
(they are on perforated pages), and complete the exercise
while referring to the text. Tests are also provided.
There are exercises which require the student to write
his own sentence as well as more objective exercises.
Part three gives several lists of spelling words. At the
end there is a short glossary of grammatical terms. The
emphasis is on grammar and usage, and the language is con
versational. This text could be used in a high school
class which is aimed at reviewing the basic rules of
English grammar and usage or in a remedial college class
as a combination textbook and workbook.

280   Morgan, Florence H. and Fred Morgan. *Experiences.* New
      York: Harcourt, Brace, Jovanovich, 1975. 370 pp.
      NPA (P)

The authors state that writing "is not primarily a matter of grammar, sentence structure, and paragraph organization." Hence, this text is a collection of essays, poems, and selections designed to teach writing through the student's own experience and to give him examples of how others have done this. Part one, Observing, includes selections under the following chapter headings: Observing Things, Observing Individuals, and Observing a Scene. Part two, Observing and Generalizing, includes essays divided into these topics-- Beginning with Direct Observation: Informal Generalizing; Beginning with Direct Observation: Explaining; Beginning with Generalized Observations; Beginning with the Observations of Others. Part three, The Direct Experience, includes essays on outward and inward experiences. Part four, Experiencing and Generalizing, includes Informal Generalizations, Expressing a View of Life, Giving Advice, and Satire and Fable. Discussion topics and brief discussion questions as well as writing suggestions follow the essays. At the end of each chapter appear plates of paintings with study questions and brief discussions. The text assumes a grasp of fundamental usage and is directed primarily to college-level students although advanced high school classes in composition could, perhaps, utilize it.

281 Morgan, Fred. *Here and Now: An Approach to Writing Through Perception.* New York: Harcourt, Brace, Jovanovich, 1968. 228 pp. $5.50 (P)

This text consists of fourteen units based on particular areas of perception or point of view. Each unit includes explorations of the particular point of view under discussion; prose readings, poems, cartoons, and illustrations are all presented in the chapters as are exercises, discussions, and writing assignments. "The book is based on the premise that good writing grows organically out of good thinking and that good thinking must begin with the materials of immediate experience." Unit topics are Perceiving Objects, Perceiving the Immediate Environment, Perceiving Emotional Attitudes, Perceiving Thoughts, Extending Awareness, Observing a Person, Evaluating Possessions, Evaluating a Person, Identifying with a Person, Looking at a Custom, Examining a Goal, Looking at an Institution, Reliving a Past Experience, and Searching for Meaning. Readings include works by E. B. White, Ray Bradbury, Katherine Anne Porter, Wallace Stevens, and Alfred Kazin. The primary audience is the standard freshman composition class.

282 Morgan, Fred. *Here and Now II: An Approach to Writing Through Perception.* New York: Harcourt, Brace, Jovanovich, 1972. 225 pp. $5.50 (P)

This college-level composition text is a revision of Morgan's *Here and Now* (listed in this bibliography) and, like the earlier version, works on the premise that good writing is based on clear thinking derived from immediate experience. It is divided into fourteen chapters all of which deal with some sort of sensory perception and how to express it. Chapter headings include Using Your Senses, Getting the Feel of Action, Observing a Person, Identifying with a Person, Evaluating a Possession, Analyzing an Institution, and Taking a New Perspective, among others. The author employs paragraphs, cartoons, paintings, poems, short stories, and essays for the student to analyze, discuss, and write about. Each section includes class writing assignments, individual writing assignments, topics for class discussion, and some sort of readings and other materials for the student to react to. For example, in the chapter on observing a person, there is an article by Gay Talese on an extended interview he had with Floyd Patterson, a poem by May Swenson called "Pigeon Woman," and a color print of the Reginald Marsh painting *High Yaller,* along with a class exercise, a writing assignment, a short discussion of emphasis, and a class writing assignment. Each chapter has a discussion of some rhetorical principle, i.e., contrast, qualification, or coherence. There is an index of artists and plates at the end.

283 Morris, Ann R. *A Short Guide to Writing Better Themes.* DeLand, Fla.: Everett/Edwards, 1968. 69 pp. $2.00 (P)

This text is divided into ten units: Choosing a Thesis and Speaking Voice, Expository Narrative, Developing a Thesis Logically, Using Examples, Defining, Classifying, Showing Cause and Effect, Comparing, Using Irony, and Experimenting. As the author states in the note to the teacher, "this text is composed chiefly of essays which the student can use as patterns for his own efforts Unlike most essay anthologies these essays are not by professional writers." All of the essays are by college freshmen. The general plan of the book is to give a short introduction to each of the units and several essays, each followed by discussion questions for the student. Individual units also end with essay assignment followed by grading sheets for the instructor's use. There is a short section at the end exlaining how to correct common errors plus a list of 200 theme subjects. All of the pages are tear-outs. The author states that this text is designed to teach "students in high school and college to write good themes."

284 Morse, J. Mitchell. *Matters of Style.* Indianapolis: Bobbs-Merrill, 1968. 318 pp. $3.25 (P)

The author states that this is a book for good students "who don't need drill in writing correctly and who therefore can profit by guided practice in writing well." The method is to analyze a variety of literary styles to discover the possibilities of English prose and to develop a consciousness of form and skill in devising form. The introduction establishes the premise that good writing comes from cultivating grace and exercising judgment and states the necessity for practice. One must go beyond correctness, the author states, and he stresses the importance of precise language use, imagination, and variation in good writing. Chapter one studies balanced styles, that is, symmetry in writing, antithesis, etc. This chapter concerns three main aspects: ancient, medieval, and early English-Renaissance authors, including Isocrates, Cicero, Seneca, Roger Ascham, and St. Augustine. The selections are short and often accompanied by brief commentary emphasizing some stylistic aspect. The second part deals with euphuism and includes John Lyly, Robert Greene, and others. The final part concerns neo-classical style, represented by such authors as Isaac Newton, Samuel Johnson, and Thomas Paine. Exercises and writing assignments follow each part. Chapter two examines varieties of poetic prose with samples from Wilde and Joyce, for example. Chapters three, four, and five study three particular styles and the variations characteristic of each type: Rabelaisian styles (Rabelais, Shakespeare, Melville, Joyce), Victorian styles (Carlyle, Dickins, Ruskin, and James), and twentieth century styles (Stein, Faulkner, Hemingway, for example). Notes precede each selection and offer brief analyses of style types, pointing out such things as the use of rhythmic repetition, visual imagery, and dead-pan solemnity. Each major section is preceded by an essay on the stylistic principles discussed. The author also provides three appendices for further study: "The Ear and the Mouth" by Andre Sprie, Sartre's "Calter's Mobiles," and an excerpt from *Finnegan's Wake*. This text is primarily aimed at advanced college writing classes.

285 Moynihan, William T., Donald W. Lee, and Herbert Weil, Jr. *Reading, Writing and Rewriting: A Rhetoric Reader*. shorter ed. New York: J. B. Lippincott, 1969. 497 pp. $4.75 (P)

The major revisions in this edition are replacements of some of the readings for more current material. The author states that "Effective writing most frequently stems from intelligent reading. Effective writing also presumes informed self-criticism. And informed self-criticism is best put into practice by learning how to rewrite." This text is divided into five sections. The first is an introductory section discussing general principles of writing and tools in compositions. The four major units in the text are Reading for Writing, Language, Form, and Argument. Each section contains brief introductory or explanatory notes with readings as illustrations. Questions and assignments after each reading provide the student with questions on reading comprehension as well as writing assignments which generally tie the readings to short compositions the student is to write. Each of these units contains a section on rewriting in which examples of writing both by students and established authors are presented before and after rewriting. Principles of good rewriting are expanded upon after the examples. The unit on form contains examples of various types of essays, including classification, comparison and contrast, analogy, cause and effect, definition, and chronology. Examples are taken from a variety of sources, including Albert Camus, Franz Kafka, Wayne C. Booth, Martin Luther King, Jr., E. M. Forster, Francis Bacon, and Jerome Ellison. This reader would be most appropriate in a freshman composition course.

286   Muller, Gill. *Comparison and Contrast: Key to Composition*. New York: Harper and Row, 1974. 31 pp. NPA (P)

This pamphlet is a part of the *Harper Studies in Language and Literature* listed in this bibliography under Shrodes, Caroline, editor.

287   Murry, J. Middleton. *The Problem of Style*. London: Oxford University Press, 1967. 133 pp. $2.25 (P)

This text consists of six lectures delivered to the school of English Literature at Oxford during the summer term of 1921. The titles of the lectures are The Meaning of Style, The Psychology of Style, Poetry and Prose, The Central Problem of Style, The Process of Creative Style, and The English Bible; and the Grand Style. The lectures are interspersed with examples from the literature of many ages. The book has no discussion questions exercises or theme topics; it is simply a discussion of the concept of style. The text would be appropriate for upper-level courses in style or literary criticism.

288   Muscatine, Charles and Marlene Griffith, eds. *The Borzoi College Reader*. 2nd ed. New York: Alfred A. Knopf, 1971. 759 pp. $6.95 (P)

The selections in this text are divided into sections according to theme: Thinking and Feeling, The Right Use of Language, The American Crisis, Race and Racism, Dissent and Civil Disobedience, The Student and the University, Technology and Human Values, The Fate of the

City, The Future of Religion, The Function of Art, and
On the Standards of Judgement. Each chapter begins with
a short introductory note which discusses briefly the
direction the selections in that chapter take. There
are no study questions or theme topics after the selections; the editors state in the introduction that "Suggesting comparison at every point, giving ready occasion
to take sides and to criticize, the book is directly
suited to generating discussion and writing." Selections
are varied in form, content, and style. There are poems,
stories, and essays by writers like Plato, Jonathan
Swift, Malcolm X, Susanne K. Langer, Mao Tse-Tung, and
Allen Ginsberg. An author and title index comes after
the last selection along with a rhetorical index of
genres, topics, and procedures. Major divisions in the
rhetorical index are Genres (fiction, public documents,
etc.), Topics (language study, style, and tone, etc.),
and Procedures (contesting argument, definition, description, etc.). This is a college-level rhetoric/reader
which is designed to be used in a composition course.

289 Muscatine, Charles and Marlene Griffith, eds. *First
     Person Singular*. New York: Alfred A. Knopf, 1973.
     343 pp. $5.95 (P)

This reader is a "collection of diary and journal
entries and letters and autobiographical selections."
In their introduction the editors state that the book is
designed to show the student how others have written
about their own experiences and to illustrate "the value
of writing for self-expression, self-discovery, and communication between people." Forty-three authors are
represented, ranging from St. Augustine and Boswell to
Jack Kerouac and Joan Baez. Each author's selection is
preceded by a brief biographical and introductory paragraph. At the end of the book an author-title index is
included along with a rhetorical and topic index. The
primary audience is college level, although it could be
utilized by classes on the advanced high school level as
well.

290 Nelson, Herbert B. *English Essentials: With Self-
     Scoring Exercises*. Totowa, N.J.: Littlefield, Adams,
     1956. 206 pp. $2.75 (P)

This text consists of a group of exercises designed
to be used as a supplement to explanations given in
another text or by an instructor. In the first part
there are short chapters and exercises in sentence completeness, subject/verb agreement, pronoun/antecedent
and case agreement, verb forms, punctuation, spelling,
and word choice. In the second part a brief review of
English grammar and exercises for subjects, verbs,

adjectives and adverbs, prepositional phrases, complement
verbals, and clauses are included. There are three tests
after the first part which cover all the sections. The
exercises are objective, and answers are listed in the
back of the book after the subject index. The explanations in this book often appear in the form of examples.
Before the first set of exercises on complete sentences,
the authors list a number of different kinds of incomplet
sentences, instructing the student to note the difference
This text would be appropriate in a high school or
remedial college English course designed to teach the
basics of making sentences.

291 Nichols, William, ed. *Writing from Experience*. New York
      Harcourt, Brace, Jovanovich, 1975. 291 pp. NPA (P)

The major premise of this text is that "most students
have undiscovered strengths as writers and that many of
those strengths can be revealed if students are encourage
to value and to write about their own experience." *Writing From Experience* is divided into seven chapters, each
of which contains essays that present some aspect of self
awareness. Chapter one deals with the journal, including
entries by Anais Nin and Thoreau. At the end of this
section the student is asked to keep, as an on-going
project, his own journal. Chapter two contains essays
dealing with Early Memory, chapter three with Person and
Place. Chapter four deals with Selfhood and Event, five
with The Self and Others, six with Art as Experience,
and seven with The Self and History. Each chapter concludes with suggested topics for different types of autobiographical writing which can be handled in short to
medium length essays. The writing topics become more
difficult as the student progresses through the text.
For students who do not need instruction in the basics
of writing, this text would be helpful and could be used
for high school and college classes.

292 Nist, John. *Style in English*. Indianapolis: Bobbs-
      Merrill, 1969. 64 pp. $1.25 (P)

This book is part of *The Bobbs-Merrill Series in
Composition and Rhetoric*. See listing under Johnson,
Falk S. for the complete annotation.

293 O'Neal, Robert and Alan C. Love. *English for You*.
      Lexington, Mass.: D. C. Heath, 1972. 220 pp. $4.95
      (P)

Designed as a freshman composition text and aimed at
raising levels of expression by increasing powers of
observation, writing experience, thought processes, and
logic, this text has a workbook format. Each chapter
deals with a writing principle (choosing words, making

sense, generating ideas, among others), often using a
diagram or photograph to help illustrate the point. The
text addresses problems of getting started, organization,
sentence variation, and outlining. Each chapter has
varied and extensive exercises designed to make the
student actively participate by writing according to the
concept discussed. The book concentrates on breaking
down barriers to and fears of writing and ends with basic
theme writing.

294   Opdycke, Leonard E. *English Manual*. Cambridge, Mass.:
      Educators Publishing Service, 1962. 46 pp. NPA
      (P)

   This brief text is divided into four sections. Section one gives the student an overview of the scope of
the text. Section two, Considerations in Reading, discusses items the student should be aware of as he reads
the various types of literature: short story, novel,
play, poem, essay, and biography. Section three, Considerations in Writing, gives specific considerations for
writing a short paper, précis, paraphrase, book report,
critical essay, or character sketch and also discusses
considerations to be kept in mind when writing a long
research paper, i.e., plagiarism, note-taking, bibliο-
graphy, footnoting, etc. Section four, English, Written
and Otherwise, has major subsections on structure,
effective composition, punctuation, spelling, form, and
correction symbols. The text is designed mainly as a
review manual, not for teaching. It is primarily aimed
at the beginning college freshman.

295   Orgel, Joseph R. *Punctuation: Handbook of English
      Reference and Study Guide*. Cambridge, Mass.:
      Educators Publishing Service, 1973. 93 pp. NPA
      (P)

   This brief handbook is divided into eight chapters,
each dealing with a different aspect of punctuation.
Chapter one is an overview of types of punctuation.
Chapter two, End Punctuation, discusses the period, the
question mark, the exclamation point, abbreviations,
punctuation of footnotes, and capitalization. The
third chapter, Punctuation to Separate, takes up the
comma, quotation marks, the semicolon, and the colon.
Chapter four, Punctuation to Link, deals with hyphens
while chapter five, Punctuation to Interrupt, focuses on
the dash and brackets. Chapter six takes up Punctuation
to Omit and discusses the apostrophe and "dots." Chapter
seven deals with Punctuation to Emphasize while the last
chapter discusses Punctuation to Numerate. Following the
last section are Final Mastery Tests. Each separate
topic contained in a chapter is followed by student practice exercises. The intended audience is those students

who need a review of punctuation or a reference handbook.

296 Ostrom, John. *Better Paragraphs*. 3rd ed. New York:
     Chandler Publishing, 1973. 89 pp. NPA (P)

This is a college-level text for basic composition
courses. It would be appropriate for the second half of
a remedial course which was ready to move from basic
grammar or sentences to paragraphs. The text could also
serve in the first half of a course designed to progress
from paragraphs to themes. There are eight chapters:
Paragraph Unity, Basic Materials of Paragraph Development
Sentence Unity, Paragraph Coherence, Sentence Coherence,
Complex Methods of Paragraph Development, The Writer's
Point of View toward his Material, and The Short Theme.
Each chapter contains explanations of principles in writing and examples and exercises. The exercises generally
lead the student from correcting or rewriting sentences
and paragraphs which are provided to writing his own
sentences or paragraphs. The chapter on sentence coherence deals with some of the basic errors in papers, such
as misplaced modifiers, parallelism, or faulty subordination. In the sixth chapter, Complex Methods of Paragraph
Development, definition, comparison, contrast, and analog
paragraphs are explained and illustrated. There are one
hundred topics for short themes listed at the end of the
text. A subject index is also included. The final chapter has a short theme as an example analyzed in marginal
notes sentence by sentence.

297 Paul, Raymond and Pellegrino W. Goione. *Perception and
     Persuasion: A New Approach to Effective Writing*. New
     York: Thomas Y. Crowell, 1973. 336 pp. $4.95 (P)

The authors state in their preface that the book is
designed to "teach two essential and inseparable skills:
perceptive reading and persuasive writing." Section one,
Thought, Imagination and Writing, discusses Situation
Paragraphs, Argumentative Paragraphs, and Propaganda
Paragraphs. Section two, The Dynamics of Language, con-
tains chapters entitled Concepts of Language; Punctuation
The White Space and the Paragraph; The Essay: A Suc-
cession of Main Ideas; Words and Meaning; Connotation;
Formal English and Slang; and Irony. Section three--
Reading, Comprehension and Logic--has chapters on Fact
and Opinion; Inferences, Assumptions and Implications;
and The Locked Room Murder Case. The fourth section,
Projects in Investigation, discusses Preparing Abstracts,
Introduction to Research, and The Independent Research
Project. Following this chapter are appendices on punc-
tuation and grammar, preparing the term paper, using the
library, and how to use a dictionary and thesaurus.
There are numerous exercises for the student to complete.
The authors state in their preface that this text is

designed for "students with substandard admission cre-
dentials" as well as for those students whose levels of
preparation are more advanced.

298 Pauley, Steven E. *Technical Report Writing Today.*
Boston: Houghton Mifflin, 1973. 324 pp. $9.95
(H)

This text could be used to particular advantage by
the student just entering technical education. Section
one is a brief introduction to the aims of technical
writing and the assumed audience. The basic idea is
that "There is no excuse for making written communication
more complex than the topic requires." Pauley also
introduces the importance of clear technical writing,
stating that "the technical man spends at least 25 percent of his time communicating, much of it 'writing up'
what he has been working on the other 75 percent of the
time." Section two, Technical Writing Techniques,
describes the basic techniques which are needed for writing in industry. Practically all technical report writing
falls into one of the categories treated in this section:
definition, description, or interpretation of statistical
data. The analysis of communication methods to be used
in technical writing, such as definition, is quite
detailed and followed by a number of examples, a writing
assignment, and several exercises. The section on describing a mechanism in operation is complete enough to include
a section on the advantage of the active voice. The
section on researching published information includes the
basic steps of library knowledge necessary for finding
information as well as complete footnote/bibliography
format. Section two also includes material on illustrating as a technique for visually reinforcing report writing, not as a substitute for clear writing. Various
types of diagrams such as the cutaway, the exploded
diagram, and the process drawing are used. Section three,
Report Formats, examines the various parts of a report
from the title page through the appendix and covers both
informal and formal reports as well as conventional and
modern formats of report writing. Section four, Types of
Formal Reports, covers proposals, feasibility reports,
progress reports, manuals, and oral reports. Assignments
and models are given for all types of reports. Section
five deals with various formats a letter might take,
style and tone in a letter, an analysis of the elements
of a letter, and a complete subsection on application
letters. The book concludes with an appendix on common
technical writing errors which is presented as a reference or trouble shooting section. An English handbook
would be necessary for more comprehensive coverage of
grammar.

299 Payne, Lucile Vaugham. *The Lively Art of Writing*. 3rd
     ed. Chicago: Follett, 1975. 223 pp. $1.25 (P)

   In her note to the student the author states that the
one purpose of this book is to help the student improve
his style. Style, in this sense, includes the whole art
of composition, not limiting the word to mean something
akin to "stylistics." The first chapter, What is an
Essay?, discusses the various purposes of essays and
includes information on how to make an essay interesting
examining the opposition, and the special aspects of a
literary paper. Chapter two, From Opinion to Thesis,
focuses on the search for a thesis while chapter three,
The Full and Final Thesis, discusses Elements of a Full
Thesis, The Psychology of Argument, Strongest Argument
Last, Form of the Full Thesis, and the Full Literary
Thesis. Chapter four is devoted to the structure of the
essay--beginning, middle, and end. The fifth chapter
makes some brief comments by way of introduction to styl
Chapter six discusses The Size and Shape of Middle Paragraphs while seven deals with Connections between Paragraphs. Chapter eight discusses The Passive Voice, and
nine deals with The Sound of Sentences. Chapter ten
examines parallel structure. Remaining chapters discuss
the use of words, use of first person, and the term pape
Each chapter concludes with questions for discussion,
writing assignments, and questions on vocabulary. The
primary audience is the college freshman needing instruc
tion in composing essays.

300 Pearlman, Daniel D. and Paula R. Pearlman. *Guide to
     Rapid Revision*. 2nd ed. Indianapolis: Odyssey,
     1974. 68 pp. NPA (P)

   This short handbook is designed to give the student
quick help in revising his papers according to the symbo
the instructor puts on them. The table of contents is
also a table of over sixty correction symbols listed in
alphabetical order. The student looks up the correction
symbol in the table of contents, turns to that page in
the text, and finds a short explanation of the problem
that symbol represents and suggestions about how to correct the problems. For example, the first symbol is "ab"
for abbreviations, and the table directs the student to
page three. On page three there is a short explanation
of the general rule to spell a word in full and a list o
exceptions to that rule. At the end of the text are
progress charts on which the student is to list the grad
and major errors in each paper and spelling charts in
which the student is to list the correct spellings of
every word he mispells. This guide could serve as a
handbook for upper-level high school students as well as
for college students.

301   Perlmutter, Jerome H. *A Practical Guide to Effective Writing*. New York: Random House, 1965. 187 pp. $6.95 (H)

This book is not specifically designed as a classroom teaching text; rather it is designed for those persons, in school or out, who wish to improve their general writing ability. The author states in his preface that "This book is based on courses that I have given to help Government officials improve their writing." The approach is practical--to see "the differences between good and bad organization, sentences, paragraphs, words, and tone." The text is divided into four parts; the first, Preparing, contains chapters on planning and organization. Part two discusses the Draft and Openers. Part three contains chapters entitled Sentences, Unity, Tone, Final Touches, and Revise--Revise--Revise. Part four, Selected Examples, contains a chapter entitled Portfolio of Good Writing. An appendix includes sections entitled Before-You-Write Check List; After-You-Write Check List; Case History of a Letter; Most Frequently Misspelled Words; and Answers to Exercises. Exercises appear at the end of each chapter. This text is a general book on effective writing and is aimed at those who have mastered basic composition skills. It could be used as a general reference and as a text for continuing education courses in effective writing.

302   Perrin, Porter G. and Jim W. Corder. *Handbook of Current English*. 4th ed. Glenview, Ill.: Scott, Foresman, 1975. 529 pp. $5.50 (P)

This edition contains new material on writing, and some of the exercises are revised in order to allow the students to write more of their own work rather than revise someone else's. The text is divided into two main parts. There is an introduction discussing the nature of language and varieties of English usage, followed by the first part--a handbook of grammar, usage, punctuation, and mechanics. There are short exercises after every section. For example, after the section on verbals the student has five sentences in which to identify the verbs as finite or non-finite and ten sentences containing misrelated or dangling modifiers to rewrite. The first section also has chapters on spelling, capitals, and abbreviations and numbers. The second section deals with practices in composition. It includes various chapters on the steps to writing a paper; chapters on sentences and paragraphs, including discussions of development, avoiding wordiness, and the need for variety; and chapters on The Writer's Work, including a discussion of the research paper. In the exercises on paragraph development the student is asked to rewrite paragraphs provided, to write a paragraph with information provided, and finally to write two paragraphs on the same topic using different types of development for the paragraphs. This text could be used either in a composition course or in a literature course as a supplement.

303 Perrin, Porter G. and Wilma R. Ebbitt. *Writers' Guide and Index to English.* 5th ed. Glenview, Ill.: Scott Foresman, 1972. 765 pp. $8.95 (P)

First published in 1939, this new edition of the text is divided into six parts and an Index to English. Part one, Writing: A Preview, begins with a chapter entitled The Writer's Resources and discusses levels and varieties of English, roles, voices, and stylistic consistency. Chapter two, Getting Started, discusses prewriting activities, types of essays, and personal narratives. In general the two chapters of part one focus on the public and private aspects of writing. Part two, Developing Ideas, contains chapters entitled Narrating, Describing, Illustrating; Making Comparisons, Finding Causes; and Dividing, Classifying, and Defining. Part three, Persuading and Proving, centers on persuasion and testing logical relationships. Finding Structure, part four, deals with essay organization: natural and logical order, transitions, beginnings and endings, and outlines and also discusses paragraph sequence, development, structure, and coherence. Part five, Elements of Style, focuses in detail on sentence structure--sentence types and variations, punctuation, separating and combining ideas, parallelism, emphasis, and economy. Also discusse in part five are dictionary use, connotation, triteness, jargon, metaphor, and allusion, among other topics. Part six is a fifty-three page section devoted to the research paper--sources to final bibliography. Each of the six parts contains from three to eleven sets of exercises. The last part of the text is a 295 page glossary which contains definitions and discussions of terms, words, concepts, and problems. This text is aimed at the colleg freshman English student and perhaps would be most appropriate for a year-long course sequence, although it could be used selectively for single term courses. It also would be useful for a variety of upper-level writing courses.

304 Pichaske, David R. *Writing Sense: A Handbook of Composition.* New York: The Free Press, 1975. 330 pp. NPA (P)

This text is a handbook that can be used in two separate ways: the student may attack his specific problems by referring to the inside of the front cover in order to locate sections of the book which address themselves to his particular problem, or the book could be used as a teaching text. The text is divided into eight sections. The first, The Sense of Organization, discusses Organization, The Tools of Rhetoric, Thesis Sentences, Outlines, and Introductions and Conclusions. The second part, The Sense of Style, includes Basic Word Sense, Sentence Sense, Paragraph Sense, and Style and Audience. Part three, The Sense of Grammar, discusses problems with sentences--fragments, comma splices, etc.--and some problems among sentence elements--verbs, pronouns, adjectives and adverbs, and miscellaneous problems such as capital letters, italics, numbers, and person. Part four is on punctuation and mechanics. Part five, The Research Paper, takes up topic selection, research, notes, organization, and footnotes and bibliography. Part six deals with Writing and Revision. Part seven contains a Glossary of Terms. The final part is a forty page section of exercises on grammar, mechanics, organization, and style and contains three sample student papers. The text is directed primarily to students who have some knowledge of basic writing skills and could be used in freshman English classes as well as serving as a handbook in more advanced writing courses.

305   Pickett, Nell Ann. *Practical Communication*. New York: Harper's College Press, 1975. 259 pp. NPA (P)

As the title indicates, this text is directed toward practical communication. Part one, Developing the Communication: Analysis, includes Analysis Defined, Classification, Partition (functional analysis and structural analysis, for example), and Classification and Partition Combined. Part two is entitled Developing The Communication: Description, and part three centers on Writing Reports. Part four covers Writing Business Letters; part five deals with Using the Library, part six with Using Visual Materials in Written Communications, and part seven with Developing Oral Communication. Student exercises are regularly included. This text assumes the student has a grasp of grammar and basic writing skills.

305   Pickett, Nell Ann and Ann A. Laster. *Handbook for Student Writing*. New York: Canfield Press, 1972. 250 pp. $2.95 (P)

This text is designed to be a reference tool; there are no exercises or theme topics. The text is divided into nine major chapters: Approaches to Writing (exposition, narration, description, and argument); The Sentence (patterns, expanding, emphasis); The Paragraph (planning, development, types of paragraphs, for example);

The Theme (planning, development, and so forth); Mechanics
Vocabulary, Spelling, and Word Choice; Grammatical Usage
(parts of speech, parallelism, prepositions, sentence
fragments, etc.); The Library Paper (selecting a subject,
research, organization, bibliographical and footnote form
following MLA style); and Business and Social Letters.
There are a glossary of grammatical terms and a subject
index at the end. In the first chapter there are examples
of each type of writing analyzed in marginal notes. In
the chapter on the theme, outlining, revision of rough
draft, considerations of audience, and point of view are
discussed briefly. The chapter on mechanics deals mainly
with abbreviations, capitalization, numbers, and punctuation. This handbook would be appropriate for use in a
freshman composition course or possibly an advanced high
school composition course.

307 Pickett, Nell Ann and Ann A. Laster. *Writing and Reading
in Technical English*. San Francisco: Canfield Press,
1970. 637 pp. $8.95 (P)

This basic text in technical writing was designed for
the beginning student in technical English, and its
authors feel its purpose is to fill needs in the two-year
college, the community college, and the technical school.
Part one "deals with basic principles and forms of writing that any student needs to know, but with emphasis on
industrial writing demands." Part one contains chapters
on Instructions and Process, Description of a Mechanism,
Definition, Analysis Through Classification and Partition,
Analysis Through Effect and Cause, The Summary, Business
Letters, Report Writing, and The Library Paper. Each
chapter contains extensive commentary, examples, and a
large number of exercises. Part two of the text consists
of a selection of readings from periodicals and formal
literature. These readings are included to stimulate
thinking and writing, and writing assignments given in
this section are correlated to the types of writing discussed in parts one and three. Readings range from
Melville (a selection from *Moby Dick* on the process of
cutting up a whale) to an article entitled "Packaging and
Labeling" from *Consumer Bulletin*. Part three of the text
consists of a handbook of accepted practices in writing
and usage. It contains chapters on The Sentence, The
Paragraph, Mechanics, Grammatical Usage, and Vocabulary
and Spelling. Exercises are given with the material.
The book also contains three brief appendices: a glossary
of grammatical terms and of words often confused and
misused, a list of suggested readings, and format directions for theme writing.

308 Pitt, Jack and Russell E. Leavenworth. *Logic for Argument*. New York: Random House, 1968. 115 pp. $1.75
(P)

The authors state in the preface that "One of the aims
of this book is to provide practice in the means of making
our researches more efficient and our arguments more
sophisticated." The text is divided into ten chapters:
Truth and Argument, Sentences and Sentence Forms, Form
and Meaning, The Logic of Definition, Form and Content in
Arguments, More Forms of Valid Argument, Complex Arguments,
Dilemmas, Complex Arguments Concluded, and Fallacies.
Each chapter contains explanations, examples, exercises,
and writing suggestions. The exercises are based on logic
and have the student identify arguments, provide omissions
which are necessary for the argument, rewrite arguments
for clarity, or eliminate other problems. The writing
suggestions generally have the student write on concepts
covered in the chapter. For example, the first writing
suggestion is to explain the differences between validity
and truth. This text uses logical notations and formulas.
It could be used alone in a one quarter course in which
the instructor wished to emphasize logic or as a supplementary text.

309   Pulaski, Mary Ann Spencer. *Step-by-Step Guide to Correct
      English*. New York: Arco, 1974. 158 pp. $3.95 (P)

This grammar workbook concentrates only on basic usage
and sentence structure. It does not address itself to
subjects such as diction, paragraphing, or spelling but
focuses on getting the student to write effective sentences by beginning with parts of speech and working up
to sentences, punctuation, and mechanics. Chapters are
entitled Subjects and Predicates, More about Nouns, Pronouns, More about Verbs, Four Kinds of Sentences,
Complete and Incomplete Sentences, Punctuation, Capital
Letters, Adjectives, Adverbs, More Punctuation, Prepositions, Still More Punctuation, Conjunctions and Inter-
jections, Letter Writing, and a Final Review. In each
chapter explanations and examples are given for the concept or rule under discussion, and immediately following
the informative material are one or more exercises for
the student to complete. For the most part these exercises consist of underlining the word under discussion,
filling in the blank, or supplying the correct or more
nearly correct word. A diagnostic text is included at
the outset with answers supplied. Also, each of the
exercises is correlated with the answer key contained at
the end of the text. The text is designed as a self-
instructional book, but it could be used as a class text.
It should be useful for students, remedial to average,
who need instruction in basic grammar and would be suitable for high school students or college freshman.

310   Quirk, Randolph, Geoffrey Leech, and Jan Svartvik. *A
      Grammar of Contemporary English*. London: Longman,

1972. 1120 pp. $26.50 (H)

This grammar is designed as a reference work, not as a teaching text. The authors state in their preface that "It will be obvious that our grammatical framework has drawn heavily both on the long-established tradition and on the insights of several contemporary schools of linguistics." They further state that "recent trends suggest that our own compromise position is a fair reflec tion of the way in which the major theories are respondin to influence from others." The text itself is divided into fourteen major sections: The English Language; The Sentence: A Preliminary View; The Verb Phrase; Nouns, Pronouns, and the Basic Noun Phrase; Adjectives and Adverbs; Prepositions and Prepositional Phrases; The Simple Sentence; Adjuncts, Disjuncts, Conjuncts; Coordin- ation and Apposition; Sentence Connection; The Complex Sentence; The Verb and Its Complementation; The Complex Noun Phrase; Focus, Theme, and Emphasis. The three appendices are entitled Word-Formation; Stress, Rhythm, and Intonation; and Punctuation. A bibliography and index are included.

311   Radner, Sanford R. and Susan G. Radner, eds. *Language and Literature for Composition*. New York: Thomas Y. Crowell, 1973. 569 pp. $5.95 (P)

The emphasis of this text, as the editors note in their preface, is on "the strategies of written communi- cation," and writing is presented as "a fascinating pro- blem of bridging the gap between writer and reader throug the writer's skillful choice of techniques from among a wide variety of rhetorical devices." Part one, Language and Personal Development, has eleven selections ranging from Yuen Ren Chao's "Personality and Language" to Melville's "Bartleby the Scrivener: A Story of Wall Street." In Part two, Language and Social Change, selec- tions by LeRoi Jones, Alvin Toffler, and Edmund Spenser appear (among others). Part three deals with the topic Language and Politics; parts four and five cover Language and Science from two distinct perspectives, and part six studies The Language of Literature. Selections range widely, including authors such as Russell Baker, Angela Davis, Jean-Paul Sartre, Noam Chomsky, and Woody Allen. Each part has a brief introductory note, and each selec- tion is preceded by a short headnote previewing its con- tent. Questions and theme suggestions after each could lead to student writing. The editors offer suggestions and ideas for the text's use in their Note to the Instruc tor. Two appendices listing selections by genre and rhetorical type are included to facilitate making assign- ments. This reader is suitable for students already well schooled in the basics of composition.

312 Rathbone, Robert R. *Communicating Technical Information: A Guide to Current Uses and Abuses in Scientific and Engineering Writing*. Reading, Mass.: Addison-Wesley, 1966. 104 pp. $4.25 (P)

This book is intended as a primary text for short in-plant writing courses for engineers and scientists and as a secondary text for college courses in engineering, science, and technical writing. As such, it is designed to serve as an inexpensive self-help reference book for both the student and the professional. Coverage includes improving the writing of abstracts, titles, technical descriptions, conclusions, and recommendations. The book also details how to eliminate semantic and mechanical "noise," how to edit someone else's writing, and how to organize subject matter effectively. A brief annotated bibliography and helpful references are included as well as a special chapter on editing intended for the technical person. An appendix contains an example of a professional journal article before and after revision.

313 Read, Herbert. *English Prose Style*. Boston: Beacon Press, 1952. 216 pp. $2.45 (P)

This text was originally published in 1928 and revised twenty years later. The introduction defines prose by examining the differences between prose and poetry, the mechanics, and the fact that "poetry is creative expression: prose is constructive expression . . . poetry seems to be generated in the process of condensation; prose is the process of dispersion." The author gives a documented discussion of these distinctions, referring to Henri Bergson, Aristotle, and others. Part one of the text concerns composition--the objective use of language which avoids the pitfalls of common speech and effectively avoids a distinctive style. Chapters in this section deal with words (focusing on word-qualities such as sound, associations, currency, and congruity); epithets ("omit all epithets that may be assumed and . . . admit only those which definitely further action, interest or meaning"); metaphor-types; and other topics--the sentence: unity, construction, word order, and punctuation; the paragraph: unity, liveliness, dignity, rhythm and configuration; and arrangement: instinctive and constructional. Part two examines rhetoric--the subjective use of language. Chapters in this section deal with exposition, narrative, fantasy, imagination or invention, impressionism, expressionism, eloquence, and unity. All illustrations of principles are classic prose models by Milton, Dryden, Lawrence, Wordsworth, and others. All instruction is geared toward classic rhetoric, not common language and writing. The purpose of the text is to delineate prose

principles; there are no suggested topics or assignments.
An appendix offers sample excerpts by Izaak Walton,
Herman Melville, John Ruskin, and others. The text would
perhaps, best serve the purposes of an upper-level Englis
course dealing in understanding style in English literature.

314 Rehder, Jessie and Wallace Kaufman. *The Act of Writing*.
     Indianapolis: Odyssey, 1969. 333 pp. $3.25 (P)

The author notes that the text is intended for freshma
composition, and the central idea is "that good writing
is an individual's reaction to the world around him" and
is possible for anyone who is "firmly convinced that he
or she is a thinking individual." The book offers specif
writing problems for study and presents possible ways of
handling them. It is designed to fit into a course which
emphasizes patterns of writing rather than the rules of
rhetoric. The emphasis is on fostering different kinds
of writing and the entire act of composition. A supplementary grammar handbook is suggested for those who have
such problems. Part one discusses the sources for the
writer, and chapter one deals with writing out of experience. A brief explanation precedes six essays by professional authors and two student essays. All are autobiographical; the student essays are brief, and each is
followed by a few questions designed to penetrate problem
of meaning, style, and methodology. All chapters close
with suggested writing assignments. Chapter two deals
with observation, including essays or excerpts by Hemingway, Thoreau, Margaret Mead, Peter Farb, and Theodore
Roethke, and ending with a student essay and writing
assignments. All chapters maintain this basic format
with commentary interspersed throughout. Chapter three
studies the function of reading as it relates to the
writing process--what we can learn about writing from
reading. Part two examines place description, revealing
personality in writing, and how to tell events that
happen. Part three deals with problems of control,
uniting idea and emotion, and its introduction deals with
moving from the abstract to the concrete. Chapters
cover anger and jealousy--controlling the destructive
force; love and delight--controlling sentimentality; and
sorrow and laughter--controlling pathos and absurdity.
Part four discusses the writer's responsibility, dealing
with writing as hard work requiring honesty, point of
view, and how to use language (economy, avoiding triteness, examining what weakens language). The author
suggests weekly assignments and emphasizes that good
writing can be done by more people than just literary
artists.

315 Renshaw, Betty. *Values and Voices: A College Reader*.
New York: Holt, Rinehart and Winston, 1975. 526 pp.
NPA (P)

This reader is designed to offer college freshmen the
opportunity to examine the values they bring to college
by offering a wide variety of statements expressed
through a number of different voices. The premise is to
have the student question his established assumptions,
to confront thorny issues, and to find answers and solutions to these problems. The author has included different views and structure forms--the expository essay, the
personal narrative, the fable, the interview, reviews,
letters, speeches, satires, and fiction. A broad cross-
section of authors has been included--contemporary and
popular writers, classic philosophers, and feminists,
among others. There are ten thematic sections: Education:
Teaching and Learning About Values; The Individual:
Finding One's Own Voice; New Voices: Defining Fresh
Values; Society: Values of Groups and Dissenters; Politics: Voices of State and Populace; Language and Thought:
Discovering Values Through Words; The Arts and Creativity:
Finding Forms for Voices; Science and Technology: Voices
of Control and Conscience; Religion: A Search for
Values; and The Future: Voices of the Imagination. Most
of the reading selections are brief, averaging four to
five pages, and are geared toward freshman reading level.
They are intended as stimuli for the student's writing.
Each selection is preceded by a headnote which offers
some biographical information and an overview of the
reading. Six questions follow each selection: two on
content, two on rhetoric, and two which provide projects
(some writing interspersed with other varied exercises).
The regular table of contents is followed by an annotated
contents offering capsulized observations on each piece
to facilitate assignment of selections. A rhetorical
contents is also included, and a title/author index concludes this text. The author suggests the possibility of
a cross-reference approach which is facilitated by the
book's design and the instructor's manual (available from
the publisher). The emphasis is on helping the student
"learn how to examine alternatives intelligently, to make
decisions about them, and to express these decisions in
a variety of forms."

316 Reyes, Raul. *Seven Steps to Theme Writing*. Glenville,
Ill.: Scott, Foresman, 1970. 226 pp. $3.85 (P)

The author states that "*Seven Steps to Theme Writing*
has one simple aim: to teach the student, by means of a
step-by-step approach, how to go about handling a written
assignment. Its premise is that writing, of the kind
demanded in college, is a practical skill that can indeed

be learned." The text, appropriate for lower-level college composition courses, is divided into three main sections. The first part consists of the seven steps which the author uses for theme writing: 1) construct a main thesis, 2) divide the main thesis into logical parts, 3) abstract from your thesis statement a good starting point for your introduction, 4) write the theme, 5) read over, checking for mechanical mistakes, 6) rewrite, and 7) repeat steps five and six. The chapters give explanations of method and examples followed by exercises. The second section gives a three step sequence to paragraph development. It includes four schemata for paragraph design. The third section is on formal organization and discusses the major types of formal theses such as classification, definition, comparison, and analysis. These types of themes are discussed using the seven steps outlined in the first part. The exercises progressively build on the chapters and each other so that after the student has completed the last exercise in a chapter he has often written or organized a short theme. A subject index is included. This text would be appropriate for basic composition courses at any level and is particular adaptable to individualized instruction.

317 Richardson, H. Edward. *How to Think and Write*. Glenvie Ill.: Scott, Foresman, 1971. 476 pp. $6.35 (P)

The preface states, "The major purpose of *How to Think and Write* is to help the student think clearly and transmit his thoughts into lucid composition. The Introduction contains an explanation of how to use the text. In addition to the Introduction, Part I of this text consis of eight chapters, each followed by a set of questions keyed to readings in Part II." The emphasis of the text is on original thinking and writing rather than on a mastery of mechanics of composition skills, and the auth suggests that any good handbook of English may be integrated with the text if necessary. Part one of the book deals with the origin and philosophy of language as well as problems of thought and style and contains chapters such as Our Changing Language; Symbols, Not Things; Words and Human Behavior; Generalizations; Common Problems in Abstraction and Logic; Verbal Confusions: The Use and Abuse of Language; and Context and Meaning. After each section in part one, there are references to appropriate readings in part two. The readings in part two are under the headings Science and the Humanities in Conflict; Language and Reality; War and Dehumanization; The Campus Today: Rebellion and Conformity; The Search for Identity; Love, Sex and Censorship; Individual Responsibility; God, Man, and Moral Consciousness; Literature and Good Writing; and Age of Controversy. The readings contain poetry, essays and prose, and a selecti of both English and American authors. Authors represented range from Herrick to Faulkner. The text might be used in an advanced high school class or a basic college composition course.

318   Rigg, Donald C. *Prentice-Hall Workbook for Writers*. Englewood Cliffs, N.J.: Prentice-Hall, 1974. 298 pp. $4.95 (P)

The author indicates the central purpose is "to provide a large variety of exercises with special emphasis upon areas that give students most difficulty." This book can be used in close conjunction with the *Prentice-Hall Handbook for Writers,* 6th ed. The author also notes that the text puts particular stress upon the generation of sentences and larger efforts which will reflect application of writing skills. The text is divided into 141 one or two page sections. All basic usage principles are covered. There are several distinctive sections: three on shifts of points of view, one on awkwardness and obscurity, one on syllabication, and one on manuscript mechanics. Section eighty- seven begins exercises on the actual writing of papers with topics such as limiting subjects, outlining, beginnings, endings, unity, coherence, development, consistency. Section 124 begins a study of miscellaneous aspects such as dictionary usage, vocabulary, synonyms, idioms, slang, and spelling. The number of exercises varies from five to twenty-five depending on the complexity and nature of the principles. All pages are tear-outs. The text is useful for review or could be used as a supplement to a composition book.

319   Rivenburgh, Viola K. *Words at Work: A Practical Approach to Grammar*. Indianapolis: Bobbs-Merrill, 1965. 371 pp. $2.95 (P)

The author states in the preface that "*Words at Work,* a combined handbook-workbook with readings, is designed to serve as the chief textbook in basic courses in English Composition." This text would be appropriate for the high school or college courses in which the student is expected to complete exercises in basic composition skills. The text is divided into four units. The first, Basic Materials of Writing, deals with parts of speech and basic sentence patterns. The second covers aspects of sentences and clauses. The third unit, Making Sentences Work, contains material on verbals, verbs, agreement, modifiers, and other basic usage problems. The fourth unit, Building the Theme, deals with the paragraph and organization, especially the outline. Each chapter has explanations designed for clear understanding of grammatical principles. There are short essays interspersed throughout the chapters, and these essays are used in the exercises. The exercises can be written on a separate sheet of paper and graded outside of class, and there are self-grading tests in the chapters. The final chapters deal more with building up to writing a theme than actual writing; the last exercises do involve writing a complete composition, but this text does not go into rhetorical types or questions of style. There are suggested writing assignments and theme topics throughout the exercises in the last half of the text; hence, the students could begin writing themes in the class before the end of the course.

320 Rivers, William L. *Writing: Craft and Art*. Englewood Cliffs, N.J.: Prentice-Hall, 1975. 214 pp. NPA (P)

In the preface the author emphasizes that writing can be learned as a craft and that "plain style is basic in most good writing." An introductory chapter, Why Learn to Write, provides discussion of writing as a craft, writing for an audience, using conventions, and how and what to revise. Chapter one deals with beginning the writing task--choosing and developing a topic, outlining and organizing, and the physical art of writing. In chapter two plain style is analyzed and discussed. Chapters three through eight examine various techniques of craftsmanship including discussions on voice, tone, and flow; making your writing visual; writing to inform and explain; description; narration; and persuasion. The chapters are essentially expository with brief examples interspersed throughout. Each one has a list of projects (at the end) which demand writing. The final section of the book is a handbook of conventions and principles for the writer. The author states in his preface that this text has a companion text which treats the research paper: *Finding Facts: Interviewing, Observing, Using Reference Sources*. *Writing: Craft and Art* is suitable for freshman composition and could be used in conjunction with some type of source book.

321 Roberts, Edgar V. *A Practical College Rhetoric: Writing Themes and Tests*. Cambridge, Mass.: Winthrop, 1975. 237 pp. NPA (P)

As the author states in his preface, this text is designed for "students who are taking their beginning courses in college English." The book is divided into two parts. The first is a general approach to organization, paragraphing, sentence structure, and diction. The second part centers on types of essays and is, in fact, the primary focus of the text. The first part begins with a chapter entitled The Complete Theme and includes discussions of theme planning, organization--body, central idea, introduction, conclusion--and the completed theme. The second chapter, The Paragraph, takes up paragraph construction and development (details, comparison and contrast, narrative example, and development by logic). This chapter also discusses concluding a paragraph, sticking to the point, and hints on how to improve paragraphs. The third chapter centers on sentence control by discussing sentence patterns: the noun; the noun group; the verbal noun phrase; the noun clause; the verb; the adverb; simple, compound, complex, compound-complex sentences; and parallelism and punctuation. Chapter four discusses diction. Part two has chapters on various types of themes: definition, description, comparison-contrast, persuasion, narration, problem themes, and writing on literature. The final part of the text examines how to take objective and subjective tests. As the author states, this text is aimed at college students and is most appropriate for students who have mastered the basics.

322 Roberts, Edgar V. *Writing Themes about Literature*. 3rd ed. Englewood Cliffs, N.J.: Prentice-Hall, 1973. 297 pp. $7.95 (H) $3.95 (P)

This book is for the student basically prepared for writing on literature and can be used in both high school and college. It concentrates on literary problems as they bear on writing themes. The aim is "to free instructors from the drudgery and lost time of making assignments and to help students by explaining and illustrating many approaches to literary technique in order to provide a sound basis for analysis." The introduction discusses how to read, literary analysis, thematic writing, topic sentences, controlling ideas, and other background material. Each following chapter deals with a type of literary theme: summary, report, character analysis, point of view, structural analysis, imagery, evaluation, the review, and many others. An appendix covers how to take exams, documentation details, and research papers. The first part of each chapter discusses problems dealing with each assignment and is followed by a sample student theme. Each chapter is relatively brief. This book would be useful in the simultaneous teaching of critical reading and analysis and writing and applies well to introduction to literature courses on the freshman level.

323 Roberts, Louise A. *Teach Yourself How to Write*. New York: Harper's College Press, 1975. 211 pp. NPA (P)

This text presents the idea that it is possible to teach yourself how to write well by using three building steps: "First, learn how to write good sentences. . . .

173

Second, learn how to organize your ideas. . . .Third, learn how to write coherent paragraphs." This text has explanations of concepts contained in these three steps, examples to read, and exercises for the student to fill out. The answers for the exercises are not given in the book. The text is divided into three units that follow the three steps mentioned in the introduction. The first, on writing and rewriting sentences, has a section on grammar and usage, a section on punctuation and sentence structure, and a final section on wordiness. The second unit, on organization, has sections on the outline form, different patterns of organization, more complex patterns of organization, and six additional writing assignments involving different types of essays. The final section in the second unit is on organizing and developing the long theme. The third unit in the text, on writing coherent paragraphs, has sections on coherence and development, writing a précis, and writing a paraphrase. There are some mini-term paper topics at the end. This text would be appropriate for use in a remedial or basic composition course. As it is set up for individual use, it could be used in a laboratory for writing skills with an answer key for the exercises.

324 Robinson, James E. *The Scope of Rhetoric: A Handbook for Composition and Literature.* Glenview, Ill.: Scott, Foresman, 1970. 366 pp. NPA (P)

The author states that "*The Scope of Rhetoric* is designed to aid the college student in two basic ways, in his writing and in his study of literature. . . .One premise of this book is that understanding various techniques of development of idea, arrangement, and style is the first step to understanding all the forms of discourse. . . .This focus is borrowed from the tradition of classical rhetoric." The text is therefore divided into three main divisions: Development of Idea (Basic Concepts, Methods of Reasoning, Processes of Association and Division); Arrangement (Parts, Continuity and Special Patterns); and Style (Perspectives, Words and Images, Figures, Forms of Irony, Sentence Patterns, and Sound Patterns). There is an appendix on Conventions and Common Difficulties (grammar, syntax, punctuation, and spelling) and an appendix which acknowledges sources and presents reference material. Each section contains explanations of the concepts involved and exercises. The exercises are not designed to get the student to write his own paper but rather to be able to analyze whatever concept is being discussed. Thus, after explaining the concept of irony, Robinson has the student analyze in his exercises the methods of irony in specific examples from literature. The text takes a classical rhetorical

approach to composition and involves quite a bit of
reading. This text would be best suited in a class in
advanced composition which uses a rhetorical approach.

325 Rockas, Leo. *Modes of Rhetoric*. New York: St. Martin's
Press, 1964. 255 pp. $5.95 (H)

In his preface the author states that "This book tries
to answer one question of rhetoric: what are the basic
modes of discourse?" Accordingly, after an initial section entitled Abstract and Concrete Sentences, the text
is divided into four sections: The Static Modes, The
Temporal Modes, The Mimetic Modes, and The Mental Modes.
Section one contains chapters on description and definition. Section two discusses narration and process.
Section three has chapters on drama and dialogue while
the last section discusses reverie and persuasion. Each
chapter begins with the author's introduction and explanation of the subject under discussion and includes a
number of readings, most about the length of the average
freshman essay. Authors represented range from Xenophon
to Shakespeare to Langston Hughes. No exercises are
included. This text would be most appropriate for a
freshman composition course.

326 Rogal, Samuel J. *The Student Critic: An Aid to Writing*.
Cambridge, Mass.: Educators Publishing Service, 1970.
113 pp. NPA (P)

As the author states in his preface, the main focus
of this text is to teach the student to criticize and
evaluate his own essays and to keep in mind that his
essay will have an audience. The text is divided into
eight chapters with each chapter being divided into a
number of sections. Following each section are student
exercises which are basically complete compositions that
the student is expected to respond to according to the
material covered in the immediately preceding section.
Chapter one is a selected list of terms and definitions.
Chapter two, The Theme Plan, takes up the guiding purpose
of an essay and discusses, with examples, the form of the
outline. Chapter three, The Paragraph, discusses topic
sentences, paragraph body and the development of concrete
details, the conclusion, the introductory paragraph, and
the concluding paragraph. Chapter four centers on the
definition and purpose of an essay and discusses descriptive, narrative, and expository presentations in addition
to containing a section on book reviews. Chapter five
attacks the sentence and includes discussions of words
and sentence structure. Chapter six, Language Lapses,
centers on common faults: faulty sentences, agreement,
punctuation, capitalization, and spelling. The final
chapter presents ten essays from outline to complete

essay for the student to judge and criticize according to the principles presented in the text. The primary audience for this text would be college freshmen in standard composition classes and in remedial classes where essays are taught. The book could be used in high school classes as an introduction to essay writing.

327 Rohrberger, Mary and Samuel H. Woods, Jr. *Reading and Writing about Literature*. New York: Random House, 1971. 189 pp. $3.50 (P)

As the title indicates, this text focuses on the problems of reading literature and then writing about it; and in their preface the authors state that their assumption is that the student using this text has conquered the problems of the fundamentals of English grammar. Chapter one, Reading Literature: The Critical Approaches, contains discussions of formalist, biographical, sociocultural-historical, mythopoetic, and psychological approaches to literature. Chapter two, Literary Genres and the Critical Vocabulary, discusses the short story, the novel, the poem, and the play. Chapter three, The Problem of Analysis and Interpretation presents Hawthorne's "My Kinsman, Major Molineux," Shakespeare's "Sonnet No. 73," Blake's "I Saw a Chapel All of Gold," and Ransom's "Philomela," each of which is followed by an analysis. Chapter four, Writing about Literature, discusses sources, introductions, development, conclusions, using secondary sources, and footnotes and bibliography. The final chapter is entitled Reports and Examinations. Two appendices are included: Glossary of Literary Terms and Index and Notes on Style. As the authors state, the primary purpose of this text is to teach students who have mastered the basics something about reading and writing about literature.

328 Romine, Jack S. *Sentence Variety: A Programmed Approach to Sentence-Writing*. New York: Holt, Rinehart and Winston, 1970. 298 pp. $4.15 (P)

In his preface the author states that this text is "Based on the assumption that students learn inductively from examples and that it is not as important for them to master a comprehensive theory of grammar as is commonly supposed. What is offered is the direct experience of writing good sentences. . . .Presented with a choice of constructions for communicating a given idea, a student is asked to rely on his intuitive good sense of what *sounds* best." This programmed text, then, presents models and exercises. In the two sections on sentence writing, the student is asked to write his own sentences. Part one, Constructions That Add Variety and Interest to Writing, centers on participial phrases, appositive group

176

appositive adjectives, absolute noun groups, shifted
word groups, indefinite pronoun groups, less common constructions, inversions, and combinations. Part two,
Avoiding Awkward Constructions, discusses fragments,
run-together sentences, lack of parallel structure,
misplaced modifiers, dangling modifiers, modifiers that
interrupt awkwardly, and awkward *which* constructions.
Also included in this section are *is when, is where, is
because,* incomplete and faulty comparisons, reducing
unnecessarily long sentence parts, and eliminating deadwood. Part three centers on some special problems with
verbs, part four on some special problems with pronouns,
part five on punctuation, and part six on capitalization.
This programmed text is most suitable for students who
need instruction in basic sentence structure. It could
be used as a supplementary text in a regular classroom
or in a writing lab.

329 Rorabacher, Louise E. *Assignments in Exposition*. 5th ed.
New York: Harper and Row, 1974. 361 pp. $4.95 (P)

This text begins with a chapter entitled The Preliminaries which gives the student an overview of essay
writing and discusses prewriting activities. Each of
the following units consists of two parts: a discussion
of a writing problem which includes a definition of the
problem, occasions that require it, and directions on
how to deal with it; and illustrative material made up
of selections showing how students as well as professional
writers have handled the problem, study questions which
emphasize the type of selection, and suggested subjects
for student practice. The first part, Aids to Exposition, includes units entitled Description, Narration, and
Analogy. Part two contains units on Process, Comparison,
and Classification. Part three discusses Analysis, Cause
and Effect, Induction, Deduction, and Definition. Part
four deals with The Character Sketch, The Familiar Essay,
The Satire, The Book Review, The Summary, The Outline,
The Research Paper, The Examination, and The Business
Letter. Although this text is addressed basically to the
college student on the freshman level, it could be used
in advanced writing courses in high school.

330 Ross, Donald H. *The Writing Performance*. Philadelphia:
J. B. Lippincott, 1973. 202 pp. $3.20 (P)

The author states in his preface that his first objective in writing this text is to shift "the approach to
composition from the concept of mimesis to organicism,"
and he therefore does not include model essays. Part
one, The Basis of Communication, contains three chapters.
The first, Attitude, discusses An Honest Approach to
Composition, Giving up Your Misconceptions, The Writing

Performance, and The Reader's Point of View. The second chapter, Subjects: What to Write About, centers on Theory and Practical Procedures. The third chapter, The Modes, discusses The Mind in Action, Description, Analysi Comparison/Contrast, and Criticism. Part two, The Architecture of Composition, contains chapters on Form (Unity, Proportion, Introductions, and Conclusions), Coherence (Orderly Sequence, Relevance), Diction, and a chapter that discusses sentence structure and syntax. Part three centers on Genres in Composition--The Essay on Personal Experience, The Essay Examination, and The Review. The appendix is a short discussion of the research paper. Each subsection of each chapter is followed by sections of discussion issues and suggestions for essays.

331   Ross, Peter Burton. *Basic Technical Writing*. New York: Thomas Y. Crowell, 1974. 349 pp. NPA (P)

This text deals almost exclusively with writing a simple, understandable technical project. The author discusses at length what he calls the "Dick and Jane" process which involves breaking any body of information down into its simplest components. His major emphasis throughout the text is on teaching the student to assemble information so that it will read in a "plain" but clear manner. Other chapters include The Three-Part Summary; The Process Description; Reporting: The Informal Memorandum, The Formal Memorandum, The Short Report; The Abstract; The Proposal; and The Long Report. Appendices include a short section on Editing the Paper--spelling, abbreviations, paragraphing, and punctuation, for example; Office Practice; Office Files; Notes, Footnotes, and Bibliography; Devising and Preparing Illustrations; and Abbreviations and Special Symbols. Each chapter begins with the goal of the chapter and the order of study. A number of exercises, examples, and study questions are included. The text does assume that the student has a firm grasp of fundamental usage and thus addresses itself primarily to the process of writing. It would be useful for students of technical writing on all levels.

332   Rothstein, Herbert M., Peter Beyer, and Frank Napolitano. *Composition Workshop*. New York: Oxford Book Co., 1975. 76, 101, and 112 pp. NPA (P)

With a premise that practice is the crux of learning, "this book focuses directly on skills and provides ways for you to develop and refine those skills." There are three different levels of the text: red, yellow, and blue. Each one contains four major parts--words, sentences, paragraphs, and longer forms. They are designed systematically, each building on the next, reinforcing

the previous principles. Emulation of model prose
writers is avoided in favor of clear and concise self-
expression. A progress chart is provided at the end of
each text to help the student define what he has done.
Each chapter has several "focuses" on writing principles,
followed by an example and writing activity with space
provided for response. The three levels often use different approaches and illustrate different points on
composition writing. *Red Level* has ten sections: Starting with Living Words, Building Better Sentences, Varying Sentences, Creating the Paragraph, Writing that
Describes, Building Better Paragraphs, Stating Your
Opinion, Writing about Yourself, Writing Letters, and
Crunchy Falls, U.S.A. *Yellow Level* contains fifteen
"skills": Using Words that Work, Writing Effective Sentences, Combining Related Sentences, Developing the Topic
Sentence, Arranging Your Ideas, Creating the Paragraph,
Writing Letters, Developing the Composition, Structuring
the Composition, Writing a Variety of Compositions, How
to Use Dialogue, How to Report, How to Get Ideas for
Stories, How to Write a Story, and How to Write Every-
thing. Finally, *Blue Level* covers the following seven-
teen topics: Using Appropriate Words, Using Power Words,
Developing the Topic Sentence, Building the Paragraph,
Writing the Descriptive Paragraph, Writing the Expository
Paragraph, Writing the Narrative Paragraph, Developing
the Composition, Writing the Narrative Composition,
Adding Description to Your Composition, Writing the
Expository Composition, How to Write a Summary, How to
Write a News Report, How to Write a Book Report, How to
Gather Information, How to Write a Research Paper, and
How to Answer a Test Question. Each level is an end in
itself and choice depends on the scope of the instructor's
intentions. The book can be used as a supplementary text
and is also well suited for high school use.

333   Rothwell, Kenneth S. *Questions of Rhetoric and Usage*.
      2nd ed. Boston: Little, Brown, 1974. 317 pp.
      $4.50 (P)

The author states in his preface that this text is
designed to be used in conjunction with an experienced
teacher in writing. It is divided into three parts:
Rhetoric, Usage, and The Writer in Action. The introduction to the first section provides discussion on the
aims and goals of a writing course. Other parts discuss
in detail prewriting and writing activities--topic
selection, outlining, beginnings, endings, titles,
paragraphing, strategies, style, logic, and so on. This
section aims at giving the student practical advice about
particular problems commonly encountered in writing an
essay and provides many examples and exercises. The
second section is a grammar that treats briefly common

problems of usage and grammar. It begins with some information on word choice, dictionary usage, and spelling, and concludes with a section on technical mechanics and manuscript preparation. This part is primarily to be used as a handbook and is constructed accordingly. The last section gives technical instruction on procedures in writing research papers then details approaches to writing on literature, including how to review a film. There is also a brief section on how to write an essay exam. The second edition includes prose models from contemporary writers and many student samples. This text provides a broad spectrum of instruction for freshman composition. The author gives detailed suggestions in his preface on how to use the text most judiciously.

334 Rougier, Harry and E. Krage Stockum. *Getting Started: A Preface to Writing*. New York: W. W. Norton, 1970. 132 pp. $1.50 (P)

This book's purpose is to help the student sort through his store of knowledge for the best subjects about which to write and to guide him through the art of saying what he wants to say. This text applies particularly to basic composition classes and could be effectively used for students with virtually no writing experience as well as for those who have had some training in the area. It is a practical manual for writing. Chapter one, Talking and Writing, discusses the common ground between talking and writing and then makes a distinction between the two in order to help the student to begin getting his thoughts on paper. The book encourages the student to develop a hypothetical reader to direct his writing to. Chapters two and three discuss how to select subjects, how to construct thesis statements, and other prewriting activities. There are diagrams, samples and experiments to facilitate the process. Chapter four deals with the physical aspects of writing and gives some practical advice about preparing to write, writing rough drafts, and preparing final copies. The text does not deal with specifics of paragraphing or any rhetorical element, nor does it supply model essays or copious writing samples. In effect, it concentrates on the purposes and acts of writing. It would be best used, perhaps, in its entirely and could serve in an introductory course on literature.

335 Rubinstein, S. Leonard. *Writing: A Habit of Mind*. Dubuque, Iowa: Wm. C. Brown, 1972. 213 pp. $3.95 (P)

The author states the intention of this book is "to investigate the convergence of all writing principles upon each individual work." The act of writing should

"make knowledge produce knowledge," causing the reader
to undergo the writer's process and reach his product.
The writer must "desire to reveal." This text is divided
into nineteen chapters which illustrate the above concepts beginning with the necessity for the writer to
discover and clarify his own view, to reveal himself each
time he writes, and to formulate his experiences into
selective, organized bodies of writing. The text continues with various discussions of the role of the
writer and the function of writing, all leading to
developing the sophisticated, creative writer. The
author often employs dramatic dialogues and other interesting expository styles to illustrate principles. Considerations for Writing are included in each chapter.
The final chapter includes famous literary works in
several genres, complete with analytic questions. The
readings include "A Clean Well-Lighted Place," T. H.
Huxley's "Method of Scientific Inquiry," and "Ode on
Melancholy" by Keats, among others. This text is suitable for advanced composition classes.

336   Ruby, Lionel and Robert E. Yarber. *The Art of Making
      Sense: A Guide to Logical Thinking.* 3rd ed. Phil-
      adelphia: J. B. Lippincott, 1974. 185 pp. $7.95
      (H) $3.95 (P)

This text is "concerned with the principles of intelligent thinking" and with applying the principles of logic
to composition. The text is divided into three parts.
Part one, The Word, opens with a general introduction to
logic and then moves on to words and their meanings. This
section contains material on ambiguity, definition, and
types of language (neutral, directive, propaganda). Part
two, The Argument, covers emotional writing in its use
and misuse and the various fallacies which crop up in
argument. The chapter on the logical argument includes
information on premises and conclusions, the syllogism,
enthymemes, chain arguments as well as dicussions of
validity and invalidity in argument. This part also
contains information on patterns of reasoning. Part
three of the text deals with Truth and Falsity and opens
with discussions on logical relativism, skepticism, and
probability. The chapter Knowing the Causes of Things
outlines the process of discovering causes and includes
material on the method of difference, the method of variations, the method of agreement, negative tests for
hypothesis, and fallacies in causal reasoning. Part
three also contains material on the truth and falsity of
generalizations and on taste and opinion. The text contains no information on the rhetoric or mechanics of
composition and does not deal with theme or essay writing as such. It could be used by an upper-division class

with an emphasis on the thinking and reasoning process.

337 Ruggiero, Vincent Ryan. *The Elements of Rhetoric*.
     Englewood Cliffs, N.J.: Prentice-Hall, 1971. 173 pp.
     $6.50 (H) $3.50 (P)

This text teaches the principles of rhetoric for
college-level composition courses. In addition, it is
designed to be appropriate for other disciplines in
which the professor wishes to teach the principles of
rhetoric and effective writing. It is not an "English"
text with exercises and paper topics but a rhetoric book
designed to teach good writing in any field. It is
divided into three units: Reasoning, Persuasion, and
Other Elements of Rhetoric (substance, organization, and
style). The chapters are subdivided. There is a brief
glossary of grammar and usage at the end dealing mainly
with common errors. The book is designed to be used as
a reference book if necessary. A detailed instructor's
manual is available which contains assignments on reasoning and persuasion and exercises on other elements of
rhetoric. The body of the text consists of explanations
of various principles of rhetoric which include short
sentences or paragraphs as examples.

338 Sachs, Harry J., Harry M. Brown, and P. Joseph Canavan.
     A Workbook for Writers. forms B and D. New York:
     D. Van Nostrand, 1970. 295 pp. $3.95 (P)

This workbook is a functional basic grammar which
teaches by exposition of material, exercises, and achievement tests to determine which types of problems need
further study. The book opens with a series of diagnostic
tests to evaluate the student's needs. An answer booklet
containing keys to all quizzes and exercises is included
for the instructor. The student is given an answer key
for thirty-three of the ninety-one exercises as an aid to
self instruction. The grammar included is basic, dealing
with those aspects of formal grammar that give the student most trouble in writing. A distinction is made
between major problems and minor problems in writing.
Space is allocated accordingly in the exercises. Regarding techniques of teaching grammar, the authors say, "We
feel that prescriptive rules per se have limited value
for the freshman, but that he does profit from descriptions of patterns." Sentence patterns, for example, are
taught according to subject, type of verb, and complement
to the verb. Part one of the text deals with sentence
patterns and parts of speech. Part two, Correct Sentences
deals with the basic problems in sentence writing--
fragments, comma splices, run-together sentences, agreement, verbs, and adjectives. Part three covers punctuation; part four, Word Study, includes use of the

182

dictionary, spelling, and faulty diction. Part five, Effective Sentences, works with dangling modifiers, reference of pronouns, misplaced modifiers, parallelism, shifts in construction, omissions, and comparisons. The book contains a number of appendices including information on conjugation of verbs, principal parts of verbs, an alphabetical spelling list, and the student's answer key.

339 Sale, Roger. *On Writing*. New York: Random House, 1970. 177 pp. $2.45 (P)

This book begins with an introduction which explains that the problems of formal papers are outside the normal course of expression. The author discusses ideas about writing that he has abstracted from his own teaching experience; therefore, the first two chapters deal with the problems of using "Good English" and writing papers. Chapter two is entitled Writing Can Be Learned but It Can't Be Taught and covers limits in the teaching of writing, the "canned essay" syndrome, and what is wrong in the traditional "English class" approach to writing. Chapters three and four deal with writing basics. The former, Organization: The Sense that Makes Writing, focuses attention on small parts--words, phrases, and sentences--rather than on the general outline approach. At the end of the chapter the author discusses introductions and conclusions as well as development. Chapter four, Style, Usage, and Grammar, focuses on these three areas and defines the nature of jargon, clichés, metaphors, and abuses of speech. A brief section on grammar rules concludes the section. The book's conclusion proposes ideas on constructing courses on writing for students. One suggestion is to choose just one book (not an anthology) like *Walden* or *The Education of Henry Adams* and intensely study it for content, style, and so on. Another is to eliminate reading altogether, suggesting thirty to fifty papers in the course of a semester. He closes by saying "we must have courses that feel no obligation to cover a certain amount of material." There are no exercises and few examples. The author states on page ten that "I think of my potential readers as teachers and students in high school and college." As the title indicates, the text centers on problems of writing and is, perhaps, not designed as the primary teaching text for a class.

340 Salem, James M. *A New Generation of Essays*. Dubuque, Iowa: Wm. C. Brown, 1972. 361 pp. $5.50 (P)

This is a collection of essays written in the main by contemporary Americans. It would be appropriate as a reader for a college freshman composition course or possibly an advanced high school composition course.

The text is divided into two main units: Methods of
Development (e.g., The Personal Voice, To Describe, To
Explain, To Classify and Divide, To Argue and Persuade,
To Narrate) and Forms of the Modern Essay (The Modern
Informative Essay, The Modern Descriptive Essay, The
Modern Autobiographical Essay, The Modern Analytical
Essay, among others). There is an alternative table of
contents which divides the essays into thematic groups
(for example, America: Ways of Living; America: The
Challenge to Higher Education; America: The Popular
Arts; America: Its Humor). An introduction discusses
basic principles of writing in terms of general rules
such as Get Rid of Obvious Padding, and Beware of the
Pat Expression. The introduction also discusses diction
at some length. Before each section of essays there is
a short introduction which describes the principles in
that unit. Discussion questions for use in class are
given after each essay and writing suggestions are includ
after the discussion questions. The writing suggestions
usually give about five topics for themes. Authors
included in this anthology are Walt Whitman, Philip Roth,
Robert Benchley, Henry Thoreau, Jessica Mitford, Mark
Twain, Erma Bombeck, and others.

341 Sanders, Thomas E. and Franklin D. Hester. *The Now Reade*
Glenview, Ill.: Scott, Foresman, 1969. 241 pp.
$6.50 (P)

The authors state, "we have attempted to present both
contemporary and timeless poems, sculpture, short stories
paintings, plays, and music in such a fashion that their
relationships to each other and to the now generation
will be apparent, meaningful, and interesting--for both
student and teacher." Three small records encased inside
the back cover include a reading of Lewis Carrol's
"Jabberwocky," and musical versions of Rodgers and
Hammerstein's "Hello, Young Lovers," among other selections. The comic strip is used widely throughout the
text for illustrating points. Readings and visual presentations are given under the general topics Reading
and Writing for the Now Generation, The Poet in You, The
Short Story--Pages From Your Life, The Play--You as
Character and Author, and The Essay--What You Have Been
Writing. The first section is divided between readings
with material on such writing techniques as emphasis and
balance as applied to all forms of art and material on
the vocabulary involved in critical discussion (symbol,
alliteration, didactic, and so on). All selections
included are broken up by or followed by questions for
thought and discussion. Writing assignments are also
included in the text. The final section on the essay
includes information and examples of definition, classification and division, example and illustration, comparison

and contrast, cause and effect, process, and description. The book is structured for more advanced freshman classes.

342 Sarris, Andrew. *The Film*. Indianapolis: Bobbs-Merrill, 1968. 64 pp. $1.00 (P)

This book is part of *The Bobbs-Merrill Series in Composition and Rhetoric*. See listing under Johnson, Falk S. for the complete annotation.

343 Saylor, Paul. *Taking Control: The College Essay*. New York: Harper and Row, 1974. 31 pp. NPA (P)

This pamphlet is a part of the *Harper Studies in Language and Literature* listed in this bibliography under Shrodes, Caroline, editor.

344 Scharbach, J. Alexander and Carl Markgraf. *Making the Point*. New York: Thomas Y. Crowell, 1975. 273 pp. NPA (P)

The authors state in the preface that this text "speaks to student-writers of whatever condition and of all ethnic backgrounds and shows them not only how to discover and bring into clear focus what they have to say but also how to make their points in language and structures most appropriate to their intended readers." Each chapter contains discussions of principles of good writing, a number of selections for the student to read illustrating the principles, and a number of questions for discussion and writing scattered throughout. Chapter titles are College Writing Now and Your Future; Your Language and Your Readers; Sentences: Word Patterns for Effectiveness; The Paragraph as Point Maker; Thinking and Feeling for Writing; Development: Putting It All Together; and Rhetoric and Style. There is an alternative table of contents listing articles according to writing principles: Language and Dialects, Paragraph Structure and Rhetoric, Exposition, Plain Style, Awareness, Analysis, Problem Solving, Socratic Dialogue, Rhetorical Tones and Styles, and Argument. An author index and a subject index end the book. Selections for student reading are by such writers as Aristotle, Saul Bellow, Eldridge Cleaver, James Joyce, Virginia Woolf, and Malcolm X, among others.

345 Schneider, Ben R., Jr. and Herbert K. Tjossem. *Themes and Research Papers*. New York: Macmillan, 1961. 77 pp. $1.95 (P)

This text is designed to give the beginning writer a basis from which to build. It is divided into two major units: Themes (planning the theme, writing the paper, format, and sample theme) and Research Papers (choosing a topic, using the library, taking notes, writing the paper, format, and sample research paper). There are no exercises or topics; this text gives brief explanations of principles of writing, and half the text is composed of examples and illustrations. There is a list of editing marks at the end with explanations of their meanings. The sample themes are printed on the right hand pages only, so marginal notes pointing up organization, content diction, and other aspects of the theme can be printed on the left hand page. The text would, perhaps, be most appropriate for a college beginning composition course in which one of the assignments is a research paper.

346   Scholes, Robert and Carl H. Klaus. *Elements of Writing*. New York: Oxford University Press, 1972. 137 pp. $1.50 (P)

The authors have intentionally kept their text brief "because reading about writing is one of the least rewarding activities known to civilized man" and a composition text should not get in the way of actually writing. This text focuses upon the sentence and the short sequence of sentences and is meant as a "point of departure" in learning the writing process. The first part, Elements of Writing, has discussions on the relationship of writing, speaking, thinking, sentences, and sentence sequence in the form of brief discussion chapters. Several exercises conclude each chapter. Part two is entitled Contents of Writing and has two chapters on the function purpose, and kinds of written work; exercises are also included. The final part consists of a number of practice writing assignments.

347   Schulman, Benson R. *English Composition: An Individual Course*. rev. ed. Palo Alto, Ca.: Westinghouse Leaing Press, 1971. 7 booklets. NPA (P)

This series of texts is designed to prepare a student for college composition. It could be used most effectively in a lower-level college composition course or in a college preparatory high school course in which the instructor wishes to give the students an unusual amount of individualized work. The text consists of "seven modules intended to help the student develop different writing skills: Orientation; Writing Skills: Getting t Idea on Paper; Logic for Writers; Logic and Illogic in Essays; Language Skills: Aspects of Form and Style in Writing; Library Skills: Finding Information and Preparing a Paper; and Evaluation." The Writing Skills module provides a pre-test so the instructor may determine which sections his students should take. The course is design so that the student can work independently and with conferences with an instructor, but it could be adapted for a classroom. There are charts of biweekly and term plan which the student fills out, indicating how he has plann

to use his time for this course. There is a form book
consisting entirely of charts for the student to fill out
indicating the grade he gets on various assignments. For
example, the first assignment is on the paragraph, and
the criteria which make up the grade include use of a
topic sentence, development, coherence, organization, and
language skills. Language skills are given a separate
chart. There are also scoring sheets for logic tests and
a list of questions for the student to answer at the end,
evaluating the course plan itself. This form book consists of perforated sheets. Each booklet contains
explanations of principles in writing and assignments in
the form of essay topics or objective pre-tests and post-
tests for the student to complete. The student can complete these assignments on his own and have the instructor
grade them, or some sort of class grading could be used.
Although this course plan calls for the student to do
much of the work on his own, it is nevertheless a structured and organized group of lessons.

348   Schuster, Mary I. *Creative Responses for Composition.*
      New York: Random House, 1973. 169 pp. $2.95 (P)

This text asserts faith in the inevitability of good
writing if the writer is given the opportunity, incentive,
and context. It stresses the value of good memory, sound
powers of observation, and a sense of wonder at the
variety of things in our universe. Each chapter gives a
brief discussion of a principle then follows it with
writing assignments. Samples of student writings are
given as well as selections by established artists.
These writings are based on the presented observation
principle and are followed by questions. Chapters
include the "Thingness" of Things, The Dimensions of
Objects, The Dimensions of Place, Creative Responses to
Persons, Creative Responses to Events, and Creative
Responses to Values. The whole text is based on writing
by experience and through experience and is geared away
from formal structure, composition, and grammar. It
could be used as a creative writing text; most of the
examples are creative pieces.

349   Seat, William R., Jr., Paul S. Burtness, and Warren U.
      Ober. *The New University Reader.* New York: American
      Book Company, 1966. 361 pp. $3.95 (P)

This text is a revised edition of *The University
Reader,* published in 1960. "The works have been selected
because they are historically significant and/or intellec-
tually stimulating statements of various issues intimately
involved in one way or another with our existence as
human beings living in a democratic society in the mid-
twentieth century." Each selection has headnotes which

include the author's dates of birth and death, a list of other works by the author in inexpensive editions, and a few shorter works which could be read with the essay involved. There is an index of rhetorical and logical devices at the back which refers the reader to specific essays in the book in which these devices occur. There is a list of general questions for close reading at the beginning of the text which apply to all the essays. The essays are generally traditional in nature and include such authors as Francis Bacon, Thomas De Quincey, John Stuart Mill, Bertrand Russell, T. S. Eliot, John F. Kennedy, and Loren Eisely.

350 Sebeok, Thomas A. *Style in Language*. Boston: The Massachusetts Institute of Technology, 1960. 470 pp. $12.50 (H) $3.95 (P)

This book is a collection of papers which came out of a conference on style held at Indiana University in 1958. Contributors include I. A. Richards, Monroe C. Beardsley, René Wellek, and Roman Jakobson, among others. The group is international and interdisciplinary. This text "reflects a genuine attempt by a group of scholars from several disciplines to bring their special resources of knowledge to bear on one problem: the nature and characteristics of style in literature." Major divisions are Poetic Process and Literary Analysis, Style in Folk Narrative, Linguistic Approaches to Verbal Art, Phonological Aspects of Style, Metrics, Grammatical Aspects of Style, Semantic Aspects of Style, Psychological Approaches to the Problem of Style, and Retrospects and Prospects. This book would be appropriate for providing a variety of viewpoints to an upper division or graduate level course on style. It could also prove a useful reference work for the teacher of composition.

351 Seltzer, Sandra and Myra Kogen. *Getting It Together: Refining Your Writing*. New York: Harper and Row, 1974. 52 pp. NPA (P)

This pamphlet is a part of the *Harper Studies in Language and Literature* listed in this bibliography under Shrodes, Caroline, editor.

352 Shaffer, Virginia. *Experiences in Writing*. Glenview, Ill.: Scott, Foresman, 1972. 186 pp. $4.25 (P)

This text is designed for the beginning college composition class, following the premise that experience leads to skill. Section topics are Writing the Theme (topic, unity, coherence), Recognizing the Sentence and Its Large Constituents, Sentence Style, Choice of Words (with a spelling section), Logical Thinking, The Research Paper, Punctuation, and Usage (subject-verb agreement, pronouns

188

modifiers, and special problems). Each section gives an explanation of a concept, an example, and exercises on perforated pages. Since many of the exercises involve actually writing an outline or paragraph, considerable workbook space is provided. The exercises are graduated in difficulty. This text would also be appropriate in a high school course designed to teach the basics in composition through having the student write as often as possible.

353 Shaw, Harry. *Punctuate It Right!* New York: Barnes and Noble, 1963. 176 pp. $1.50 (P)

The author notes in his preface a substantial list of manuals consulted in comprising this text on punctuation. In areas of uncertain usage, the more prevalent usage is suggested. Part one of the text is a brief survey of what punctuation is and does, including information on the history of punctuation and its modern trends and purposes. Part two is a reference section, arranged alphabetically, of individual punctuation marks, from abbreviations to the semicolon. Part three consists of two glossaries: one of terms, another of applied punctuation. There are no exercises; the text is for basic reference.

354 Shaw, Harry. *20 Steps to Better Writing*. Totowa, N.J.: Littlefield, Adams, 1975. 140 pp. $1.95 (P)

This text would be appropriate in any class, English or otherwise, in which the teacher wishes to teach writing in conjunction with other course work. It consists of twenty short chapters which give basic steps to producing good writing. The author states in the preface that this book "offers practical comment on the attitudes with which everyone should approach writing . . . tries to remove some of the false notions about writing that have been developed and expanded in recent years . . . seeks to single out, define, and explain the essential steps-- and only the essential steps--that everyone must take in attempts to make writing not only literate but competent." These steps include Preplan Everything You Write, Choose and Use Words Carefully, Make Sentences Complete, Punctuate Sentences Correctly, various suggestions in style and development, Spell It Right, Revise Everything You Write, Proofread Everything You Write, and Pay Attention to Manuscript Form, among others. There is a list of trite expressions in the section on avoiding tired language, a list of inflated expressions which can be cut down in the section on making your writing concise, and a list of common editing marks in the section on proofreading. Steps and rules are given in easy-to-read, concise chapters. This text could be used at any level.

355 Shaw, Harry. *Writing and Rewriting*. 5th ed. New York: Harper and Row, 1973. 360 pp. $4.50 (P)

This text is based on the premise that "one can write effectively only when he knows the fundamentals of writing" and that learning to write is a process of writing, rewriting, and reading. It is designed specifically for freshman English classes. Part one, A Brief Manual of Rhetorical Principles, discusses prewriting activities and topic selection, paragraphing, the complete essay, and style. These discussions are brief and systematicall arranged, assuming the student has had some experience in composition. Part two, the main section of the text, discusses basic grammar, sentence structure, punctuation and mechanics, usage, and word choice, with exercises. Part three is a guide to terms and usage. This text, originally published in 1937, provides a review of fundamental writing aspects with succinct and basic discussion and exercises. There are no sample writings or suggested writing topics. It can also be used as a handbook or general reference text.

356 Shefter, Harry. *Short Cuts to Effective English*. New York: Pocket Books, 1955. 286 pp. $.95 (P)

On the cover of this book below the title is the advertisement: "Learn how to speak and write correct English without memorizing rules and terms. This grammarless grammar book is a home-study course that will work for you." This text is not really designed for the class room but for someone who wishes to improve his English on his own. The text is divided into four major units: Common Sense and Your English!, Serious Errors You Should Avoid!, Keeping Your Language Habits in Good Shape!, and Review Material to Help You Practice! There are exercises throughout the chapters with answers directly afterward. An appendix offers review sentences and paragraphs for more practice. This text has no formal or conventional order; it is to be read in one's spare time to improve language and writing skills. The appendices have excerpts from tests in English usage from city, state and federal civil service examinations. The text is aimed at the average person who wants to get ahead by improving his English.

357 Shepherd, Ray. *Alpha: A First Course in College Writing*. Chicago: Science Research Associates, 1974. 247 pp. $4.95 (P)

This text is written for students who have already had problems with English. It has pre-tests, exercises, post-tests, and evaluation forms for themes in each section. Answers for the exercises are at the back of the book. Part one deals with description of people and places (emphasizing detail), part two with reading and writing a narrative; part three concerns writing to explain (including control, development, and the paragraph), and part four is a grammar (with a diagnostic test) to be used simultaneously with the other chapters. This text would be used best in individualized instruction; it is not designed for classroom teaching. It is probably best suited for high school or very basic college composition courses.

358   Sherman, Theodore A. and Simon S. Johnson. *Modern Technical Writing*. 3rd ed. Englewood Cliffs, N.J.: Prentice-Hall, 1975. NPA (H)

This new edition retains the same overall format that was used in the first two editions. However, much of the material is updated or rewritten, and the material on oral presentation is entirely new. Part one, Technical Writing in General, introduces the topic then offers individual chapters on effective style, organization, mechanics, special problems (definitions, technical descriptions, explanation of a process, etc.) and tables and figures. Part two covers reports, proposals, and oral presentation, focusing on form, purpose, procedure, language, and many other aspects. Part three studies business correspondences --general principles, special types of letters, and letters of application. The final part is a handbook of fundamentals with information on paragraphing, standard usage, punctuation, etc. Two appendices on abbreviations for scientific and engineering terms and helpful publications for technical writers are also included. Exercises and assignments conclude each chapter. Numerous specimens of technical writing, graphs, illustration, etc., are included to illustrate principles. This very comprehensive text addresses many aspects of technical writing and could be employed in a wide range of technical courses.

359   Shores, David L., ed. *Contemporary English: Change and Variation*. Philadelphia: J. B. Lippincott, 1972. 380 pp. $5.25 (P)

This text would be most appropriate for an advanced English course in which the instructor wishes to teach principles of language along with composition or literature. It could be used in an advanced composition course with an emphasis on language theory, but it would perhaps be most appropriate in a course on the English language. It is a collection of essays by a variety of experts in language, and the editor "has hoped to provide a book that will serve the needs of college students, prospective teachers and practicing teachers at all levels in the understanding of the problems of language diversity in society." There are three major parts to this text:

Standard and Nonstandard English: Temporal, Regional, and Social Variations, with an introduction by Roger Shuy; Standard English: The Problem of Definition, with an introduction by Philip Gove; and Standard and Nonstandard English: Learning and Teaching Problems, with an introduction by Irwin Feigenbaum. Essayists include Morton Bloomfield, Raven I. McDavid, Jr., Virginia F. Allen, and Roger Shuy, among others. There are notes to the essays and a selected bibliography of other material in this area at the end.

360 Shostak, Jerome and Alfred E. Chant. *Read Write React.* New York: Oxford Book Co., 1974. NPA (P)

This is a series of workbooks (levels green, 152 pp.; blue, 161 pp.; and orange, 176 pp.) "designed to provide a developmental program for the improvement of reading ability, word mastery, and language communications skills with a special focus on students with previous difficulti in Standard English. Each book is divided into short units; most contain a brief reading selection as a basis or springboard for additional activities. Some of the themes dealt with are aspects of urban living, problems and achievements of minorities, incidents in American history, sports, boy-girl relations, and humor. The authors have tried to make them relevant to the concerns and interests of young Americans. Some units are designe to help students respond better to their environments and themselves. Students are asked to react to familiar situations then compare their reactions to those of others. Character and behavior charts are often provided so that the students can measure the way they handle themselves in these circumstances. A third set of units helps to sharpen awareness of the use of humor, with riddles, puzzles, puns, and word games. In their preface the authors list several other sets of student activities which follow the core section of this unit: group activities based on ideas and vocabulary from the reading exercises in usage, pronunciation, and spelling; and activities designed to help students plan careers. The authors suggest that the exercises can be used selectivel or completely. These texts are specifically designed for secondary school use but could be used for remedial college-level classes.

361 Shrodes, Caroline. *Definition: Explorations in Meaning.* New York: Harper and Row, 1974. 35 pp. NPA (P)

This pamphlet is a part of the *Harper Studies in Language and Literature* listed in this bibliography under Shrodes, Caroline, editor.

362 Shrodes, Caroline, ed. *A Rhetoric Reader: An Inductive Approach*. from the *Harper Studies in Language and Literature*. New York: Harper and Row, 1974. NPA (P)

This is a series of seven booklets approximately thirty-five to forty pages each. The editor states in the forward to *A Rhetoric Reader: An Inductive Approach* that "Each contributor to the series focuses on a single rhetorical principle in full recognition that no single method of organization is discrete but rather relates to, depends upon, merges with, or supplements another or several others. . . .Accordingly, the student who works through the entire series will consistently review principles to which he or she has previously been introduced in a variety of different contexts." Each pamphlet consists of selections for "introducing and illustrating the rhetorical principles under consideration," questions for projects or discussion, and writing topics for the student to practice with. Selections which are used for the student to study as examples of rhetorical principles are from a variety of styles and sources and include such writers as David Brinkley, Eldridge Cleaver, Arthur Miller, W. H. Auden, Thomas Kuhn, James Dickey, and H. L. Mencken. The titles of the pamphlets and authors in the order in which the general editor suggests they be used are *Comparison and Contrast: Key to Composition,* Gil Muller; *Classification: The Forms of Experience,* Niel K. Snortum; *Definition: Explorations in Meaning,* Caroline Shrodes; *Illustration: All Knowledge is Particular,* James R. Wilson; *Analysis: From Detail to Discovery,* Patrick Hartwell; *Description: Using the Mind's Eye,* Rita Fuhr and Cyra McFadden; *Argument and Persuasion: From Direct Attack to Seduction,* James R. Wilson. In addition to these seven pamphlets which form a series, there are six pamphlets using the same general organization, some with exercises and more detailed writing assignments, which deal with other aspects of writing. They are, in alphabetical order of author, *Euphemism,* Walker Gibson; *Turning on to Writing,* William A. Knox; *Technical Writing,* Norman Levine; *Taking Control: The College Essay,* Paul Saylor; *Getting It Together: Refining Your Writing,* Sandra Seltzer and Myra Kogen; *Revising the Theme: Theory and Practice,* Theodore F. Simms.

363 Shrodes, Caroline, Harry Finestone, and Michael Shugrue. *The Conscious Reader: Readings Past and Present.* New York: Macmillan, 1974. 1,037 pp. $5.95 (P)

The authors state in their preface that "Believing that the development of writing skills depends on the heightening of consciousness, the editors . . . invite the examination of possible and probable futures of man and society

and concentration on the basic questions that writers
since Plato have posed." The text is divided into nine
sections: The Search for Self; Personal Relationships:
Parents and Children; Personal Relationships: Men and
Women; Art and Society: Popular Culture; Art and Society
The Cultural Tradition; Freedom and Human Dignity; The
World of the Future; The Examined Life: Science and
Humanism; and The Examined Life: Personal Values. Each
section contains readings in the form of essays, fiction,
and poetry; and many contain more personal forms such as
letters, reminiscences, and interviews. Approximately
two-thirds of the selections are expository. A selected
rhetorical table of contents arranges selections into
the areas of identification, comparison and contrast,
definition, analysis, illustration, argument and persuasion, and diction and tone. At the end of the text are
suggestions for discussion and suggestions for writing
for each selection. This long reader could be used in
both beginning and advanced college writing courses.

364 Shrodes, Caroline, Clifford Josephson, and James R. Wilson
      Reading for Rhetoric: Applications to Writing. 3rd ed
      New York: Macmillan, 1975. 638 pp. NPA (P)

This reader contains forty-nine selections, basically
essays and short fiction and is divided into eight sections of four to nine readings. Authors represented
include Jonathan Swift, Joyce Carol Oates, Mark Twain,
George Orwell, and Norman Mailer, among others. The eight
sections are entitled Identification, Definition, Classification, Comparison and Contrast, Illustration, Analysis
Argument and Persuasion, and Diction and Tone. A glossary
of rhetorical terms is included which refers the student
to one of the essays which illustrates the term. Each
selection is followed by a set of student exercises:
Purpose and Structure, Diction and Tone, and Applications
to Writing. This text could be used in basic college-
level writing or advanced composition courses.

365 Siegel, Howard and Roger Boedecker, et al. *A Survival
      Kit.* San Francisco: Canfield Press, 1971. 351 pp.
      $5.95 (P)

This textbook is a reader designed to bring students
to greater awareness of their own states of being. "The
authors believe that without awareness, without action on
the part of committed individuals, there will be no meaningful survival--and maybe none at all--for individuals
or society." The text is organized in the form of a
play--Act One: Sleeping Man has "scenes" on Invisible
Man, Processed Man, and Alienated Man, each with a variety of readings to illustrate these states in men.
Act Two: Dreaming Man has scenes on A Dream of Heroes,

The American Dream, and The Celluloid Fantasy. Act
Three: Awakening Man has scenes on Your Potential and
Your World. There is an Epilogue which "offers some
areas for hope and faith." The readings include poems,
essays, excerpts from plays, stories, speeches, and
other types of literature. There are questions for discussion and suggestions for writing after every few selections. Fifty photographs are scattered throughout the
text. The authors discuss the concepts presented in the
selections in short introductions to each scene, but this
is mainly a text of readings and does not teach composition as a separate discipline. The readings would be
appropriate for a lower-level composition course in a
college or an advanced composition course in a high
school.

366   Simms, Theodore F. *Revising the Theme: Theory and Prac-
       tice.* New York: Harper and Row, 1974. 35 pp. NPA
       (P)

   This pamphlet is a part of the *Harper Studies in Language and Literature* listed in this bibliography under
Shrodes, Caroline, editor.

367   Simonson, Harold P. *Writing Essays.* New York: Harper
       and Row, 1966. 134 pp. $3.50 (P)

   The author states in his preface that "This is a book
about writing essays. It sets forth three essential
steps: self, subject, and style. It is intended to be
used as a text either by itself or with a rhetoric handbook." The first section, Finding Your Self, discusses
the problems of finding one's self in an attempt to gain
a clearer focus when writing an essay. Section two,
Finding Your Subject, has chapters entitled Reminiscence,
The Present Scene, Ideas and Reading, Special Subjects,
Originality, and Summary. Section three, Finding Your
Style, includes chapters on Structure (explicit and
implicit) and Tone (words, figurative language, word
patterns). Each of the three sections ends with student
exercises for discussion and application, most of which
call for the student to write essays and paragraphs of
varying length. Primarily this text is for those who
have mastered the basics or who are studying the basics
in conjunction with essay writing.

368   Sklare, Arnold B. *The Technician Writes: A Guide to
       Basic Technical Writing.* San Francisco: Boyd and
       Fraser, 1971. 314 pp. $5.50 (P)

   The Technician Writes is a guide to writing for the
technical student on all levels. It may be used to equal
advantage in a college or technical institute. The text

is neither a freshman English handbook nor a rhetoric nor a book of readings: "it attempts to incorporate and adapt to the needs of the technical student some of the usual features of each of these standard tools." This text has four parts. Part one is comprised of ten chapters on the technical report. Information is included on defining the objective of the report and differentiating among the levels of technical writing as determined by audience, and there is a list of guidelines adapted to each level. Levels given are non-technician, technician, advanced technician or junior engineer, engineer' level and advanced engineer's or scientific level. Section one also includes preliminary plans, bibliography and outlining, a guide to library usage, lists of reference books, and guides to the encyclopedias. Two chapter of part one cover ways of organizing technical material for presentation and developing the material in a logical manner. The final chapter of this section discusses in detail, with illustrations, the types of visual aids which may be used in report presentation. Part two devotes four chapters to other modes of technical communication--letters, memoranda, articles, and abstracts. Examples are given in each category. In part three, four chapters deal with some of the refinements of technical writing--functional English, sentences, paragraphs, and matters of grammar. Style and word choice, as they lend themselves to voice and the problem of padding, are also covered. Part four contains two reference guides, one to good usage and the other to grammatical terms. The book contains no standardized exercises for classroom use, but Sklare has selected and included a number of articles from various journals on aspects of technical writing. These additional readings are interspersed throughout the text to supplement the traditional textbook information.

369   Skwire, David, Frances Chitwood, Raymond Ackley, and
        Raymond Fredman. *Student's Book of College English*.
        Beverly Hills, Ca.: Glencoe, 1975. 369 pp. NPA
        (P)

As the authors state, this text is based on four "important guidelines": 1) most writing should state a central idea, 2) the main purpose is to prove or support that idea, 3) the best way to prove or support that idea is by being specific, 4) writing needs to be logically organized. Part one, Fundamentals: The Principles of Good Writing, includes discussions on finding a thesis, supporting the thesis, outlining, and an overview of actual writing. Part two discusses patterns of development: example, classification, process, definition, cause and effect, comparison and contrast, argument, description, and analysis of literature. Part three, Style, discusses denotation, connotation, economy, parallelism, subordination, and repetition, for example. Part four is a handbook and glossary of approximately fifty pages. Each of the first three parts contains essays and short fiction as well as many student essays. Questions for discussion and writing assignments are in the first three parts; exercises are in all four parts. This text is aimed at standard freshman composition classes, gives instruction about each idea under discussion, readings illustrating the idea, and student essays as models and, thus, with the included handbook, is designed to be the sole text for a class.

370 Smart, William. *Eight Modern Essayists*. 2nd ed. New York: St. Martin's Press, 1973. 380 pp. NPA (P)

This text "holds to the principle that the best way to learn to write is by studying outstanding writers in depth." The main idea is to convince the reader that good writing comes not from following strict rules but extends from personal and unique experience. The eight essayists included are E. M. Forster, Virginia Woolf, D. H. Lawrence, Edmund Wilson, E. B. White, George Orwell, Norman Mailer, and James Baldwin. A biographical sketch of each writer, with information about the writer's style and major contributions to the history of ideas included, precedes each group of essays; and the essays are listed chronologically. Each author is represented by three to five essays of varying length. An appendix on style concludes the book, with single essays by Ben Jonson, Swift, Hazlitt, Alexander Smith and F. L. Lucas. There are no questions, exercises, or discussion topics included. The text is exclusively a collection of exemplary essays, perhaps best suited for more advanced studies in rhetoric.

371 Smith, Charles Kay. *Styles and Structures: Alternative Approaches to College Writing*. New York: W. W. Norton, 1974. 436 pp. $4.25 (P)

This is a college-level composition book in which composition is taught by using different approaches and styles for the student to evaluate and imitate. The author states in his preface that "The premise of this book is that patterns of writing enact patterns of thinking, that by finding and practicing different ways of writing we can literally think different things. The book is designed to help people learn to do this by analyzing many diverse writing patterns and suggesting how students can practice them to achieve new ways of thinking." Major unit headings are Descriptive and Narrative Styles (How Form and Content Work Together in an Objective Style, Using Metaphors and Parallel Constructions, How Form and Content Work Together in a Psychological Style, etc.), Writing and Thinking with Definitions

(How Form and Content Work Together in a Defining Style, Contextual and Stipulative Defining, etc.), Writing and Thinking with Assumptions (How Form and Content Work Together in an Assumptive Style, Discovering Criteria, etc.), A Rhetoric of Reperception (How Form and Content Work Together in a Reperceptive Style, Evaluating and Recommending Original Ideas, etc.). Each major unit contains readings to illustrate particular points. Readings are by Paul Shepard, Edward Carr, Dorothy Lee, Jonathan Swift, Richard Wright, John Donne, and Ernest Hemingway. The text of the book discusses what comprises each particular style, analyzes the style, provides exercises which give students writing tasks using the components of each style, and finally tells the student to write a brief essay in each particular style. The text presents the approach that different styles are used to present an idea differently, thus creating fresh ideas with new forms. Illustrations are included.

372   Smith, William F. and Raymond D. Liedlich. *From Thought to Theme: A Rhetoric and Reader for College English.* 4th ed. New York: Harcourt, Brace, Jovanovich, 1974. 413 pp. NPA (P)

The authors state in their preface that the purpose of this fourth edition is essentially the same as the first-"to show through both precept and practice just how the raw materials of experience, ideas and opinions can be shaped into clear and convincing expository or argumentative prose." Part one, Rhetoric, contains five chapters: paragraph unity, development, coherence, argumentation, and the theme. More than seventy examples of paragraphs are used to illustrate rhetorical principles, and more than seventy-five exercises on tear-out sheets encourage immediate application. Part two, Reader, includes eight sections with rhetorical and thematic groupings: The Aims of Education (First Person Narrative), The Changing Times (Description), The Media and Their Messages (Combination of Expository Methods), Male and Female (Analysis Division and Classification), Pride and Prejudice (Definition), The Limits of Language (Reasons, Cause/Effect), The Web of Life (Illustration, Factual Detail), and In Quest of Value (Comparison and Contrast). Most of the selections are brief and are done primarily by noted authors such as Erich Fromm, Stefan Kanfer, James Thurber, and Norman Cousins. The first three selections of the four included in each section are accompanied by introductory notes pointing out rhetorical techniques and devices to look for. Questions on language and rhetoric follow these selections, including suggestions for theme assignments. Three indices conclude the text, one classifying the selections by rhetorical type, another by methods of development, and a final one by questions on

language and rhetoric. This text is suitable for a freshman composition course perhaps to be taught over a two-
semester sequence. It is also applicable to more advanced
courses and can be assigned selectively.

373   Smith, William F. and Raymond D. Liedlich. *Rhetoric for
      Today*. 3rd ed. New York: Harcourt, Brace, Jovano-
      vich, 1974.   214 pp. $4.50   (P)

      Emphasizing exposition and argument, this text "con-
centrates on basic rhetorical principles, beginning with
the paragraph and concluding with the complete theme."
Chapters include discussions of paragraph unity, topic
sentences, controlling idea, development of different
types, transition, argumentation, and the theme as a
whole.   Special focus is given to the paragraph, which is
viewed as a theme in miniature, emphasizing exposition
and argumentation.   The text presents a step-by-step
approach to problems of composition, and the section on
the theme as a whole rounds out the discussion by employing previously illustrated principles.   Each chapter concludes with a review of the points covered as well as
ample exercises on tear-out sheets.   More than seventy
sample paragraphs illustrate the rhetorical principles
discussed, and they are designed as models and oppor-
tunities for discussion.   Many of the exercises allow for
writing; others are brief fill-in-the-blank types.   This
text does not deal with basic grammar and sentence structure; hence a supplementary handbook might be useful.
Its basic format and style make the text applicable to
all levels of college writing classes, particularly freshman composition.

374   Snortum, Niel K. *Classification: The Forms of Exper-
      ience*. New York: Harper and Row, 1974.   39 pp.
      NPA   (P)

      This pamphlet is a part of the *Harper Studies in Lan-
guage and Literature* listed in this bibliography under
Shrodes, Caroline, editor.

375   Snortum, Niel K. *Contemporary Rhetoric*.   Englewood
      Cliffs, N.J.:   Prentice-Hall, 1967.   285 pp. $4.25
      (P)

      This text is designed "as a foundation for the college
writing course," and the author suggests selective use
according to the needs of the instructor.   Each chapter
systematically addresses a rhetorical problem, giving
explanations then "applications" (periodic exercises
based on principles explained).   Chapter one gives a
brief review of communication--how to make yourself under-
stood; chapter two studies the sentence, making comparisons between speech and writing; chapter three, The Kinds

of English, discusses levels of usage; chapter four,
Words and Meaning, covers diction and word choice; chapters five through seven comprise a three-chapter section
on planning and developing, especially in regard to paragraphs and classifying ideas, covering description,
narration, explanation, argument and persuasion. Chapter
eight deals with research papers: how to start, note-
taking, outlining, bibliography, and footnote information.
Chapter nine covers punctuation, emphasizing trouble
spots and spelling. The author takes pains to develop
logical explanations based on classical rhetorical theory.
The format is an integration of explanation and exercises.

376   Sparke, William, ed. *Prisms: A Self Reader.* New York:
      Harper's College Press, 1975. 305 pp. NPA (P)

      This text is divided into eight parts, each written
by a different author. The eight sections are Woman of
Valor, Man of Honor; The Thought of Writing: Self Discovery; Asian Ways to Awareness; Writing for and About
Film; Nature Designs: Ecology and the Awareness of Self
Self-Awareness through Community Awareness; Journey
toward Self; and Models of the Future. This text is, in
large part, a workbook in which the student is asked to
respond to and write about ideas, statements, pictures,
word games, and essays. The text is not designed to provide instruction in basic composition. That is, there i
no real discussion of basic organization, development,
etc. The premise appears to be that if the student is
stimulated to respond to and write about interesting
subjects, he will find himself more able to compose.
Certainly, the student is required actively to participa
in the learning process. The primary audience is the
student fairly well grounded in basic grammar, but who i
not, perhaps, ready for a standard composition class. I
used with a grammar handbook, it could be appropriate
for more remedial instruction.

377   Sparke, William and Bernice Taines. *Doublespeak: Lan-
      guage for Sale.* New York: Harper's College Press,
      1975. 195 pp. NPA (P)

      This text is an examination of what happens to langua
in commercial contexts: a study of propaganda. Part on
defines what propaganda is; how to recognize it; its use
in schools, home, on the news, in advertising, in politics, in art; and the bias against minorities manifeste
in language. Part two studies the evolution of propaganda, starting with the American Revolution, the consti
tution, and the slavery debate. Part three covers "whe
we are going," investigating the possibilities of
language trends. The first section looks at a number o
excerpts from utopian or anti-utopian books in order to

examine their persuasive impact. Other sections investigate the possible uses of propagandistic methods. The text is a montage of photographs, illustrations, cartoons, excerpts, and editorial comment about the various popular uses of language, its manipulation, and the ramifications of propaganda. In a sense, the book raises one's consciousness to media use of language--past, present and future. Here are some sample assignments: "What do you think of the TV commercials you currently watch? Select some that you dislike and some that you like, and explore your reasons for disliking or liking each"; "Think about a movie you have seen recently, and write a short analysis of the various facets of propaganda you have noticed in it." The book is filled with slogans, clichés, popular mottoes, etc. Most of the material is self-instructive, although the text lends itself to discussion. It could be appropriate for lower-level classes because it is based on the premise of rapid movement--never trying the student's patience.

378   Stageberg, Norman C.   *An Introductory English Grammar.*
      2nd ed.   New York: Holt, Rinehart and Winston, 1971.
      473 pp. $6.95   (P)

      In 'To the Instructor the author states: "This is a college textbook of English grammar.   It is essentially a structural grammar, supplemented by occasional borrowings from transformationism.   At the end it gives the student a brief glimpse of the theory and practice of transformational grammar.   The book is designed for a three-hour, one-semester course for the undergraduate."   Part one, The Phonology of English, includes chapters covering The Production and Inventory of English Phonemes, Assimilation and Other Phonetic Processes, Spelling and Pronunciation, Stress, Pitch Levels and Terminals, Internal Open Juncture, and Phonotactics.   Part two, The Morphology of English, contains chapters on Morphemes, Words, Inflectional Paradigms, Six Processes of Word Formation, and Determiners and Prepositions.   Part three discusses The Syntax of English--Noun and Verb Phrases, Basic Sentence Patterns, Modification, Constituents, and Some Syntactic Details.   Part four, Transformational Grammar by Ralph M. Goodman, is an introduction to this approach to grammar. There are 325 student exercises, and the answers to these are contained at the end of the text.

379   Stevens, Martin and Charles H. Kegel.   *A Glossary for
      College English.*   New York: McGraw-Hill, 1966.   245
      pp. $4.50   (P)

      This glossary "is designed to provide the college student with concise, practical definitions of grammatical, linguistic, and literary terms as well as readable, up-to-date discussions about acceptable practices in written English." The text is divided into four main sections: Common Usage Problems, Conventions of Editorial English, Linguistic, Stylistic, and Grammatical Terms, and Literary Terms. There is a short introduction preceding each section which discusses the range of terms included in the section. The terms are cross-referenced where appropriate. There is an index at the end which lists entries individually and by subject matter.

380 Stewart, Donald C. *The Authentic Voice: A Pre-Writing Approach to Student Writing*. Dubuque, Iowa: Wm. C. Brown, 1972. 151 pp. $2.95 (P)

The author states in his preface that this text is designed for the first term of freshman composition classes. "It proceeds from the conviction that the primary goal of any writing course is self-discovery for the student and that the most visible indication of that self-discovery is the appearance, in the student's writing, of an authentic voice. It proceeds from a second conviction that the techniques of pre-writing . . will best help the student develop this authentic voice." Each of the six chapters contains a detailed discussion of the particular aspect of prewriting presented, and each--except for the chapter on the journal--concludes with exercises and suggested topics for papers. The chapters are entitled The Writer's Attitude; The Seeing Eye; The Journal: Birthplace of an Authentic Voice; Conquering the World of Abstractions; The Art of Divine Meditation; and Analogy--A New Way of Looking at Things. This text does not approach the subject of prewriting by way of discussions of topic selection, thesis sentence, outlines, etc. Rather, it centers on student perception and expression. Nor does it address itself to the essay as a whole, assuming that these matters will be taught in the following term. It could be used as a single text or as a supplementary text; and, although it is addressed primarily to the college freshman, it could be handled by high school students.

381 Stockwell, Richard E. *The Stockwell Guide for Technical and Vocational Writing*. Menlo Park, Ca.: Cummings Publishing, 1972. 296 pp. $6.50 (P) $2.95 (Workbook)

This text is intended for the vocational high school and/or community college. The contents deal with the common forms needed by technical writers, and the book places a strong emphasis on the printed form and its uses reproducing such forms repeatedly throughout the informative material. The book begins with a brief introduction to various types of writing style and then moves immediately into chapters on the forms of technical writing. There are chapters entitled The Memorandum; Letters; Employment Applications and Resumés; Work Orders and Other Job-Related Forms; Job, Operation, and Maintenance Records; Description of Materials and Equipment; Organizing Notes to Improve Speaking; Reading and Taking Notes before Writing a Report; Organizing and Outlining Information before Writing a Report; Illustrations for a Written Report; and a final chapter which covers the written report in detail with complete examples. The text concludes with a list of useful reference works and a series of brief appendices on such topics as abbreviations, grammar, handwriting, punctuation, readability, spelling, and so on, along with a form for evaluating the oral report. The student who has problems with grammar and mechanics would probably require an additional basic handbook of writing skills.

382   Stonberg, Selma F. *From Start to Finish*. Boston: Houghton Mifflin, 1970. 201 pp. $4.95 (P)

The author states that this book is "the logical outgrowth of an intensive involvement in the teaching of composition to freshmen through concentration on the psychological aspects of the process." The techniques presented "teach the student effective ways of generating ideas out of his own interests, beliefs, and opinions." The author also states that the text is not as concerned with rules and requirements as it is with "thinking, organizing, and correcting." The text is divided into three main parts: Pre-Writing, Writing, and Rewriting. The sixteen chapters are entitled Getting Started; Finding Facts and Ideas; Building Paragraphs; Types of Paragraphs: Taking a Stand; Types of Paragraphs: Pro and Con; Types of Paragraphs: Change of Mind; Types of Paragraphs: Story with a Point; The Longer Paper; Revising the Paragraph; Words and Exact Words; Too Many Words; Transitions; Some Tips on Grammar; Developing Sentences; Spelling; and The Role of Punctuation. Each chapter is followed by exercises, many of which require the student to write his own sentences, paragraphs, and outlines. The exercises are on tear-out pages.

383   Stone, Wilfred and J. G. Bell. *Prose Style: A Handbook for Writers*. 2nd ed. New York: McGraw-Hill, 1972. 316 pp. $6.95 (H) $4.95 (P)

In their preface the authors state the freshman of today "has had more training in the fundamentals of English composition" than the student of ten years ago. It is assumed, then, that this text will be a review text, not one that teaches "from the ground up." Hence, it is intentionally brief and designed to be read, not just referred to. It is a "guidebook to style, to

research strategies, and even to the kind of person the
writer ought to be" and goes beyond basic matters such as
syntax, diction, and usage. The author conceives of
writing as a three-way liaison between writer, reader, and
written work. The text is divided into four parts. The
first deals with the writer and his message, including
subsections on audience, logic and evidence, and tone.
Part two deals with writing technique--paragraphing,
sentences, word usage, making images, and what good prose
is. A substantial part on mechanics follows, and the
final section provides basic instruction on research
papers. An index to current usage, investigating modern
language idiosyncracies, follows. The text is a handbook
aimed at the college freshman who has had experience with
writing and would probably be best used in conjunction wi
a supplementary rhetoric or reader. No exercises are
included.

384 Stovall, Sidney T., Virginia B. Mathis, Linda C. Craven,
G. Mitchell Hagler, and Mary A. Poole. *Composition:
Skills and Models*. Boston: Houghton Mifflin, 1973.
449 pp. $6.95 (P)

This text is basically a reader with each chapter
introduced by explanations of basic techniques of composition followed by from four to six stories and essays.
Chapter one, Getting an Idea on Paper, discusses choosing
a topic, finding a central idea, outlining, and revision
and is followed by pieces by Christian Barnard, Ralph
McGill, Eldridge Cleaver, and E. B. White. Chapter two,
Starting and Stopping, takes up thesis statements, unity,
introductions, and conclusions. The third chapter,
Outlining, includes authors such as Deems Taylor, John
Ciardi, and Genevieve Millet Overstreet. Chapter four
discusses the paragraph while chapter five, Joining Mode
to Purpose, focuses on the best method, e.g., comparison-
contrast, for developing a given subject. Chapter six
continues this discussion. Seven centers on sentence
structure--fragments, types, and sentence flexibility.
Chapter eight discusses diction, word choice, and usage.
Chapter nine deals with revision, and the last chapter
discusses Forming Your Own Style. An appendix is include
on writing essay exams. A glossary and an index are also
included. One student-written essay appears in each
chapter. This text is basically a freshman composition
text/reader but could be used for more advanced students.

385 Strong, William. *Sentence Combining: A Composing Book*.
New York: Random House, 1973. 205 pp. $3.95 (P)

This text is based on principles of transformational
grammar and is totally exercise-oriented. The student
writes out the exercises on separate sheets of paper.

The first section of the text, Phase One, has the student
produce complicated sentences from lists of very simple
sentences which, to a certain extent, actually represent
the deep structure of the complicated sentence. For
example, the first exercise involves taking the sentences "French fries are loaded into a basket. The
french fries are white. The basket is wire." and combining them in as many ways as the student can think of into
complicated sentences. The student then chooses the
combination he likes best. There are suggested topics
for papers scattered throughout these exercises, but this
is the format which the student follows throughout the
first section of the book. In the second section the
student is provided with models to imitate in forming his
sentences so that he can develop more diverse style.
These kernel sentences, from which the student is to
produce transformed sentences, make up the entire book.
This textbook would be appropriate for a high school or
lower-level college composition course designed to teach
the sentence.

386 Strunk, William and E. B. White. *Elements of Style*. 2nd
     ed. New York: Macmillan, 1972. 78 pp. $2.95 (H)
     $.95 (P)

This brief text is a handbook on style, probably most
appropriate for an advanced composition course. It is
divided into five units: Elementary Rules of Usage,
Elementary Principles of Composition, A Few Matters of
Form, Words and Expressions Commonly Misused, and An
Approach to Style with a list of reminders. There are no
exercises or theme topics; this is a book of information.
Its style is simple and clear. Short discussions of
some element of style are preceded by a statement of the
rule involved: under chapter one--Do not break sentences
in two; under chapter two--Use the active voice, and so
forth.

387 Sturges, Clark. *Witnesses*. Berkeley, Ca.: Glendessary
     Press, 1974. 139 pp. $3.50 (P)

As the author states in his preface, this text is "a
collection of papers written by college students enrolled
in required freshman composition classes." The text
offers none of the traditional suggestions for writing or
discussion as the author believes the book "can be used
most profitably when the instructor creates his or her
own critical and analytical methods." Thirty-four student essays with photographs interspersed throughout are
included. The author states that most of the essays have
been printed without change but that some misspellings
and matters of phrasing have been corrected. This text
is primarily a source book/reader. As such it would be

appropriate for any composition class--high school
through college--as a supplementary text.

388 Swanson, Roger M. *The Freshman Writes*. Indianapolis:
Odyssey, 1973. 422 pp. $5.95 (P)

   This textbook is a reader of good freshman themes for
the student to read and criticize. It would be appropriate for advanced high school, junior college, or
university composition courses which deal with teaching
beginning theme writing. The essays are divided according to rhetorical type: Analysis; Exemplification and
Illustration; Definition; Comparison, Contrast, and
Analogy; Classification and Division; Description; Narration and Dialogue; Autobiography; Irony, Satire, Parody,
and Burlesque; and The Literary Theme and Research Paper.
There is a short introduction before each unit which discusses the methods involved in employing the rhetorical
type illustrated in the unit. After each selection there
is an analysis which asks the student questions about the
theme paragraph by paragraph. These questions could be
used for class discussion or for writing assignments.
After each unit there is a list of suggested theme topics
for the student to choose from for his own writing. The
essays were chosen to give the student good examples of
writing which are possible to emulate, analyze, and discuss in class. The author feels this method could be
more effective than giving the student professional
models which he cannot emulate and which require some
background in critical theory to analyze.

389 Tate, Gary, ed. *From Discovery to Style: A Reader*.
Cambridge, Mass.: Winthrop, 1973. 372 pp. $4.95
(P)

   The editor states in his preface that "the organizing
principle of this book is an informal and modernized
version of the classical framework." The text is divided
into four main units: Discovery (In Experience, In
Reading, In Reflection), Audience (Emotional Appeal,
Appeal to Reason, Ethical Appeal), Arrangement (Beginnings,
Middles, Ends; Developing the Middle), and Style. Each
unit begins with a short note to the student explaining
what direction he should be headed in as he reads the
examples. Each example has a list of three to six discussion questions afterward. These questions could be
used in class, or some of them could be used as writing
assignments, but they are not specifically designed as
such. Such theme topics would have to be worked out by
the instructors from the readings. Selections are by such
authors as James Agee, Marya Mannes, Jonathan Swift,
Martin Luther King, Jr., and E. B. White, among others.
This reader would be appropriate for composition classes
on the advanced high school or lower college level.

390 Taylor, Karl K. *Stages in Writing*. New York: McGraw-Hill, 1973. 317 pp. $5.50 (P)

The author states in his preface that this text integrates "grammar, mechanics, rhetoric, and writing in a single book." Thus, items of grammar, for example, are presented one or two items at a time. Further, the text deals only with the gross and common errors. The six stages are Describing a Small Object, Describing a Place, Describing a Person, Describing How People Talk (Dialogue), Writing a Profile, Writing about an Experience, and On to Exposition. Each of these chapters begins with sections on selecting, narrowing, and organizing the subject. Each chapter also contains stylistic requirements, sets of questions dealing with such things as underlining the subject and verb in the student's writing assignment. The student is expected to meet each of these requirements in the paper he will be writing. Following each of these sections are detailed explanations of the requirements just presented. Writing assignments begin with short, simple assignments; and as the text progresses, these become longer and more complex. The text is aimed at college freshmen, particularly for "those students who are not prepared for college English."

391 Taylor, Karl K. and Thomas A. Zimanzl. *Writing from Example: Rhetoric Illustrated*. Englewood Cliffs, N.J.: Prentice-Hall, 1972. 271 pp. $4.25 (P)

The authors state in their preface that this text is "designed to combine the merits of the new inspirational texts dealing with the 'now' culture and the traditional features which we consider worth preserving from more conventional texts." To this end, they have preserved the traditional rhetorical divisions but have drawn their materials from unusual sources such as *Christian Century* and *Consumer Reports*. The text is divided into two basic parts: Basic Structures of Composition and Basic Purposes for Writing. The first chapter of part one, Organizational Patterns, includes subsections entitled Chronology and Space, Deduction, Induction, and Comparison/Contrast. Chapter two, The Introduction, includes sections entitled The Paragraph, Direct Introductory Paragraphs, Delayed Introductory Paragraphs, Polishing the Introduction, Describing with Details, and Describing with Examples. Chapter three, The Middle, discusses middle paragraph development; chapter four, The Conclusion, centers on kinds of concluding paragraphs, special effects, and polishing the conclusion. Part two begins with the fifth chapter, Exposition, which focuses on Illustration, Solution, Analysis, Definition, and Interpretation. The final chapter, Argumentation, addresses Logical Argument and Emotional Argument. Each chapter is briefly introduced, and most of the subsections of the chapters are illustrated by a reading selection. The reading selections are followed by student exercises, questions for discussion, topics for composition, and an assignment guide.

392 Thomas, Earl W. *Preparation for Better Writing*. Dubuque, Iowa: Wm. C. Brown, 1973. 172 pp. $3.95 (P)

This is a college or high school level workbook "intended for students who have encountered problems in writing clearly and expressing their ideas forcefully." The author takes the inductive approach to learning. There are five chapters in the text: Sentences; Sentence Patterns; Compound and Complex Sentences; Paragraphs; and Mechanics: Capitalization and Punctuation. The chapters are set up so that the student reads short explanatory notes with examples then writes answers to exercises in the text. All the pages are on tear-out sheets. The student is required to begin constructing whole sentences according to patterns. The chapter on paragraphs includes different types of paragraphs such as argumentative, descriptive, story, and quotation paragraphs. This chapter also includes a section on revision and short papers. The student is required to write many paragraphs of his own from a list of topics. Answers to the exercises are not provided in the text; however, most of the exercises would produce different answers from different students.

393 Thomas, Owen. *The Structure of Language*. Indianapolis: Bobbs-Merrill. 1967. 64 pp. $1.00 (P)

This book is part of *The Bobbs-Merrill Series in Composition and Rhetoric*. See listing under Johnson, Falk S. for the complete annotation.

394 Thompson, Ruth and Marvin Thompson. *Critical Reading and Writing*. New York: Random House, 1969. 179 pp. $3.50 (P)

This advanced high school or college-level text is designed to be used in an English course which teaches both literature and writing. It would be most appropriate in a freshman-level college composition course which uses an anthology of literature as topic material for paper assignments. Its chapters are entitled Writing about Literature; Theme; Action, Structure, and Plot; Characterization; Point of View; Irony, Symbol, and Tone; and Poetry. There are study guides in the form of summary outlines at the end of each major section. These outlines can be used to form paper topics by using the points and questions outlined. The text includes literary selections by W. H. Auden, Stephen Crane, William Faulkner, Robinson Jeffers, and Wallace

Stevens, for example; but the examples are brief and probably could not substitute for an anthology or selection of books to read. The authors state in the preface that "We have deliberately narrowed our focus in the belief that it is better for the beginning student to concentrate on a few elements, such as plot, character, and point of view, and to learn how to handle them well, rather than to try to learn and apply a host of critical approaches. . . .we have placed our primary emphasis on organization of content rather than on mechanics."

395   Tibbetts, A. M. and Charlene Tibbetts. *The Critical Man: Reading, Thinking, Writing*. Glenview, Ill.: Scott, Foresman, 1972. 391 pp. $5.95 (P)

This rhetoric/reader is designed to perform two tasks, "first, teaching students to read various forms of non-fiction prose accurately and critically, and second, providing students with topics for discussion, and more importantly, for writing." In part one the problems of critical reading and thinking and their relationship to writing are discussed. This section begins with seven samples of the types of prose given in the reader. These samples are marked by marginal comments and reactions and followed by analysis and discussion to indicate what discoveries critical reading might bring. Section one also includes a survey of the steps necessary for the critical writer in forming opinions for composition. Pitfalls posed by metaphor, faulty premise, and cant are discussed. Exercises are given at the conclusion of this section. Part two consists of readings gathered under the headings The Young vs. The Old; On Getting (and Keeping) Money; The Proper Uses of Language and Rhetoric; On Politics and Governing; The Individual and the Law; Of Love, Marriage, and the Family; Man and His Religions; The "Solution" of War; The Values of Science; and Craftsmanship and Art. All the selections are nonfiction, and most are contemporary. Part three, A Gathering of Styles, gives a selection of readings from letters, autobiographies, and fictional works. No discussion questions or theme topics are included with the readings, and the book contains no specific information on composition. This text is applicable to college-level courses but could be used on the advanced high school level.

396   Tibbetts, A. M. and Charlene Tibbetts. *Strategies of Rhetoric*. rev. ed. Glenview, Ill.: Scott, Foresman, 1974. 383 pp. $5.95 (P)

This is a comprehensive text which is designed to address fundamental problems in writing skills, specific problems of various types of writing, and to solve some grammatical problems. There are four major sections to the book. The first is Solving Early Problems. Individual chapters in this section deal with establishing a writing stance, forming a thesis, making an outline, and seven strategies of developing themes--experience, definition, cause and effect, process, analogy, classification and comparison-contrast. Part two presents information on how to write better themes, dealing with organization, content, word choice, style, and variations on structure and meaning. Part three covers special assignments--the persuasive argument, research papers, the literary paper, and business and technical writing. The concluding section is A Short Guide to Better Writing Skills which focuses on grammar errors, clear punctuation, dictionary usage, rules for quotation and paraphrasing, and revision and proof-reading. Each principle is discussed generally then broken down into systematic rules, hints, or general points to remember. At least half of each chapter is practice, a number of exercises in varying forms that illustrate principles. Examples are used throughout, and the text avoids the traditional model-essay approach. The author often employs diagrams or logical constructs to illustrate principles. The text is aimed at basic composition and can be used selectively considering its large scale.

397 Tighe, David J. and Lloyd A. Flanigan. *Source, Idea, Technique: A Writer's Reader*. 2nd ed. Boston: Holbrook Press, 1974. 587 pp. $6.95 (P)

In their preface the authors state that the purpose of this book is to show the student the problems writers face and how to solve them and to stimulate discussion and writing by including a broad spectrum of essays, stories, and poems. The text proper is divided into six expansive sections. Section one, Sources and Idea, is followed by a section entitled Idea and Method which includes chapters on narration, description, exposition, and argument. The third section, Development, contains chapters entitled Examples, Particulars and Details, Comparison and Contrast, and Cause to Effect. The fourth section, Organization, has chapters entitled Time and Space Order and Logical Order. The fifth section deals with coherence and the sixth with diction. Each of these larger sections is briefly introduced, and most of the individual readings are followed by exercises and writing assignments. Authors represented range from John Steinbeck to Eldridge Cleaver to Nathaniel Hawthorne, and there are over twenty-five student essays included. The primary audience of this text is college-level students, from basic to advanced writing classes; and it is designed, for the most part, to be used in conjunction with other texts.

398 Trimble, John R. *Writing with Style: Conversations on the Art of Writing*. Englewood Cliffs, N.J.: Prentice-Hall, 1975. 143 pp. NPA (P)

This high school or college-level composition text is a short, easy-to-read review of fundamentals in composition writing. The author states in his preface that it is not intended to be inclusive; rather it "answers the wish for a 'survival kit'" for bewildered students in college composition classes. He also states four aims: to explain how experienced writers think, give useful tips, address technical considerations, and encourage brevity. The text is basically expository, containing limited examples or illustrations. The book is divided into two major sections: Fundamental (beginning the writing task, thinking well, diction, revising, proofreading, etc.) and Odds and Ends (punctuation, conventions regarding quotations, tips on usage, etc.). There are no exercises, discussions of manuscript form, or rules of grammar presented. The text is designed as a refresher course and discusses the fundamentals of writing an essay in an informal style.

399 Troyka, Lynn Quitman, ed. *Guide to Writing*. New York: Harper's College Press, 1975. 198 pp. NPA (P)

This text is a workbook and guide to basic composition. Each of the five sections is written by a different person. Chapter one, Turning On, deals with how the student gets ideas to write about by turning on to What You Know, Your Experiences, the Unusual, Your Intellectual Power, Proper Point of View, and Proper Balance of Method and Content, and turning on to other sources--books, magazines, and satire, for example. The second chapter, Taking Control, discusses the structure of the essay and deals with coordinating materials into cohesive essays. Chapter three discusses paragraphs--Topic Sentences, Support: Paragraph Development, Strategies (general to particular, cause and effect, and definition, for example), and Introductory and Concluding Paragraphs. Chapter four deals with refining--transition devices, subordination, and connecting paragraphs. Chapter five covers revising, from the whole theme to paragraphs to sentences and words. Each chapter has numerous exercises for the students to complete. Its primary audience is students from high school through college who need instruction in basic essay writing. A grammar handbook would, perhaps, be desirable as a companion text.

400 Tufte, Virginia. *Grammar as Style*. New York: Holt, Rinehart and Winston, 1971. 280 pp. $5.50 (P)

This is not a "composition text" as such but a book on stylistics as it relates to grammar. The author states

in the preface that "Each chapter, except the first, concentrates on a major syntactic structure or concept and
considers its stylistic role in sentences from twentieth-
century fiction and nonfiction. In all, the book include
fifteen major grammatical topics and more than a thousand
samples of modern prose." The analyses of the grammatica
structures in relation to style are descriptive--"I hesi-
tate even to use the word *conclusions*; *observations* is
more accurate." This is a book of information; there is
a workbook, *Grammar as Style: Exercises in Creativity*,
which accompanies it and guides the student in writing
based on models provided. Some grammatical classifications included as separate chapters are Kernel Sentences,
Verb Phrases, Prepositions, Dependent Clauses, Free Modifiers, The Appositive, The Passive Transformation, and
Cohesion. The last chapter, Syntactic Symbolism:
Grammar as Analogue, discusses the symbolism in syntax.
There are many short examples from literature throughout
this text, and at the end there is a Bibliography-Index
of Authors and Editions Quoted. An index of terms follows the bibliography. This book would be most appropriate as a text in an advanced course on stylistics or
as a reference book for teachers of English, stylistics,
literary criticism, or composition.

401 Ulman, Joseph N., Jr. and Jay R. Gould. *Technical Report*
     ing. 3rd ed. New York: Holt, Rinehart and Winston,
     1972. 419 pp. $9.95 (H)

     In their preface the authors state "This book is
addressed primarily to students and practitioners of
engineering and the sciences who have reached the point
at which they have reporting jobs to do and have something to say . . . Only at this stage are most of them
receptive to instruction in technical reporting, and only
then do they have genuinely realistic subject matter to
work with." They recommend the book specifically to
upperclassmen, graduate students, and those already in
industry. Section one of the book, Basic Issues, begins
with a survey of the importance of technical writing and
an examination of its major virtues: clarity, brevity,
and accuracy. Basic background material such as knowing
your audience, emphasizing the significant, organizing
for logic and brevity are given as well as material on
openings, conclusions, consistency, and the inclusion of
opinion in technical writing. This section also includes
material on the general procedure of report writing such
as gathering the data, developing an outline, writing and
revising the rough draft, and the physical details of the
report, i.e., proofreading and typing. The final chapter in Section one is entitled Technical Description and
deals with a variety of descriptions used in technical
writing such as description of machines and mechanisms,

description of processes, and description of theories. Most of the chapters contain an ample selection of exercises. Section two, The Report, is the core of the book and covers report writing at length. It begins with an introductory chapter on reports in general and contains chapters on Informal Reports, Formal Reports, Laboratory Reports, The Thesis, Instructions, Proposals, Technical Papers and Articles, and Oral Reports and Speaking in Public. All these chapters, with the exception of Oral Reports, contain exercises. Section three, Tools and Methods, covers considerable material found in traditional writing courses such as chapters on style, grammar, punctuation, and mechanics. It also contains material more specifically aimed at the technical writer such as a chapter on the use of tables and one on the visual presentation of information. The appendices include a list of abbreviations for scientific and engineering terms and specimens of most types of technical writing, including all types of reports and business letters.

402 Van Ghent, Dorothy, and Willard Maas, eds. *The Essential Prose*. Indianapolis: Bobbs-Merrill, 1965. 1225 pp. $7.50 (H)

The editors state in the foreward that "*The Essential Prose* has two general aims: to provide materials for the teaching of discursive writing, and at the same time to give the student a fairly broad and various acquaintance with his cultural heritage." The text is divided into three units according to the themes of the selections. The first unit is called The Individual Experience and has sections with writings on Private Lives, Fathers and Sons, Men and Women in Love, The Extreme Situation, and Attitudes Toward Death. The second unit is on The Collective Experience and has sections on The Human Condition, The Historical Dimension, and The Example of Perfection (utopian writings). The third unit is on The Orders of Knowledge and contains sections on The Order of Nature, The Order of the Mind, The Spiritual Order, The Order of Art, and The Process of Learning. There is an alternative table of contents arranged by rhetorical forms and elements, with units on Methods of Exposition, Argument and Persuasion, Description and Narration, Informal Discourse, Diction and Style, and Research (writings which give possibilities for research papers). A list of questions for discussion and writing follows each selection. The exercises calling for student writing vary in length, but there is a suggested assignment for an essay-length paper given after each selection. Writers included in this reader are Maxim Gorky, Homer, John Keats, Loren Eiseley, James Baldwin, and Joan of Arc, among many others.

403 Van Ghent, Dorothy and Willard Maas, eds. *The Essential Prose*. alt. ed. Indianapolis: Bobbs-Merrill, 1966. 748 pp. $3.95 (P)

This text is virtually identical to *The Essential Prose* (1965) with the following exceptions: the third part deletes the section entitled The Process of Learning and combines other sections; there are fewer readings.

404 Waddell, Marie L., Robert M. Esch, and Roberta R. Walker. *The Art of Styling Sentences*. Woodbury, N.Y.: Barron's Educational Series, 1972. 106 pp. $1.50 (P)

This high school or college-level basic composition text is appropriate in classes in which composition with emphasis on sentence structure and variety will be taught. It is divided into five chapters. The first chapter gives a short explanation of the basic parts of a sentence. The second chapter, which takes up over half the book, consists of twenty patterns for style and variety for the student to learn and imitate. There is space provided in the text for the student to make up sentences of his own when imitating the patterns, but the text is not a workbook of exercises. The different sentence patterns taught consist of compound constructions, sentences with series, repetitions, aspects of modifiers, inversions, and an assortment of further patterns. The third chapter deals with combining and expanding these sentence patterns. The fourth chapter discusses figurative language in the sentence, including simile, metaphor, analogy, and allusion. The fifth chapter contains some examples of the twenty patterns in published writers' works. There are suggested review questions at the end and a short section on punctuation, though punctuation is generally taught within the sentence patterns.

405 Wagner, Geoffrey and Sanford R. Radner. *Language and Reality: A Semantics Approach to Writing*. New York: Thomas Y. Crowell, 1974. 255 pp. NPA (P)

This text is divided into two broad sections: Signs and Symbols. The first unit contains chapters on The Human Animal (communication, body language, and the human face, for example), The Extensions of Man (gesture, silence, listening, feedback), and The Reality of Words. Part two has unit headings of In Search of Meaning, Language and Reality, Language Structure and Thought, On Abstraction, Reasoning Systems, Contexts, and Taboo. Each chapter ends with exercises over key concepts presented and topics for discussion and for writing. Short-answer quizzes are presented, and extensive overview discussions and exercises are included at the end of each

unit. The individual discussions address themselves
primarily to contemporary issues. The text is suitable
for both standard and advanced composition courses.

406 Waldo, Willis H. *Better Report Writing*. 2nd ed. revised
     and enlarged. New York: Reinhold Publishing, 1965.
     276 pp. $10.95 (H)

This text is largely an expanded analysis of report
writing with emphasis on the use of a readable, interesting style. The text opens with three chapters of basic
introductory material on the content, tone, style, and
audience with which the report writer works. The third
chapter gives an overall view of taking technical or laboratory notes, analyzing data, producing a clear statement, a rough draft, and finally achieving a completed
report. Chapter four and the following chapters move
into the technical aspects of report writing and include
standard information on the division of a report, use of
tables and illustrations, bibliographical reference, and
punctuation and grammar in technical English. Chapters
thirteen and fourteen define the various types of reports
by characteristics they possess. There are also chapters on specialized definition, word usage, and the oral
report. The final two chapters deal with the use of the
computer and other modern methods for the storage and
retrieval of technical information and with the new technique of technical report writing by computer. The book
concludes with appendices on abbreviations, tables and
figures, and compound technical terms. There are no
assignments or exercises in the text and relatively few
examples of points made. The basic English material
included, particularly that on punctuation, is slanted
strongly towards needs exclusive to technical writing.
The text presupposes that the student has a grasp of basic
elements of English.

407 Wasson, John M. *Subject and Structure: An Anthology for
     Writers*. 5th ed. Boston: Little, Brown, 1975. 491
     pp. NPA (P)

The fifth edition of this standard reader is divided
into nine sections, and every selection in individual
sections is on the same general subject and illustrates
the same rhetorical principle. The selections include
Example, Description, Comparison and Contrast, Process,
Cause and Effect, Definition, Argument, Persuasion, and
Evaluation. The first selection in each section is a
short essay which approximates the length of a student
essay and attempts to illustrate clearly the rhetorical
technique under consideration. The remaining selections
are arranged in increasing order of difficulty with short
stories and poems last. The introductions to the

sections discuss "the philosophy, importance and utility of each rhetorical technique" and offer instruction in general principles of theme writing. After each selection appear study questions which are divided into two groups: subject and structure. The premise is that students are to see the interrelation between form and content. The structure questions in particular are aimed at solutions to specific writing problems. The thematic divisions are Turning Points, The World Around Us, America's Entertainment, The Computer-Card Culture, Work in an Alienated Society, Language and Style, Freedom and Responsibility, A Matter of Faith, and Lessons for the Future. Most reading selections are of substantial length. The selections range from classical examples to more contemporary ones. The inclusiveness of the text makes selectivity necessary, yet even selectivity does not reduce the amount of material for class discussion. The text applies to classes of basic or advanced composition, and a supplementary handbook is advisable in the former instance.

408   Wasson, John M. *Subject and Structure: An Anthology for Writers*. alt. ed. Boston: Little, Brown, 1972. 571 pp. $5.95 (P)

This reader would be appropriate for beginning or advanced composition courses on the college level. It is divided into nine units, each of which has both theme and rhetorical form common in all its readings. The units are entitled Growing Up In America: Example; Looking at People: Description; The Movies: Comparison and Contrast; Work in an Alienated Society: Cause and Effect; Problems of Postcivilization: Process; Works of the Imagination: Definition; Where the Power Is: Argument; The Liberation of Women: Persuasion; and Where Are We Now?: Evaluation. Thus, the rhetorical forms are the same as those illustrated in the fifth edition (see previous annotation); this alternative edition offers different thematic groupings and selections in the same format as the fifth edition. Introductions at the beginning and questions at the end of the selections are handled in the same way. The artists included in this reader are Samuel Beckett, E. B. White, Norman Mailer, Marya Mannes, John Stuart Mill, and Richard Brautigan, among others.

409   Watkins, Floyd C., William B. Dillingham, and Edwin T. Martin. *Practical English Handbook*. 4th ed. Boston: Houghton Mifflin, 1974. 353 pp. NPA (P)

This handbook is intended as a "brief but practical guide" to writing English prose and is aimed at the standard college-level student. It can be used as the basis

216

for classroom teaching or for student self-help. The
text opens with a brief explanation of how the instructor
or student may grade or evaluate a paper by indicating
the section number and subsection letter which explains
and teaches material the student has missed. For
example, the marking 1/7/f would send the student to the
section on Sentence Errors and grammar/subject and verb
agreement/indefinite pronouns. The tutorial sections of
the book are divided under six main headings: Sentence
Errors and Grammar, Sentence Structure, Punctuation,
Mechanics, Diction and Style, and the Process of Composition. The latter section covers logical thinking, how
to write good paragraphs, how to write good themes,
writing about literature, and creative writing. A brief
section of exercises covers each grammatical principle,
and a complete sample term paper with a detailed explanation is included in the rear of the text. The book
concludes with a glossary of usage and terms.

410   Watkins, Floyd C. and Karl F. Knight, eds. *Writer to*
Writer: Readings on the Craft of Writing. Boston:
Houghton Mifflin, 1966. 243 pp. $5.25 (P)

In their forward the editors state that "In this book
practicing writers talk about writing. . . .The common
theme of the selections in this volume is down-to-earth
advice about writing." This text consists of essays by
respected published writers on writing. Major selections are On Not Writing; The Job of Writing; Interviews,
Conferences, Notes; The Seeing Eye and the Thinking Mind;
Writing Truly; Gobbledygook and Pompous Writing; Language:
Art, Belief, and Behavior; Particular Problems; and The
Last Word. Contributors include Jesse Stuart, Alan
Devoe, Aldous Huxley, Norman Cousins, Ernest Hemingway,
Stephen Leacock, and others. This text has no discussion
questions, introductory essays, and no suggested topics
for student themes. Although a teacher of basic composition would probably want some kind of handbook to use
in conjunction with this text, the readings would be
appropriate as source material for advanced high school
or college-level composition classes. Though there are
no specific leads for paper topics, in the text, comparing
and contrasting different writers' views on writing could
produce enough possibilities for papers.

411   Weathers, Winston and Otis Winchester. *The Strategy of*
Style. New York: McGraw-Hill, 1967. 262 pp. $6.95
(H) $4.95 (P)

The authors state that this book takes up where most
composition texts leave off and that the aim is to develop
"a more provocative, stimulating kind of writing than has

been fostered in recent years." The idea is to help the student overcome dull writing, clumsiness, and aridity. The premise of the book is that style is "the choosing between alternatives," and the book seeks to guide the student in making appropriate stylistic choices from all the possibilities available to him. The introduction stresses the importance of flexibility in style and suggests that learning to read with an eye toward style, practicing various stylistic techniques, and developing the habit of revision and rewriting are essential to sound writing. Chapter one concerns subject and thesis--getting the proper subject for the purpose then establishing a focal point. The discussion also looks into placement of thesis, remaining consistent, and concludes with a sample essay. In chapter two classification and order are discussed; then following chapters deal with introductions and conclusions, expansion, momentum, emphasis, level of rhetorical sophistication, paragraphs, sentences, words, metaphor, sound and rhythm, and punctuation. Each chapter provides explanation interspersed with examples; a list of questions to keep in mind while writing; a sample essay (usually by an established writer like George Orwell or Dylan Thomas); and a series of exercises which involve critical reading, grasping principles, and writing. All principles are dealt with in regard to their practical stylistic application; therefore, sections on punctuation, paragraphing, etc., do not emphasize rules but the rationale for proper usage. The book presupposes a grasp of fundamentals and would serve accomplished freshmen or more advanced rhetoric students.

412 Webster, J. Rowe. *Planned Paragraphs: Examples from Various Sources.* Cambridge, Mass.: Educators Publishing Service, 1956. 48 pp. NPA (P)

This text begins with a general overview of the purpose and plan of the theme. It then discusses twelve points to keep in mind while revising the theme--for example, avoiding unnecessary use of the passive voice, using economical language, proofreading, and making the theme neat. The author then discusses The Planned Paragraph, its unit, coherence, and emphasis, moves to Order of Statement then to six classifications of themes--definitive description, exposition, argument, artistic description, narration, and appreciation or criticism. The author then discusses, with examples followed by student exercises, the Seven Common Orders of Progression in Written Work: Chronological Order--The Order of Sequence in Time; An Order of Aptly Chosen Progress in Space; Tapering Order--Progress from the Most Significant to the Least Significant; Climax--Progress from the Least Significant to the Most Significant; The Order

of General or Topical Statement; The Order of Natural
Division, Branching, or Ramification; and The Order of
Alternation in Themes of Comparison Involving Contrast or
Resemblance and Contrast. Discussions of simple, compound, and complex paragraphs, verb tense, précis writing, pronouns, and miscellaneous paragraphs follow. The
text does not contain a table of contents. Its primary
audience would be students who need specific work with
various methods of constructing paragraphs.

413   Webster, James E. *Combining Reading and Writing.*
      Dubuque, Iowa: Kendall/Hunt, 1974. 155 pp. NPA
      (P)

      The author states in the preface to this workbook
that most writing deficiencies extend from reading difficulties; that is, if the student does not understand what
he has read, how can he write on it? He goes on to say
that developing the student's self-expression by allowing
him to write on personal experience as a method to improve
writing really does not address itself to the college
student's needs and demands--responding in writing to the
ideas of others. Hence, the author contends that close
reading stimulates ideas for the student to write about
while encouraging him to imitate good writing technique.
This text, then, focuses on both levels of this reading/
writing relationship, beginning with words and leading
to the development of composition writing skills. The
introduction provides a quotation to respond to for a
student writing sample, and pages are provided for all
writing assignments. Seven chapters follow: Words and
Sentences; Main Idea in a Paragraph: Topic Sentence;
Paragraph Development; Paragraph Analysis: Writing the
Complete Paper; Use of Facts: The Library and Selecting Books; Reading Magazines and Newspaper Reports; Inferences and Judgements: Slanting and Loaded Words; and
Argument and Persuasion. Each chapter contains readings
always given in the context of exercises. These exercises vary greatly depending on the nature of the lesson;
some entail fill-in-the-blank, summarizing main ideas,
essay writing, or responding to a given topic sentence,
for example. The instructional chapters are followed by
five Writing Workshops which consist of student compositions based on the writing assignments from the preceding
chapters and grammar exercises based on common errors.
A space for notes is provided at the end. This text can be
as a supplement to a literature course or as a writing
text in a composition course. It is aimed primarily
at the college level with a remedial orientation but
could easily be used in high school.

414   Weintraub, Stanley. *Biography and Truth.* Indianapolis:
      Bobbs-Merrill, 1967. 64 pp. $1.25 (P)

This book is part of *The Bobbs-Merrill Series in Composition and Rhetoric*. See listing under Johnson, Falk S. for the complete annotation.

415   Weisman, Herman M. *Basic Technical Writing*. 3rd ed.
       Columbus, Ohio: Charles E. Merrill, 1974. 453 pp.
       $11.95 (H)

This text is one of the most inclusive texts in the field of technical writing. It is intended not only for students in colleges and technical institutes but also for practicing scientists and engineers who must use written communication as a part of their professions. The book is set up in two parts each of which may be complete in one semester, according to Weisman. Part one concentrates on the principles and techniques of writing reports; part two concentrates on advanced elements of technical writing. Included in each chapter are summaries of the material, illustrative examples and models, discussion problems, and exercises to be integrated as teaching aids. A selected bibliography and advanced readings are also included. Part one begins with a chapter defining technical writing, giving the history of technical writing, and isolating the problems of factual communication. Chapter two deals generally and at length with the scientific method and approach, including sections on the origins of science, how man learns, and the definition of logic. Chapter three is an analysis of technical correspondence from planning through physical format and stationery. Specialized correspondence such as application letters, letters of inquiry, claim and adjustment letters, the letter of instruction, etc., are included. Chapter four begins a three-chapter sequence on report writing discussed at length in the following entry. Chapter seven surveys graphic presentations in technical writing by type and usage. Part two of *Basic Technical Writing* discusses Semantics and the Process of Communication. A two-chapter sequence dealing with special expository techniques in technical writing--definition, description, explanation, and analysis--follows. Chapter eleven deals with the technical article and paper. The text works with all levels of writings about science and technology, from work for professional and trade publications to popular pieces for the general public. The final chapter consists of forty pages on technical style, mechanics, and grammar which should suffice as an aid to the student who has a basic understanding of English grammar and syntax. An appendix gives examples of the various forms of technical writing covered in the text.

416   Weisman, Herman M. *Technical Report Writing*. 2nd ed.
       Columbus, Ohio: Charles E. Merrill, 1975. 181 pp.

NPA (P)

This text is an abridged version of the 3rd edition of
Basic Technical Writing. *Technical Report Writing* begins
with a discussion of the elements and history of technical
writing. Chapter two discusses the background of Semantics
and the Process of Communication. A brief look at the
origin and nature of language leads into a more technical
discussion of the process of communication and the
abstract concept of semantics. A bibliography of additional works on semantics and language theory is included.
Chapter three begins a three-chapter sequence on report
writing by discussing report writing as the reconstruc-
tion of an investigation. A general look at report writing discusses reports as informational or analytical.
The chapter begins with suggestions for investigating the
problem such as library research, observation, or experi-
mentation and discusses methods for these types of
investigation. A section of discussion problems and
exercises follows each chapter. Chapter four suggests
methods of organizing the report data according to chronological patterns, order of importance, simple to complex, cause and effect, etc. This chapter also goes into
outlining in some detail. Chapter five, Writing the
Elements of the Report, briefly covers all the elements
of a report from the letter of transmittal through
cover, title page, and so on down to index and distribution lists. Examples are given as well as suggestions
for format and the treatment of equations, headings,
documentation, and footnotes/bibliography. Chapter six
introduces graphic aids to report presentation. Chapter
seven is on technical style and stresses the fact that
"technical style is plain, impersonal, and factual."
Weisman touches on clarity, preciseness, active and
passive voice, sentence structure, readability, and how
to write a paragraph. A reference index and guide to
grammar, punctuation, style, and usage is included as
well as a bibliography of other works in grammar, language background, and technical writing.

417 Wells, C. Michael, Alan R. Velie, and Donita Williams
     Walker. *Appleseeds and Beer Cans: Man and Nature in
     Literature*. Pacific Palisades, Ca.: Goodyear, 1974.
     304 pp. NPA (P)

This reader is primarily an anthology of works which
apply to ecology. "The selections are not tightly
reasoned scientific articles; most are works of art:
poems, essays, short stories, and selections from novels.
Their appeal is not primarily to the reason, but to the
imagination and the feelings." The selections are grouped
under four major headings: The Ecological Attitude;
Failures; Where Did We Go Wrong?; and Solutions:

Variations on a Theme of the Simple Life. The selections range from Gerard Manley Hopkins to Richard Brautigan and include some essays from Eastern literature as well. There are no exercises or study questions included in the book.

418 White, Edward M., ed. *The Writer's Control of Tone: Readings, with Analysis, for Thinking and Writing about Personal Experience.* New York: W. W. Norton, 1970. 221 pp. $1.95 (P)

This text is designed to enable the writer who has something he believes is significant to say about some personal experience to be able to express it so other people will want to read it. The editor states in his introduction that "I am convinced that the most important job before teachers of writing is to resist and protest against the dehumanizing effect of materials and essay assignments that turn writing into academic gamesmanship." The text is divided into three main sections: Controlling Attitudes: Child and Adult; Controlling Analysis: Schools and Institutions; and Controlling Meaning: Large Small Experiences. There is an appendix entitled Rewriting for Control of Tone which contains a first and second draft of a student paper. Each section beings with a brief discussion of the sort of problem approached in the section, usually focusing on tone. Readings illustrating the problems follow; a short biography of the writer and discussion questions follow each reading. The readings are generally "literary," by such authors as e. e. cummings, Henry Adams, Mary McCarthy, and George Orwell. Papers written in a class using this text would be personal; the first section would suggest a paper describing an adult the student knew as a child, conveying an attitude as well as information. This text does not prepare the student to write formal college papers; the editor specifically believes such papers should be de-emphasized. This text would be best used in college-level composition classes designed to help the writer write effectively in the "real world."

419 Whitten, Mary E. *Creative Pattern Practice: A New Approach to Writing.* 2nd ed. Harcourt, Brace, Jovanovich, 1975. 349 pp. NPA (P)

This textbook would be appropriate for college remedial courses in composition or high school composition courses which also deal with fundamentals. The author states in the preface that "The first edition of *Creative Pattern Practice* grew out of the belief that modern advances in the teaching of foreign languages could be profitably applied to the teaching of the forms and structures of English. This second edition reaffirms that belief, as it

incorporates many of the recent discoveries about language.
The principles of pattern practice, the derivation of rules
from examples, the oral and written imitation of models, and
step-by-step learning are here put to constructive use."
This text is a workbook consisting almost entirely of exercises. It is divided into three main sections plus an appendix on spelling and punctuation. The first part is entitled
Forms in English (agreement, verbs, nouns and pronouns, modifiers and connectives); the second part covers structures
in English (different types of sentences, clauses, appositives, series, connectors, ellipsis, etc.); the third part
deals with single and combined paragraphs. The appendix on
spelling and punctuation has exercises in spelling but only
rules in punctuation. The pages are all tear-out sheets.
The exercises on paragraphs have the student write his own
paragraphs modeled on types the book presents, for example,
"write a paragraph making and developing a classification" (a
suggested structure and some suggested topics are given).

420   Whitten, Mary E. *Decisions, Decisions: Style in Writing.*
      New York: Harcourt, Brace, Jovanovich, 1971. 241 pp.
      $4.95 (P)

This workbook-style composition text could be used in
high school or freshman level college composition courses.
It is designed to make the student see the choices offered
in the English language in developing style and to imitate
some of these choices. The first section is entitled
Patterns within Sentences and Patterns of Sentences. The
student is taught the concept of style through learning
sentence patterns and doing exercises imitating those
patterns. The second section, Ways to Develop Paragraphs,
provides twenty paragraphs for study. The paragraphs are
analyzed in questions after each one in which the structure is briefly pointed out, vocabulary is studied, and
assignments which involve writing paragraphs are made.
The third section deals with various types of compositions such as the personal experience, description, classifying information, argument, definition, analysis, etc.
Each section contains short essays as examples, questions
analyzing the essays, vocabulary lists, and finally suggestions for writing. Selections are by such authors as
Marshall McLuhan, James A. Michener, Arthur Schlesinger,
Jr., and Corey Ford, among others. There are photographs
for illustrations throughout the latter half of the text.

421   Wiener, Harvey S. *Creating Compositions.* New York:
      McGraw-Hill, 1973. 494 pp. $5.95 (P)

This text is a comprehensive workbook based on the
concept that good writing comes from responding to personal experience; hence, the exercises are designed to

help the student recreate his experiences in writing, moving gradually into the formal college essay by focusing initially on the well-developed paragraph. Part one includes six chapters on paragraphing, covering the subjects of description, narration, writing on a past experience, comparison-contrast, detailing, and writing about images. Part two deals with the longer composition with separate chapters on expanding the paragraph into a theme, argumentation, describing a familiar person, professional writing (resumés, letters of application, etc.) and definition. The final section is a "minibook" listing and discussing thirteen special skills needed for composition writing, e.g., spelling, vocabulary, note-taking, using a thesaurus. Three appendices conclude the text--vocabulary exercises, a theme progress sheet, and a record for student-teacher conferences. Each chapter is organized around an experience meaningful to the student's life--family moments, the automobile, etc. Each is subdivided into a brief introduction, drills on pertinent vocabulary, a section entitled Building Composition Skills explaining different techniques in the construction of a paragraph or essay, another on solving troublesome problems in writing (run-ons, fragments, etc.), another involving writing either a paragraph or essay which offers specific goals for the writing exercise followed by illustrative writing samples from important authors (e.g., Philip Roth, Thomas Wolfe, Germaine Greer). Each chapter concludes with a section entitled Reaching Higher which involves review or further practice in composition. Occasional charts and photographs are employed to facilitate instruction. All pages are tear-out. This text is suitable for freshman composition or the high school level. Its scope requires a lengthy time commitment.

422 Wiener, Harvey S. and Rose Palmer. *The Writing Lab: An Individualized Program in Writing Skills.* Beverly Hills, Ca.: Glencoe, 1974. NPA

The Writing Lab is a modular approach to writing which consists of nine booklets presenting "basic material in rhetoric and mechanics for the student with minimal skills in composition." The booklets teach composition skills; all information on mechanics appears on twenty-four cards to which the student can refer when he has a problem. The teacher's manual suggests various ways of using the packet tutorially, as a classroom text, as writing laboratory, and so on. Students may work on the various booklets in any order according to their individual or collective needs. Module one, A Job You Did, contains exercises in developing ideas, observation, establishing a topic sentence, how to use transitions, and paragraphing following the topic discussion. The discussion uses photographs, stories, and other means to elicit response. Module two, Describing Someone You Know, uses a sensory approach to raise awareness then leads the student through basic composition development. Other modules are entitled Comparing Two Teachers, How to Write Definitions, The Language of Faces and Figures, Cause and Effects, Giving and Following Directions, You as Correspondent, and Note-taking and Summarizing. Each unit illustrates basic principles with photographs, illustrations, and writing exercises which are designed to build from impressions to organized thoughts. The sample essays are brief.

423 Williams, Barbara. *The Well-Structured Paragraph*.
Columbus, Ohio: Charles E. Merrill, 1970. 163 pp.
$2.95 (P)

As the title indicates, this text attacks the problem of composition through a focus on the paragraph. Part one, Paragraph Elements, contains chapters entitled Food for Those Hungry Paragraphs (supportive facts), Unity through the Topic Sentence and Controlling Idea, and Coherence through Order and Transition. Part two, Methods of Paragraph Development, contains chapters on process, narration, detail, illustration, comparison and contrast, analogy, analysis, definition, reasoning, and combination of methods. The Whole Composition, part three, discusses developing a thesis statement, outlines, and beginnings and endings. Part four, Fundamentals of English Prose, has a glossary of usage and a list of symbols for correcting themes. Each chapter is followed by brief exercises that usually require the student to write his own paragraph on one topic to be selected from a list. The text is short enough to be used in conjunction with other books and would, perhaps, be applicable to remedial as well as basic composition.

424 Williams, John B. *Style and Grammar: A Writer's Handbook of Transformations*. New York: Dodd, Mead, 1973.
200 pp. $4.75 (P)

This text takes a generative-transformational grammar approach to constructing effective sentences. The author states in A Note to the Teacher that this book "is an attempt to present such a grammar with the minimum essentials of technical information." The text consists of six chapters. Chapter one, Language and the Sense of Order, has subdivisions entitled Sentence Sense, What Is a Sentence?, Kernel Sentence Patterns, and Qualities of Kernel Verbs. Noun Phrases and Verb Phrases, chapter two, discusses morphemes, building the noun phrase, types of noun phrases, building the verb phrase, and forms of verbs. Chapter three includes negatives, questions, imperatives, and inversions. Chapter four presents compounds and insertions; chapter five discusses more insertions: noun substitutes, modifiers, complements, and comparatives. The last chapter takes up sentences in sequence. Each section of each chapter is followed by exercises which focus on identifying the various elements presented by that section and on writing, connecting, and rearranging sentences.

425 Williams, Joseph M. *The New English: Structure/Form/ Style.* New York: The Free Press, 1970. 421 pp. $8.50 (H)

In the preface the author emphasizes that he does not teach rules but questions: "we have to realize that in language and rhetoric, there are no predetermined right answers. There are only better or worse questions, inter esting and uninteresting answers." He points out that awkward or unclear sentences are much more serious errors than minor grammatical points. The text is divided into two main sections. The first contains two chapters: Grammar: A Theory of Language and A Sketch of a Grammar of English. There are exercises throughout these sections designed to help the student see the language structurally, using a transformational approach. The second section concerns rhetoric and discusses The Proble (intention, audience, subject), Form (inductive and deductive approaches, ways of organization, and movements in form), and Style (sentences, transition, diction, and tone). A glossary of key terms is given at the beginning of the text. The main audience is the freshman English student, but the text might be used for the advanced high school student.

426 Willis, Hulon. *Basic Usage, Vocabulary, and Composition* 2nd ed. New York: Holt, Rinehart and Winston, 1975. 340 pp. NPA (P)

This text has a basic workbook format and is divided into three parts. The first covers troublesome aspects of usage with thirty-two different lessons presented on a practical basis rather than theoretically. Part two consists of eighteen reading selections "chosen for thei general interest and their provision for vocabulary buil ing." The selections primarily treat issues oriented topics written by such authors as Henry Steele Commager, C. S. Lewis, Peter Farb, and George Orwell. Each selection has an accompanying vocabulary test, and most have short sentence-writing exercises based on words that hav some similarity or that are often confused. The third part consists of ten writing assignments on various expository types--description, personal narrative, character sketch, familiar essay, and précis--with specific instruction on how to execute them. Tips and "mini-exercises" are interspersed throughout. All pages are on perforated sheets. The author notes the importance of the Instructor's Manual which provides keys to exercises plus additional exercises. This text is particularly suitable for freshman composition and can be used selectively.

427 Willis, Hulon. *A Brief Handbook of English.* New York: Harcourt, Brace, Jovanovich, 1975. 251 pp. NPA (P)

This text is a guide to usage and grammar. The author states in his preface that he has restricted himself to discussing basics, giving "concise rules and instructions without splitting hairs." The text is divided into five sections. The first, Grammar, discusses parts of speech, sentences, phrases, clauses, modifiers, appositives, coordination, subordination, and ambiguity. Longer sections in the first chapter deal with sentence fragments, comma splices and run-together sentences, misused modifiers, pronoun case forms, subject-verb agreement, shifts, and verb forms. Section two, Punctuation and Mechanics, includes chapters which deal with all aspects of punctuation. The third section, Spelling, discusses spelling rules and covers capitalization, the apostrophe, and the hyphen. Section four, Diction, includes several chapters dealing with word choice. The last section, Effective Sentences, addresses itself to faulty sentence structure, pronoun reference, faulty comparison, and well-formed sentences. The primary audience would be students needing basic instruction or students needing only a reference.

428 Willis, Hulon. *Logic, Language, and Composition.* Cambridge, Mass.: Winthrop, 1975. 372 pp. NPA (P)

As the title indicates, this text is divided into three parts: Logic, Language, and Composition. There are a total of thirty-six separate chapters, and each presents some aspect of the three main divisions. Each chapter ends with a Usage Lesson which is followed by student exercises centering only on the problem of usage just discussed. For example, the first chapter, Definitions of Logic and Related Terms, is followed by Usage Lesson 1: A Spelling Rule, which is in turn followed by exercises. Chapters under part one are entitled Induction, or Establishing Generalizations; Scientific Inductions; and Different Kinds of Major Premises, for example. Part two, Language, contains eleven chapters, each of which centers on some aspect of language; part three contains twelve chapters, ranging from chapters on audience to basic organization to paragraphs and style. This text is designed for students who need some work on fundamentals of grammar, usage, and composition. The text takes a workbook approach, and the pages can be torn out.

429 Wilson, James R. *Argument and Persuasion: From Direct Attack to Seduction.* New York: Harper and Row, 1974 33 pp. NPA (P)

This pamphlet is a part of the *Harper Studies in Language and Literature* listed in this bibliography under Shrodes, Caroline, editor.

430 Wilson, James R. *Illustration: All Knowledge is Particular.* New York: Harper and Row, 1974. 35 pp. NPA (P)

This pamphlet is a part of the *Harper Studies in Language and Literature* listed in this bibliography under Shrodes, Caroline, editor.

431 Wilson, Smokey. *Struggles with Bears: Experience in Writing.* New York: Canfield Press, 1973. 334 pp. NPA (P)

This is a college-level text in composition based on experiences in an actual writing class. The first section of each chapter is about some learning experience in that class. The author states in the preface that "The text moves from free-form writing (Part I) to the writing of narratives (Part II); and then from the specific, 'the well-told tale,' to the general (Part III." Part four concerns diction, and part five deals with rewriting. There is a short glossary of terms after the fifth section and an index at the end. The preface holds that some of the writing suggestions would be incomprehensible without the teaching manual to accompany instruction. Writing examples are given throughout and include such writers as Dick Gregory, Lewis Carroll, Andrew Marvell, and Yevgeny Yevtushenko. Chapters contain discussions of concepts, examples, writing suggestions, and blank pages for the student to record his learning experience on. The five parts of the text are entitled Free Flow: Finding a Style; Reflections: Recollecting the Past; Significance: Discovering Meaning in Events; Imaginary Gardens: Looking Inward; and Polish: Revising the Essay. Black and white photographs and sketches are scattered throughout. The text is intended to encourage free expression in college-level writing.

432 Winchester, Otis and Winston Weathers. *The Prevalent Forms of Prose.* Boston: Houghton Mifflin, 1968. 167 pp. $4.95 (P)

The authors state in their preface that this text is for "the college writer who wants to understand the prose forms he reads in magazines and journals by writing them himself." Chapter one provides an overview of the essay

Discussions include A Sense of Form, Clarity and Effectiveness, The Writing Process, and The Readable Manuscript. Chapter two, The Popular Article, deals with
the form of this type of prose, how to write a popular
article, and gives an example from *Fortune* which is followed by an analysis and ten assignments for discussion
and writing. Chapter three, the Professional Article;
chapter four, The Personal Essay; chapter five, The
Formal Essay; and chapter six, The Critical Review all
follow the same format as chapter one. This text is
designed for those students who have mastered basic
writing skills and for those who wish to look beyond
"college writing." Its approach is practical and how-
to-do-it.

433 Winkler, Anthony C. and Jo Ray McCuen. *Rhetoric Made
     Plain*. New York: Harcourt, Brace, Jovanovich, 1974.
     324 pp. NPA (P)

In their preface the authors state, "We have tried to
answer squarely, and helpfully, such . . . student questions as: 'What's a thesis?' 'How do I organize?' 'How
do I get from outline to paragraph?'" The text addresses
basic questions frequently raised by freshman composition
students. Part one discusses prewriting questions about
the meaning of rhetoric, word choice, organization, etc.
Part two examines various principles of writing: outlining, consistency, making sense, polishing, etc. The
final part, Special Assignments, has individual chapters
on the research paper, writing about literature, science
writing, and report writing. These chapters are interspersed with numerous examples and exercises, most requiring writing. This text is applicable to freshman composition and could be supplemented with a handbook or
readings.

434 Winterowd, W. Ross. *Contemporary Rhetoric: A Concept-
     ual Background with Readings*. New York: Harcourt,
     Brace, Jovanovich, 1975. 380 pp. NPA (P)

The author in his preface states that this text has
three purposes: "First, it brings together some of the
most significant recent work in the field of rhetoric.
Second, it interprets that work. . . .Third, it develops
new theoretical material concerning invention, style, and
form." Following a thirty-seven page introduction entitled
Some Remarks on Pedagogy appears a chapter entitled Invention which contains a ten page introduction/explanation
and eleven readings. The second chapter, Form, contains
an introduction and six essays while the last chapter,
Style, contains an introduction and seven essays. Most
of the essays are by professional teachers and writers.
The author states that the text "is aimed at a broad and

varied audience: composition students at all levels (wh
can use it as their reader and theoretical base); those
who are in training to be instructors of writing at any
level (who can use it as their textbook); students of
rhetoric; and scholars in the field of rhetoric."

435 Winterowd, W. Ross. *The Contemporary Writer: A Practical Rhetoric.* New York: Harcourt, Brace, Jovanovich, 1975. 542 pp. NPA (H)

The author states that this rhetoric/handbook has a
rich and unified conceptual basis in addition to its
completeness, reliability, modernity, and practical use-
fulness. It is divided into four major sections. The
first part discusses The Uses of Writing, beginning with
writing as a mode of expression and continuing with writ
ing as a composing process; it has sections on prewritin
developing ideas in paragraphs, exposition, writing abou
literature, research writing, the persuasive essay
and creative writing. Each of these subdivisions begins
with a summary of the chapter then has brief subsections
on various aspects of the rhetorical principle being dis
cussed. Each chapter contains a series of discussion
topics and activities. Part two, Style, begins with a
chapter on language--its nature and function, meaning
and structure, the dynamics of language change, etc.
Separate chapters on the sentence, words, figurative lan
guage, and style follow; each has basically the same
format as the preceding chapters. Part three is entitle
A Spectrum of Student Essays, and part four is a Reference Guide which defines and illustrates rhetorical
terminology. The text could serve as a comprehensive
reference text, a writing supplement, or a text for a
class. It would best serve students on the college leve
especially in an introduction to literature or survey of
literature course.

436 Winterowd, W. Ross. *Structure, Language, and Style: A
Rhetoric Handbook.* Dubuque, Iowa: Wm. C. Brown,
1969. 290 pp. $5.95 (H)

This text is designed for a college composition class
but could be used in an advanced high school college
preparatory composition course. There are large units o
Writing an Essay: An Overview; The Paragraph; The
Grammars of English; The Sentence; Punctuation; The
Word; Thinking Straight; The Long Paper; The Growth of
English; and A Checklist of Writing Problems. The unit
on the word defines many of the classic figures of speech
after discussing the appropriateness of slang, jargon,
neologisms, etc. The grammar section gives a history of
the development of grammar theory in the English language
and ends with discussions on structural, transformational

and generative grammar. Each section has numerous subdivisions and several sets of exercises. There are no
model essays, but examples are included in each discussion of principles. Although the units form a progression, each is self-contained so the text could be
used simply on specific problems. This text would be
appropriate for a teacher who wishes to use modern
approaches to grammar but does not want to confuse those
students with backgrounds in more traditional grammar.

437 Wolff, Cynthia Griffin, ed. *Other Lives*. Pacific Palisades, Ca.: Goodyear, 1973. 383 pp. $6.95 (P)

This text is a collection of readings and is based "on
the assumption that it is not only interesting but also
genuinely informative to understand how other people's
experience has affected them." Because college freshmen
have usually had limited experience, there is a need to
read of experiences and ideas of others to stimulate
ideas for writing. Six different situations are offered
as topics of consideration: Being Married, Being Insane,
Being Powerful, Being in Prison, Aging and Dying, and
Being in Touch with the Infinite. Each section has an
introduction, a sort of synopsis of the issue, and readings to follow. Essays, stories, and poems done by many
different types of authors are included. Works by
authors such as W. B. Yeats, William Shakespeare, and
Alfred Lord Tennyson are intermixed with selections by
George Jackson, Timothy Leary, Anne Sexton, etc. Discussion questions conclude each section with questions
directed at the readings and the situations in reference
to the student's own life. This reader can be used at
any level of college English. There are no formal writing assignments listed though issues raised in the discussion questions could easily evolve into paper topics.

438 Wubben, John. *Guided Writing*. New York: Random House,
1971. 343 pp. $5.50 (P)

This is a workbook of composition designed to teach
the student through analysis of other themes and writing
and analysis of his own theme. It would be most appropriate in a high school or college freshman composition
course. It is not a book of grammar or mechanics, and
a handbook of some sort which deals with those problems
could be used as a supplement. There are eight chapters:
Fundamentals of Composition; Outlining the Composition;
Paragraphing the Composition; The Autogiography; Building
on Experience: Exposition; Recreating Experience:
Description; Recreating Experience: Narration; and
Interpreting Experience: Argumentation. In each chapter
the student reads explanatory material concerning the
principles covered in the chapter. The student then reads

one or two model compositions. There are questions to answer and charts to fill out which thoroughly analyze that model composition. For example, in the first chapter for the first model composition, the student is supposed to quote from the work illustrating the writer's experience with his subject, answer questions on limiting the subject, quote from the work illustrations of how he has limited his subject, quote illustrations of how he has kept the central idea in mind throughout the essay, quote examples of concrete and specific detail, quote examples of various kinds of diction, quote transitions illustrating coherence, and find errors in many areas of punctuation, mechanics, grammar, and spelling. In other chapters the student must do other types of analysis such as filling in an outline of the model composition. After the student works on these models, he writes his own composition and puts it through the same analysis process, filling in the same questions and charts he had to work on in the model compositions. All the pages are on tear-out sheets. This text teaches composition through minute analysis. Examples are taken from such authors as Thomas Wolfe, Richard Wright, Sherwood Anderson, and Arthur Mizener, among others.

439   Wyld, Lionel D. *Preparing Effective Reports*. Indianapolis: Odyssey, 1967. 198 pp. $3.25 (P)

A brief handbook which offers a quick reference for those who wish to review aspects of technical writing, this text is designed for the university course in technical writing or for someone already employed in industry. For classroom use the book does incorporate discussion questions or exercises following each chapter. The major emphasis of the text is on style in the technical report. Chapter one, Writing and Reports, emphasizes audience, purpose, and report prose structure and style. Chapter two deals with semantics, and chapter three covers sentence and verb structures which contribute to writing a readable report. Chapter four concentrates on the design of the paragraph; chapter five covers tables and graphs of all types. Examples are given. Chapter six discusses documenting the report by footnote, bibliography, and reference lists. Chapter seven is devoted to the short report in its various forms, and chapter eight is a lengthy look at the long report. The final chapter of the handbook discusses operations research and report editing. The report editor in this case is considered a separate individual from the report writer. The chapter also contains a bibliography of further works on report writing as well as manuals on grammar and style and specialized dictionaries and glossaries. The appendices include Notes on Business Correspondence, Writing Essentials and Manuscript

Mechanics, USAECOM Standards for Technical Reports, and Sample Reports.

440 Yarber, Robert E. and Barbara Heyward. *Breakthrough: Contemporary Reading and Writing*. 2nd ed. Menlo Park, Ca.: Cummings Publishing, 1973. 343 pp. $5.75 (P)

The authors state that this text "gives the English instructor a tool with which to capture students' attention, hold their interest, and help them deal constructively with their concerns through discussion and writing" and is designed for freshman English in particular. The text revolves around "issues" and has four major parts. Part one is divided into three sections: Dissent--Why and How, with selections by Arlo Guthrie, Art Buchwald, and others; The Learning Experience, including a selection from *Mad Magazine*; and Sports and the Supernatural, including a satiric piece and an excerpt from *Scholastic Scope*. Part Two deals with relationships and includes sections on individuals, brotherhood, and society, with primarily contemporary selections. Part Three, Turning In: Identity and Values, has selections from literary figures like Malamud, Updike, and Yevtushenko as well as contemporary social critics like Joni Mitchell and Eugene McCarthy. The final part, which deals with the future, has sections on career planning, love, and marriage. Each major part begins with a brief introduction which is meant to stimulate thinking on the forthcoming topic, and the individual chapters have essay questions directed at specific issues and selections. Following the questions in each chapter are writing guidelines (such as Writing a Summary, Describing a Person, or Narrating a Personal Experience) which give instruction in writing. Each set of guidelines is followed by a writing assignment which integrates ideas stimulated by the readings with the rhetorical principles discussed. A black and white photograph precedes each chapter, and the authors include a gallery of four-color art in a center-fold, each illustration more complex than the preceding one. A series of questions accompanies the paintings. The authors state that this edition includes revisions in reading selections and introductions and has eliminated unpopular or unteachable sections from the first edition.

441 Yarber, Robert E. and J. Burl Hogins. *College Reading and Writing*. New York: Macmillan, 1968. 498 pp. $4.95 (P)

This reader, as the authors state in their preface, contains "thirty-six essays that cover a wide range of interests--from the need for a college education to sex in Sweden. The essays themselves will serve as models

for writing your own work and as stimuli for discussion."
Each of the twelve sections that deal with writing contains three essays, each of which is followed by a section of student exercises connected to the essay. These
exercises include divisions on vocabulary, discussion of
rhetorical principles, discussion of the essay's theme,
and suggestions for writing. The sections are entitled
Organization: The Main Idea; Diction: There's a Word
for It; Sentence Variety; Paragraph Development: The
Topic Sentence; Paragraph Development: Definition;
Paragraph Development: Example; Paragraph Development:
Comparison and Contrast; Paragraph Development: Reason
and Evidence; Beginning and Ending a Theme; Transitions;
The Whole Theme; Practical Pointers: Some Reminders for
the Student; Using the Dictionary; Vocabulary Building
(1); Vocabulary Building (2); and Improving Reading
Skills. The appendix contains a glossary of rhetorical
terms, a list of recommended readings, and one hundred
theme topics. The primary audience for this reader seems
to be freshman composition and advanced writing classes.

442   Young, Richard E., Alton L. Becker, and Kenneth L. Pike.
       Rhetoric: Discovery and Change. New York: Harcourt,
       Brace, Jovanovich, 1970. 383 pp. $7.50 (H)

       This text utilizes the linguistic theory of tagmemics
to "make a much more extensive and fundamental contribu-
tion by supplying the theoretical principles and problem-
solving procedures necessary for a distinctly new approac
to rhetoric." The text, however, does not teach linguistic theory but composition. The authors hold that
rhetoric involves all the processes of writing from prewriting to editing and base the text on that principle.
The first chapter discusses the history and domain of
rhetoric. The second through seventh chapters deal with
"invention"--the processes one goes through before
actually writing. Chapters eight through twelve deal
with the problem of audience or the relationship between
writer and reader. Chapters thirteen through fifteen are
devoted to language and revision. The last chapter discusses the problems of style. Each chapter discusses the
problems involved in its areas at some length and ends
with a group of exercises. The exercises often involve
analyzing examples given by professional writers such as
"Crossing into Poland" by Isaac Babel or "Letter from
Birmingham Jail" by Martin Luther King, Jr. The exercise
also have the students rewrite sentences provided and
write themes of their own. The text ends with a subject
index referring the reader to points covered in the
chapters. This college-level text could be used in
advanced composition courses or advanced courses in style
and rhetoric.

443 Young, William L. *Teach Yourself English*. Woodbury,
     N.Y.: Barron's Educational Series, 1968. 127 pp.
     $1.85 (P)

This programmed workbook is designed for high school
and college students, secretaries, non-native speakers
learning English, and for preparation for English Proficiency Examinations. There are sections on the parts
of speech, pronoun problems, verb tense and agreement,
modifiers, subordination and coordination, style, punctuation, and spelling. A short index at the back and an
appendix conjugating *to be* and *to choose* are included. A
brief explanation of a rule and examples are on left-hand
pages while exercises for the rules are on right-hand
pages. Answers for exercises are placed for easy grading on the next right-hand page. Though this text is
designed for individual use by a student, tutorial gui-
dance would be helpful.

TITLE INDEX

237

Autobiography. Maurianne Adams. (1)

Awareness: Exercises in Basic Composition Skills. Suanne Mac
    and Dorothy Patterson. (250)

Barnet and Stubb's Practical Guide to Writing. Sylvan Barnet
    and Marcia Stubbs. (23)

Basic Grammar for Writing. Eugene Ehrlich and Daniel Murphy.
    (111)

Basic Technical Writing. Peter Burton Ross. (331)

Basic Technical Writing. 3rd ed. Herman M. Weisman. (415)

Basic Usage, Vocabulary, and Composition. 2nd ed. Hulon
    Willis. (426)

Basic Writer and Reader. new alt. form. Irwin Griggs and
    Robert Llewellyn. (161)

Better Paragraphs. 3rd ed. John Ostrom. (296)

Better Report Writing. 2nd ed. Willis H. Waldo. (406)

Biography and Truth. Stanley Weintraub. (414)

Black Americans: Images in Conflict. P. M. Banks and V. M.
    Burke. (20)

The Bobbs-Merrill Series in Composition and Rhetoric. Falk S.
    Johnson, James Kreuzer, and Franklin Norvish, general eds
    (215)

The Borzoi College Reader. 2nd ed. Charles Muscatine and
    Marlene Griffith, eds. (288)

Breakthrough: Contemporary Reading and Writing. 2nd ed.
    Robert E. Yarber and Barbara Heyward. (440)

A Brief Handbook of English. Hulon Willis. (427)

The Bright Blue Plymouth Station Wagon. Robert E. Moore.
    (279)

*Building Writing Skills: A Programmed Approach to Sentences
    and Paragraphs*. Alan Casty. (70)

Checking Your English. Harry M. Brown and Karen K. Colhouer.
    (58)

The Christensen Rhetoric Program: The Student Workbook.

Francis Christensen and Marilynn Martin Munson.   (74)

City Life: Writing From Experience.   William Makely, ed.
(265)

Classical Rhetoric for the Modern Student.   2nd ed.   Edward
P. J. Corbett.   (89)

Classification: The Forms of Experience.   Niel K. Snortum.
(374)

Clear Technical Reports.   William A. Damerst.   (100)

Clear Technical Writing.   John A. Brogan.   (55)

Clear Thinking for Composition.   2nd ed.   Ray Kytle.   (231)

Clear Writing.   Marilyn B. Gilbert.   (144)

College Reading and College Writing.   rev. ed.   Willoughby
Johnson and Thomas M. Davis.   (216)

College Reading and Writing.   Robert E. Yarber and J. Burl
Hogins.   (441)

The College Writer's Handbook.   Suzanne E. Jacobs and Roderick
A. Jacobs.   (214)

College Writing.   2nd ed.   Harry H. Crosby and George F.
Esty.   (98)

Combining Reading and Writing.   James E. Webster.   (413)

Coming to Terms with Language: An Anthology.   Raymond D.
Liedlich, ed.   (244)

*Commanding Sentences: A Chartered Course in Basic Writing
Skills*.   Helen Mills and Wayne Hersh.   (277)

*Communicating Technical Information: A Guide to Current Uses
and Abuses in Scientific and Engineering Writing*.   Robert
R. Rathbone.   (312)

Communitas of College and Community.   Louis T. Grant.   (155)

The Comp Box.   Ray Kytle.   (232)

Compact Handbook of College Composition.   2nd ed.   Maynard J.
Brennan.   (53)

Comparison and Contrast: Key to Composition.   Gill Muller.
(286)

The Contemporary Writer: A Practical Rhetoric. W. Ross Winterowd. (435)

Correct Writing. Form D. Edwin M. Everett, Marie Dumas, and Charles Wall. (123)

Counterpoint: Dialogue for the 70's. Conn McAuliffe, ed. (251)

The Craft of Writing. Thomas Elliott Berry. (37)

A Crash Course in Composition. Elizabeth McMahan. (259)

Creating Composition. Harvey S. Wiener. (421)

Creative Pattern Practice: A New Approach to Writing. 2nd ed. Mary E. Whitten. (419)

Creative Responses for Composition. Mary I. Schuster. (348)

The Critical Man: Reading, Thinking, Writing. A. M. Tibbetts and Charlene Tibbetts. (395)

Critical Reading and Writing. Ruth Thompson and Marvin Thompson. (394)

Decisions, Decisions: Style in Writing. Mary E. Whitten. (420)

Definition: Explorations in Meaning. Caroline Shrodes. (361)

Description: Using the Mind's Eye. Rita Fuhr and Cyra McFadden. (136)

Destination Tomorrow. Jack Carpenter. (69)

Developing Style: An Extension of Personality. Lloyd A. Flanigan and Sylvia A. Holladay. (128)

A Dictionary of Usage and Style: The Reference Guide for Professional Writers, Reporters, Editors, Teachers and Students. Roy H. Copperud. (88)

Doublespeak: Language for Sale. William Sparke and Bernice Taines. (377)

Ecology: A Writer's Handbook with a Full Glossary of Ecological Terms. Mary Travis Arny and Christopher R. Reaske. (14)

Effective Communications for the Technical Man. John M. Campbell and G. L. Farrar. (64)

Effective English: A Guide for Writing. P. Joseph Canavan. (65)

Eight Modern Essayists. 2nd ed. William Smart. (370)

Elements of College Writing and Reading. P. Joseph Canavan. (66)

The Elements of Rhetoric. Vincent Ruggiero. (337)

Elements of Style. 2nd ed. William Strunk and E. B. White. (386)

Elements of Technical Writing. Marva T. Barnett. (21)

Elements of Writing. Robert Scholes and Carl H. Klaus. (346)

English Composition: An Individualized Course. rev. ed. Benson R. Schulman. (347)

English Essentials: With Self-Scoring Exercises. Herbert B. Nelson. (290)

English for You. Robert O'Neal and Alan C. Love. (293)

English Fundamentals. 5th ed. form B. Ronald W. Emery and John M. Kierzk. (120)

English Grammar: A Handbook for Everyday Usage. Frances M. Briggs. (54)

English Grammar: Forms and Structures. Harold Fleming. (129

English Language Arts Workbook. Joseph Bellafiore. (31)

The English Language: Form and Use. William S. Chisholm, Jr. and Louis T. Milic. (73)

English Manual. Leonard E. Opdycke. (294)

English Prose Style. Herbert Read. (313)

English Review Manual: A Program for Self-Instruction. James A. Gowen. (151)

English Simplified. rev. ed. Blanche Ellsworth. (116)

English Skills for Technicians. Jack Block and Joe Labonville. (48)

English 3200: A Programmed Course in Grammar and Usage. 2nd ed. Joseph C. Blumenthal. (50)

English 2600: A Programmed Course in Grammar and Usage. 4th ed. Joseph C. Blumenthal. (49)

The Essay: Structure and Purpose. Richard L. Cherry, Robert J. Conley, and Bernard A. Hirsch. (71)

The Essay: Subjects and Stances. Edward P. J. Corbett. (90)

The Essayist. 2nd ed. Sheridan Baker. (17)

Essays. 2nd ed. Fred L. Bergmann. (34)

Essays by the Masters. M. B. McNamee. (260)

The Essential Prose. Dorothy Van Ghent and Willard Maas, eds. (402)

The Essential Prose. alt. ed. Dorothy Van Ghent and Willard Maas, eds. (403)

Essentials of English. rev. ed. Vincent F. Hopper, Cedric Gale, and Ronald C. Foote. (198)

Essentials of English Workbook. Joseph Bellafiore. (32)

Euphemism. Walker Gibson. (141)

Experience in Writing. Virginia Shaffer. (352)

Experiences. Florence H. Morgan and Fred Morgan. (280)

Exposition. 2nd ed. Jerome W. Archer and Joseph Schwartz. (13)

Exposition and Literature. Carson Gibb. (140)

The Film. Andrew Sarris. (342)

Finding a Voice. Jim W. Corder. (92)

First Person Singular. Charles Muscatine and Marlene Griffith, eds. (289)

First Principles of the Essay. 2nd ed. Robert Miles. (274)

The Five-Hundred-Word Theme. 2nd ed. Lee J. Martin, revised by Harry P. Kroitor. (268)

Focusing on Language: A Reader. Harold B. Allen, Enola Borgh, and Verna L. Newsome, eds. (6)

Forms of Rhetoric: Ordering Experience. Tom E. Kakonis and James C. Wilcox, eds. (219)

The Freshman Writes. Roger M. Swanson. (388)

From Discovery to Style: A Reader. Gary Tate, ed. (389)

From Experience: A Basic Rhetoric and Reader. Monte M. Hart
and Benson R. Schulman. (172)

From Experience to Expression: A College Rhetoric. Joseph
Comprone. (86)

From Start to Finish. Selma F. Stonberg. (382)

*From Thought to Theme: A Rhetoric and Reader for College
English*. 4th ed. William F. Smith and Raymond D.
Liedlich. (372)

Fundamentals of English: Reading, Writing, Grammar. H. G.
Allen. (5)

Getting It Together: Refining Your Writing. Sandra Seltzer
and Myra Kogen. (351)

Getting Started: A Preface to Writing. Harry Rougier and E.
Krage Stockum. (334)

A Glossary for College English. Martin Stevens and Charles H.
Kegel. (379)

Grammar as Style. Virginia Tufte. (400)

Grammar in Context. form B. Leo Hamalian and Edmond L.
Volpe. (166)

A Grammar of Contemporary English. Randolph Quirk, Geoffrey
Leech, and Jan Svartvik. (310)

Guide to Rapid Revision. 2nd ed. Daniel D. Pearlman and Paul
R. Pearlman. (300)

*A Guide to Technical Literature Production: A Concise Hand-
book of Productin Methods*. Emerson Clarke. (77)

Guide to Writing. Lynn Quitman Troyka, ed. (399)

Guided Writing. John Wubben. (438)

The Handbook for Basic English Skills. Richard M. Bossone and
James M. Reif, Jr. (51)

Handbook for Student Writing. Nell Ann Pickett and Ann A.
Laster. (306)

245

Image: Reflections on Language. Clark McKowen. (258)

In Phase: Sentence, Structure, Style. Emil Hurtik and
   Thomas Lillard. (207)

An Introduction to Modern English Grammar. Jean Malmstrom.
   (267)

An Introductory English Grammar. 2nd ed. Norman C. Stageberg. (378)

Insight: A Rhetoric Reader. 2nd ed. Emil Hurtik. (206)

Invention and Design: A Rhetorical Reader. Forrest D. Burt
   and E. Cleve Want. (62)

Just Rhetoric. Harry H. Crosby and George F. Estey. (99)

Juxtaposition, Encore! James Burl Hogins and Gerald A.
   Bryant, Jr. (186)

Keys to American English. Constance Gefvert, Richard Raspa,
   Amy Richards. (139)

Language and Literature for Composition. Sanford R. Radner
   and Susan G. Radner, eds. (311)

Language and Reality: A Semantics Approach to Writing.
   Geoffrey Wagner and Sanford R. Radner. (405)

Language Awareness. Paul A. Eschholz, Alfred F. Rosa, and
   Virginia P. Clark, eds. (121)

Language in Thought and Action. 3rd ed. S. I. Hayakawa.
   (177)

Language in Uniform: A Reader on Propaganda. Nick Aaron
   Ford, ed. (132)

Language: Introductory Readings. Virginia P. Clark, Paul A.
   Eschholz, and Alfred F. Rosa, eds. (76)

The Language of Argument. 2nd ed. Daniel McDonald. (256)

Literary Style of the Old Bible and the New. D. G. Kehl.
   (222)

Literature and Aesthetics. Monroe C. Beardsley. (27)

A Little Casebook in the Rhetoric of Writing. Richard
   Braddock. (52)

The Little English Handbook: Choices and Conventions. Edward P. J. Corbett. (91)

The Lively Art of Writing. 3rd ed. Lucile Vaugham Payne. (299)

Logic for Argument. Jack Pitt and Russell E. Leavenworth. (308)

Logic, Language, and Composition. Hulon Willis. (428)

The Making of Style. James Howe. (202)

Making the Point. J. Alexander Scharbach and Carl Markgraf. (344)

Matters of Style. J. Mitchell Morse. (284)

The Mature Students' Guide to Reading and Composition: Book I. Delores H. Lipscomb, Judith I. Martin, and Alice J. Robinson. (247)

Miss Thistlebottom's Hobgoblins: The Careful Writer's Guide to the Taboos, Bugbears and Outmoded Rules of English Usage. Theodore M. Bernstein. (36)

Mixed Bag: Artifacts from the Contemporary Culture. Helene D. Hutchinson. (209)

Models for Writing. James Burl Hogins and Robert Earl Yarber. (189)

Modern English Handbook. 5th ed. Robert M. Gorrell and Charlton Laird. (148)

Modern English Reader. Robert M. Gorrell, Ronald Freeman, and Charlton Laird. (149)

Modern Rhetoric. shorter 3rd ed. Cleanth Brooks and Robert Penn Warren. (56)

Modern Technical Writing. 3rd ed. Theodore A. Sherman and Simon S. Johnson. (358)

Modes of Argument. Monroe C. Beardsley. (28)

Modes of Rhetoric. Leo Rockas. (325)

The Most Common Mistakes in English Usage. Thomas Elliott Berry. (38)

Multimediate: Multi Media and the Art of Writing. Warren L. Clare and Kenneth J. Ericksen. (75)

The Nature of Literature: Writing on Literary Topics.
William F. Irmscher. (211)

The New Conservatives. Leonard Lief. (245)

The New English: Structure/Form/Style. Joseph M. Williams,
(425)

A New Generation of Essays. James M. Salem. (340)

New Preface to Writing: Series One, Two, or Three. Harlan
H. Hamilton. (167)

A New Reading Approach to College Writing. Martha Heasley
Cox, ed. (95)

The New University Reader. William R. Seat, Jr., Paul S.
Burtness, and Warren U. Ober. (349)

The Norton Reader: An Anthology of Expository Prose. 3rd
shorter ed. Arthur M. Eastman, et al. (109)

The Now Reader. Thomas E. Sanders and Franklin D. Hester.
(341)

The Odyssey Reader: Ideas and Style. Newman P. Birk and
Genevieve B. Birk. (41)

The Odyssey Reader: Ideas and Style. shorter ed. Newman P.
Birk and Genevieve B. Birk. (42)

On Writing. Roger Sale. (339)

1001 Pitfalls in English Grammar Spelling and Usage. rev.
ed. Vincent F. Hopper. (196)

Options: A Program for English. John Bigby and Russell Hill.
(39)

Other Lives. Cynthia Griffin Wolff, ed. (437)

Outside-In. Madelon E. Heatherington. (179)

The Oxford Reader: Varieties of Contemporary Discourse.
shorter ed. Frank Kermode and Richard Poirier, eds. (223)

The Paragraph in Context. Virginia M. Burke. (61)

Paragraph Patterns: A Program for Self-instruction. Blair
Barrett, programmer. (26)

Paragraphs and Themes. 2nd ed. P. Joseph Canavan. (67)

248

Pattern Practices to Learn to Write By: Level II. Marilyn
Birkley, James Birkley, and Louis Rivers. (47)

Patterns for Composition. Joseph P. Collignon. (84)

Patterns for Prose Writing: From Notes to Themes. Nelle
Francis and J. Warren Smith. (133)

Patterns of Exposition. 4th ed. Randall E. Decker. (102)

Patterns: Readings for Composition. James D. Lester.
(241)

*People and Words: A Visual Rhetoric and Resource Book for
Writing.* James Burl Hogins. (184)

*Perception and Persuasion: A New Approach to Effective Writ-
ing.* Raymond Paul and Pellegrino W. Goione. (297)

Perceptions and Reflections: A College Reader. Diane Tomcheff Callin, Gilbert Tierney, and Daniel Tomcheff. (63)

Person to Person: Rhetoric, Reality, and Change. Irving
Deer, Harriet A. Deer, and James A. Gould. (103)

Persona: A Style Study for Readers and Writers. Walker
Gibson. (142)

The Personal Voice: A Contemporary Prose Reader. shorter ed.
Albert J. Guerard, Maclin B. Guerard, John Hawkes, and
Clair Rosenfield, eds. (162)

Phase Blue: A Systems Approach to College English. annotated
ed. James Burl Hogins and Robert E. Yarber. (190)

Phase Blue. rev. annotated ed. James Burl Hogins and Robert
E. Yarber. (191)

Phase Blue, Too. rev. ed. James Burl Hogins and Robert E.
Yarber. (192)

Plain English Please. 2nd ed. Gregory Cowan and Elizabeth
McPherson. (94)

Plain Style. John Durham and Paul Zall. (108)

Planned Paragraphs: Examples from Various Sources. J. Rowe
Webster. (412)

*Popular Writing in America: The Interaction of Style and
Audience.* Donald McQuade and Robert Atwan. (261)

Pouring Down Words. Suzette Haden Elgin. (114)

A Practical College Rhetoric: Writing Themes and Tests.
Edgar V. Roberts. (321)

Practical Communication. Nell Ann Pickett. (305)

Practical English Handbook. 4th ed. Floyd C. Watkins, Willia
B. Dillingham, and Edwin T. Martin. (409)

A Practical Guide to Effective Writing. Jerome H. Perlmutter.
(301)

Practical Rhetoric. O. B. Hardison. (170)

A Practical Rhetoric. John Hurley. (205)

The Practical Stylist. 3rd ed. Sheridan Baker. (18)

Practice for Effective Writing. rev. ed. Vincent F. Hopper
and Cedric Gale. (197)

Practice for Understanding and Using English. Newman P. Birk
and Genevieve B. Birk. (43)

*Précis Writing Practice: Exercise to Improve Reading Compre-
hension and to Strengthen Communication Skills.* Richard
F. Hood, ed. (194)

Preface to Critical Reading. 4th ed. Richard D. Altick.
(8)

Prentice-Hall Handbook for Writers. 6th ed. Glenn Legett, C.
David Mead, and William Charvat. (240)

Prentice-Hall Workbook for Writers. Donald C. Rigg. (318)

Preparation for Better Writing. Earl W. Thomas. (392)

Preparing Effective Reports. Lionel D. Wyld. (439)

The Prevalent Forms of Prose. Otis Winchester and Winston
Weathers. (432)

Principles of Rhetoric. Richard E. Hughes and P. Albert
Duhamel. (204)

Principles of Technical Writing. Robert Hays. (178)

Prisms: A Self Reader. William Sparke, ed. (376)

Probing Common Ground: Sources for Writing. James Burl

250

Say What You Mean. Rudolph Flesch. (131)

The Scope of Rhetoric: A Handbook for Composition and Literature. James E. Robinson. (324)

Seeing and Writing: Fifteen Exercises in Composing Experience. 2nd ed. Walker Gibson. (143)

Sentence Combining: A Composing Book. William Strong. (385)

Sentence Strategies: Writing for College. Jacqueline P. Griffin and G. Howard Poteet. (160)

Sentence Variety: A Programmed Approach to Sentence Writing. Jack S. Romine. (328)

Seven Steps to Theme Writing. Raul Reyes. (316)

The Shapes of Prose: A Rhetorical Reader for College Prose. Charles M. Cobb. (79)

Shaping College Writing: Paragraph and Essay. 2nd ed. Joseph D. Gallo and Henry W. Rink. (137)

Short Cuts to Effective English. Harry Shefter. (356)

A Short Guide to English Composition. 2nd ed. William A. McQueen. (262)

A Short Guide to Writing a Critical Review. rev. ed. Eliot D. Allen and Ethel B. Colbrunn. (3)

A Short Guide to Writing about Literature. 3rd ed. Sylvan Barnet. (22)

A Short Guide to Writing Better Themes. Ann R. Morris. (283)

So You Have to Write a Technical Report: Elements of Technical Report Writing. Dwight E. Gray. (157)

Someone Like Me: Images for Writing. 2nd ed. Sheena Gillespie and Linda Stanley. (145)

Source, Idea, Technique: A Writer's Reader. 2nd ed. Donald J. Tighe and Lloyd A. Flanigan. (397)

Stages in Writing. Karl K. Taylor. (390)

Step-By-Step Guide to Correct English. Mary Ann Spencer Pulaski. ·(309)

The Stockwell Guide for Technical and Vocational Writing.
Richard E. Stockwell. (381)

Strategies of Rhetoric. rev. ed. A. M. Tibbetts and Charlene
Tibbetts. (396)

The Strategy of Style. Winston Weathers and Otis Winchester.
(411)

Structure, Language, and Style: A Rhetoric Handbook. W. Ross
Winterowd. (436)

The Structure of Language. Owen Thomas. (393)

The Structure of Writing. James Burl Hogins and Thomas
Lillard. (187)

Structures for Composition. Bernard A. Drabeck, Helen E.
Ellis, Virginia Low, and Hartley Pfeil. (107)

Struggles with Bears: Experience in Writing. Smokey Wilson.
(431)

Student Activism. Irving Howe. (201)

The Student Critic: An Aid to Writing. Samuel J. Rogal.
(326)

The Student Critic: Thinking and Writing about Literature.
David R. Cox and Stephen Lewis. (96)

*The Student Speaks Out: A Rhetorical View of Typical Freshman
Essays.* Alfred J. Lindsey and Arthur C. Donart. (246)

The Student Writer's Guide. rev. ed. Eliot D. Allen and
Ethel B. Colbrunn. (4)

Student's Book of College English. David Skwire, Frances
Chitwood, Raymond Ackley, and Raymond Fredman. (369)

A Student's First Aid to Writing. Theodore Grieder and
Josephine Grieder. (159)

Studies in Prose Writing. 3rd ed. James R. Kreuzer and Lee
Cogan. (229)

Style and Grammar: A Writer's Handbook of Transformations.
John B. Williams. (424)

Style: Diagnosis and Prescriptions. Stoddard Malarkey, ed.
(266)

Style in English. John Nist. (292)

Style in Language. Thomas A. Sebeok. (350)

A Style Manual for Written Communication. Arno F. Knapper and
    Loda I. Newcomb. (226)

Style: Writing as the Discovery of Outlook. Richard M.
    Eastman. (110)

*Styles and Structures: Alternative Approaches to College
    Writing*. Charles Kay Smith. (371)

Subject and Structure: An Anthology for Writers. 5th ed.
    John M. Wasson. (407)

Subject and Structure: An Anthology for Writers. alt. ed.
    John M. Wasson. (408)

A Survival Kit. Howard Siegel and Roger Boedecker, et al.
    (365)

Taking Control: The College Essay. Paul Saylor. (343)

Teach Yourself English. William L. Young. (443)

Teach Yourself How to Write. Louise A. Roberts. (323)

Technical and Business Writing. Clarence A. Andrews. (10)

Technical Communication. George C. Harwell. (175)

Technical Report Writing. 2nd ed. Herman M. Weisman. (416)

Technical Report Writing Today. Steven E. Pauley. (298)

Technical Reporting. 3rd ed. Joseph N. Ulman, Jr. and Jay
    R. Gould. (401)

Technical Writing. David E. Fear. (124)

Technical Writing. Norman Levine. (243)

Technical Writing. 3rd ed. Gordon H. Mills and John A.
    Walter. (276)

The Technician Writes: A Guide to Basic Technical Writing.
    Arnold B. Sklare. (368)

The Techniques of Writing. 2nd ed. Paul L. Kinsella. (225)

*The Technologist as Writer: An Introduction to Technical
    Writing*. Peter Coleman and Ken Brambleby. (83)

Technology and Social Change. Emmanuel G. Mesthene. (271)

Telling Writing. Ken Macrorie. (263)

Themes and Research Papers. Ben R. Schneider, Jr. and Herbert K. Tjossem. (345)

Thirteen Types of Narrative. Wallace Hildick. (181)

--30--: A Journalistic Approach to Freshman Composition. C. Jeriel Howard and Richard Francis Tracz. (200)

Time In: A Guide to Communication Skills. Kim Flachmann and Henry A. Bamman. (127)

Thought and Statement. 3rd ed. William G. Leary, James Steel Smith, and Richard C. Blakeslee. (238)

Thought in English Prose. J. C. Dent. (105)

Tradition and Dissent: A Rhetoric/Reader. 2nd ed. Florence Bonzer Greenberg and Anne P. Heffley. (158)

The Triumph of Style: Modes of Nonfiction. John R. Knott and Reeve Parker, eds. (227)

TRRPWR: Think, Read, React, Plan, Write, Rewrite. Royce W. Adams. (2)

Turning on to Writing. William A. Knox. (228)

Twenty Questions for the Writer: A Rhetoric with Readings. Jacqueline Berke. (35)

20 Steps to Better Writing. Harry Shaw. (354)

Understanding and Using English. 4th ed. Newman P. Birk and Genevieve B. Birk. (45)

Using English Effectively. Newman P. Birk and Genevieve B. Birk. (46)

Values and Voices: A College Reader. Betty Renshaw. (315)

Viewpoints. Burton J. Fishman, ed. (125)

Ways of Writing. William F. Irmscher. (212)

The Well-Structured Paragraph. Barbara Williams. (423)

What's the Usage: The Writer's Guide to English Grammar and Rhetoric. C. Carter Colwell and James H. Knox. (85)

Who Needs Nature? Dixie S. Jackson, ed. (213)

Witnesses. Clark Sturges. (387)

Word for Word: The Rewriting of Fiction. Wallace Hildick. (182)

Word, Self, Reality: The Rhetoric of Imagination. James E. Miller. (275)

Words and Ideas: A Handbook for College Writing. 4th ed. Hans P. Guth. (163)

Words at Work: A Practical Approach to Grammar. Viola K. Rivenburgh. (319)

A Workbook for Writers. Forms B and D. Harry J. Sachs, Harry M. Brown, and P. Joseph Canavan. (338)

Working Sentences. Robert Allen, Rita Pompian, and Doris Allen. (7)

Workouts in Reading and Writing. O. B. Davis. (101)

The World of Informative-Persuasive Prose. Keith F. McKean and Charles Wheeler. (257)

The Would-be Writer. 3rd ed. Clinton S. Burhans, Jr. (60)

Write Me a Ream: A Course in Controlled Composition. Linda Ann Kunz and Robert R. Viscount. (230)

Write Now!: Substance, Strategy, Style. Gary L. Harmon and Ruth F. Dickinson. (171)

The Writer and the Worlds of Words. Robert Bain and Dennis G. Donovan, eds. (15)

Writer to Writer: Readings on the Craft of Writing. Floyd C. Watkins and Karl F. Knight, eds. (410)

The Writer's Control of Tone: Readings, with Analysis, for Thinking and Writing about Personal Experience. Edward M. White, ed. (418)

Writers' Guide and Index to English. 5th ed. Porter G. Perrin and Wilma R. Ebbitt. (303)

A Writer's Guide to Literature. Walter J. De Mordaunt. (104)

Writing: A Habit of Mind. S. Leonard Rubinstein. (335)

Writing a Technical Paper. Donald H. Menzel, Howard Mumford Jones, and Lyle G. Boyd. (270)

Writing about Imaginative Literature. Edward J. Gordon. (147)

Writing About Literature. rev. ed. B. Bernard Cohen. (81)

Writing about Literature and Film. Margaret B. Bryan and Boyd H. Davis. (59)

Writing and Reading in Technical English. Nell Ann Pickett and Ann A. Laster. (307)

Writing and Rewriting. 5th ed. Harry Shaw. (355)

Writing by Patterns. Helen E. Lefevre and Carl A. Lefevre. (239)

Writing: Craft and Art. William L. Rivers. (320)

Writing Essays. Harold P. Simonson. (367)

Writing Essays about Literature: A Literary Rhetoric. Joanne Cockelreas and Dorothy Logan. (80)

Writing for Occupational Education. Ann A. Laster and Nell Ann Pickett. (237)

Writing for the Fun of It: An Experience-Based Approach to Composition. Robert C. Hawley and Isabel L. Hawley. (176)

Writing from Example: Rhetoric Illustrated. Karl K. Taylor and Thomas A. Zimanzl. (391)

Writing from Experience. William Nichols, ed. (291)

Writing: Growth Through Structure. Clarence A. Andrews. (11)

The Writing Lab: An Individualized Program in Writing Skills. Harvey S. Wiener and Rose Palmer. (422)

Writing Modern English. Robert M. Gorrell and Charlton Laird. (150)

The Writing Performance. Donald H. Ross. (330)

Writing Prose: Techniques and Purposes. 3rd ed. Thomas S. Kane and Leonard J. Peters. (220)

Writing Scientific Papers and Reports. 6th ed. W. Paul Jones. (218)

Writing Sense: A Handbook of Composition. David R. Pichaske. (304)

Writing Skills I: A Program for Self-instruction. Blair Barrett, programmer. (24)

Writing Skills II: A Program for Self-instruction. Blair Barrett, programmer. (25)

Writing: The Personal Voice. Jill Wilson Cohn. (82)

Writing Themes about Literature. 3rd ed. Edgar V. Roberts. (322)

Writing Through Understanding. Nancy Arapoff. (12)

Writing to be Read. Ken Macrorie. (264)

Writing to the Point: Six Basic Steps. William J. Kerrigan. (224)

Writing Well. Donald Hall. (165)

Writing with a Purpose. 5th ed. James M. McCrimmon. (253)

Writing with a Purpose. short ed. James M. McCrimmon. (254)

Writing with Style: Conversations on the Art of Writing. John R. Trimble. (398)

Writing without Teachers. Peter Elbow. (113)

You. Joseph Frank. (134)

Your Future in Technical and Science Writing. Emerson Clarke and Vernon Root. (78)

WITHDRAWAL